ESSEX BOYS, THE NEW GENERATION

This book is dedicated to the memory of
Dean Fergus Boshell
Resting where no shadows fall
13 April 1976 – 28 February 2001
'I won't ask for forgiveness, my sins are all I had'

To my late beautiful wife and friend Emma,
my loss is an open wound that will never heal

ESSEX BOYS

BOYS

The New Generation

Bernard O'Mahoney

MAINSTREAM
PUBLISHING

EDINBURGH AND LONDON

First published in Great Britain in 2008 by
MAINSTREAM PUBLISHING COMPANY
(EDINBURGH) LTD
7 Albany Street
Edinburgh EH1 3UG

ISBN 9781845963125

A catalogue record for this book is available
from the British Library

Typeset in Badhouse and Palatino

Printed in Great Britain by
Clays Ltd, St Ives plc

ACKNOWLEDGEMENTS

Dicky Rutter RIP

My mother Ann, my sons Adrian and Vinney and my little girl Karis have inspired me in writing this book. I am also most grateful to the following people, who have assisted me or in some other way helped in telling this story: Natalie, the Bump, Michael, Carol, Finn, Lily, Paul, Colleen, Ami, Michael, Miles, Leanne, Tino and family, Debra King, Bilbrook Earl and Martin 'Whizz Kid' Moore; the intensive care staff at Selly Oak hospital, Birmingham; Father O'Connor; Dr Hull of Harborne; Dr Wilson of Market Deeping; Shane Smith, Gilly, Ross, Bingley, Rachie, Hughie, The Cowleys, Mike West, Mad Andy, Battersea Steve, Brett Dunn, Wez, Shanae and Zoe the 'geezer bird' (according to Jade Goody), Champagne Steve and Beverley Boshell; Danny, David, Sandy and Ricky Percival, Kevin Walsh, Gavin and Sue, Carl Eve, Gina Marsden, David Giles, Ronnie Tretton, Nipper Ellis, the lady who tends (so graciously) to plot 7 on the Manchester Drive allotments and Southend Sarah; Martin, Steve and Storming Norman Hall, Stacie Harris, Sean Fallon, Carla Shipton, Ann Lippett and Steve 'Penfold'.

A very special thank you to those of you who have assisted me but asked for your names not to be mentioned in this book. Your admirable courage is appreciated. Too many others have chosen to stand by and do nothing, an attitude that permits lies and evil to prosper.

Last, but by no means least, Jacquelyn Lippett, for friendship, guidance, photography and partially made cups of tea. Thank you, Lippy. I wish you luck and happiness.

For more information about this case and other books written by Bernard O'Mahoney, please visit:

www.bernardomahoney.com

CONTENTS

Introduction

THE SOUNDS OF SILENCE

Tuesday, 3 April 2007. The prison warder unlocked the door and pointed towards the street. 'Sorry, Mr O'Mahoney,' he said, 'I regret to inform you that you cannot come into this prison. You have been listed as a banned visitor.'

I had just travelled 130 miles from my home in Birmingham with an approved visiting order to meet twenty-seven-year-old Ricky Percival, who is serving four life sentences with a recommendation that he is not considered for parole until he has completed at least twenty-eight years. There was little opportunity to argue: after taking just one step out of the visitor's centre, the door slammed shut behind me.

It had been my intention to sit down with Percival in the hope that I could begin to make sense of the case against him, but it was not to be. Security staff at HMP Chelmsford in Essex had denied me access and so I had no choice other than to get in my car and retrace the long journey home.

I spent the majority of the following rain-drenched day staring out of my window, then back at a blank computer screen. It's not that I was suffering from writer's block or that I didn't have sufficient material to write this book; my problem was that I didn't know where to begin. How was I to unravel a web of lies and deceit that was so well constructed it managed to fool not only the police but also a judge and jury? How was I to explain in simple terms a complicated, well-thought-out weave of fact and fiction so that you, the reader, could understand fully the enormity of one man's deception? This has undoubtedly been the most challenging story I have ever attempted to tell.

Every conceivable hurdle that could have been erected to try and prevent me from learning the truth has been put in my path. A grieving mother who is desperate to learn the truth about her son's murder was advised by the police not to talk to me. Security staff and the governor at HMP Chelmsford sent me a visiting order but then did an inexplicable U-turn and banned me when I arrived. After appealing that decision and, at the governor's request, signing a lengthy undertaking not to discuss, disclose or publish anything other than matters related to the case, access to Percival was still denied. Despite never being given a reason for this ban, I was then informed that no further appeals from me would be considered. 'As far as Bernard O'Mahoney is concerned,' one officer told me, 'the gates of Her Majesty's Prison Chelmsford are to remain closed.'

In 1999, five Law Lords ruled that a ban on journalists visiting prisoners and writing about their cases was an unlawful interference with free speech. They said that prisoners who protested their innocence often had no other means of searching out the fresh evidence needed to have their cases looked at again. Their decision was strongly influenced by an affidavit from Gareth Peirce, a solicitor who has acted for more than 20 miscarriage-of-justice victims. She pointed out that there was no legal aid available to prisoners for investigations and more than 90 per cent of applicants to the Criminal Cases Review Commission had no solicitor. The resources available to the national and local media provided the best chance of discovering new evidence, she added. Concluding their judgment, the Lords said that freedom of speech was 'the lifeblood of democracy', acting 'as a brake on the abuse of power by public officials'.

In Percival's case, the brake appears to have been firmly re-applied; but, despite the ban, which has made progress slow, my thirst for the truth has never diminished.

Tracing and interviewing witnesses in sensational cases involving murder is normally a time-consuming but relatively simple task because people feel a need to unburden themselves and talk about their experiences. However, many of the potential witnesses that I have contacted to interview for this book have either been advised against assisting me or have instructed their solicitor to request that I do not contact them again. A message on my website requesting people to contact me who might have been able to contribute to the book was viewed by 2,785 people, but not one responded. One witness whom I approached at his place of work was so reluctant to talk to me he leapt over his shop counter and fled down the street.

After several meetings in the most unusual of places, and after convincing people that my intentions were completely honourable, I have managed to uncover what I believe is the truth about one of the most vicious crime waves in Essex's bloody gangland history. Now that I know the truth, I am not surprised that certain people actively tried to prevent me from ever discovering it.

This is a story of senseless murder, psychotic violence, drug dealing and deceit that has culminated in an unparalleled miscarriage of justice occurring. I am not saying that I know Ricky Percival is innocent and I am certainly not saying that he is guilty – nobody is in a position to do either because he was not given a fair trial. Until such a trial takes place, nobody should level an accusing finger in Percival's direction.

The beginning of this remarkable story is, I guess, at the end of another equally disturbing yet remarkable story, so perhaps I should begin there.

In December 1995, Patrick Tate, Tony Tucker and Craig Rolfe were lured to a deserted farm track by the promise of a lucrative drug deal. They died from multiple gunshots to the head as they sat in their Range Rover. Two farmers, who discovered the bodies in the blood-spattered vehicle, initially thought the men were asleep. The executions had been carried out so swiftly and with such ruthless efficiency that the victims had no time to react. A seven-year reign at the top of the criminal heap – which had resulted in the deaths of three teenagers who had taken drugs supplied by the gang, numerous beatings, stabbings and shootings, and the murder of a young man for his part in a botched drug deal – was finally over. The two men jailed for life for the triple murders, Michael Steele and Jack Whomes, have always protested their innocence. They were convicted on the word of a former friend turned supergrass named Darren Nicholls. A self-confessed drug dealer, liar and thief, Nicholls himself was accused of the killings before he turned on his friends.

The murders and the trial of the accused unleashed a bout of tortured hand wringing by politicians and community leaders, who pledged to wage war on drug barons and their minions. The events dominated the news, causing the county of Essex to come under intense media scrutiny. An area that has produced more than its fair share of hoodlums, Essex was branded as 'Crime County' and the 'Drug Capital of England'. Its law-abiding citizens were horrified and complained bitterly about their unwanted badge of dishonour. Some even suggested that the extraordinary amount of adverse publicity the county's criminals were attracting would cause house prices to plummet.

Nina Stimson, MP for Southend West at the time, complained that the drug capital label was yet another insult to a county that has had to put up with being branded 'sleazy'. She said, 'A few years ago, we had the silliness which suggested that all Essex men went around wearing shell suits and medallions, and Essex girls were brainless bimbos in white stilettos. That was rubbish, and it is just as far from the truth now to portray Essex as being a crime- and drug-ridden area.'

But not everybody in Essex reacted to the publicity in the same way. Young up-and-coming criminals in the county revelled in their new-found fame. To be an Essex Boy meant that you were a top boy, a geezer, a real somebody amongst the criminal fraternity. Impressionable teenagers who had never even heard of the trio before they were executed began claiming that they used to do business with them or were 'close personal friends'. Any link, exaggerated or fabricated, that associated them with the now glorified Essex Boys firm enhanced their reputations within the circles they moved.

The death of such powerful, prominent gang members left a huge vacuum in the drug-distribution network in the south-east of England. Detective Inspector Ivan Dibley, who led the investigation into the murders, told a press conference: 'There is not a villain in this country who isn't talking about these murders. The void these three men have left will be filled very quickly because there is big money to be made.'

Unfortunately for the good people of Essex, DI Dibley was correct in his assumption. Like the head being cut from the Hydra, evil quickly replaced evil. The older, wiser and more hardened criminals in the county were suddenly presented with an army of gullible, willing, but, more importantly, expendable young wannabes who were eager to make a name for themselves in the murky criminal underworld. One such impressionable youth was Dean Boshell. He was in his late teens at the time of the Rettendon killings and was striving, like many of his naive teenage friends, to gain a reputation as a hard man in the area where he lived. The main thrust of Boshell's efforts revolved around a wannabe gangster named Damon Alvin, whom he had met in HMP Chelmsford. Alvin was a drug dealer with a fearsome reputation whom Boshell described as a 'kind of older brother'.

INTRODUCTION

The respect and admiration shown to Alvin by Boshell was, however, not reciprocated – it was ridiculed. Boshell would be publicly taunted and humiliated, apparently 'to keep him in his place'. Alvin's cruel, sadistic streak was an invaluable asset in the violent drugs world that he inhabited and controlled, but it was his weakness that inflicted the most pain upon people. Whenever Alvin faced a crisis or was accused of wrongdoing, it would always be somebody else's fault and someone other than Alvin was always made to pay, regardless of innocence or guilt.

This is the true story of when Percival and Boshell met Alvin. It is a story many people never wanted you to read.

1

A MOTHER'S TALE: BEVERLEY BOSHELL

Thursday, 1 March 2001. Basildon, Essex. Ten people dead and a further eighty injured in a rail crash was the news that dominated the headlines that day. Beverley Boshell, a mother of two sons, took particular interest in the story because her eldest, Wayne, was a train driver. She was saddened by the terrible loss of life but relieved to learn that the crash had taken place the previous day in Selby, North Yorkshire. Wayne was employed in London. Putting her newspaper to one side, Beverley sat back to relax, but she was soon disturbed by the sound of her front gate being opened and people arriving at her door.

'The knock on my front door was firm and somehow alarming,' Beverley recalled. 'It was mid-morning and I had no idea who it could have been, as I wasn't expecting any visitors. When I opened it, two ashen-faced police officers – one male, one female – stood before me.

'I was asked if I was Mrs Beverley Boshell, and when I confirmed that I was they said they needed to come into my house to talk to me. My heart sank. I just knew they weren't going to give me anything other than bad news. "Why do you need to come in?" I asked. "Anything you have to say, you can tell me here and now." The male police officer assured me that it would be better for me if I invited them into my home.

'I relented and showed them into my lounge. "You had better take a seat, Mrs Boshell," the WPC said. I remained standing – my heart was pounding. I told them that I was OK as I was and asked them to say whatever it was they had come to say.

'The WPC glanced momentarily at her colleague, who gave a shrug of his shoulders, as if to say, "OK then, tell her." Looking back at me, the WPC drew a breath and said, "I regret to have to inform you that your son is dead, Mrs Boshell."

'My first thought was of Wayne. I automatically assumed that he had been involved in an accident on the railways or some sort of terrorist incident, like a bombing. I felt as if I was falling at speed, but everything in the room appeared to be moving in slow motion. I slumped down into a chair and kept asking the officers what had happened.

'"Your son, Dean, has been shot," they said. "His body was discovered in allotments in Manchester Drive, Leigh-on-Sea, at 9.20 yesterday morning. A murder investigation is now under way."

'It had not occurred to me for one moment that this news would have anything to do with Dean. I cannot describe how I felt at that moment, nor could I repeat what I said because I simply don't recall.

'After informing Wayne of the news by telephone and asking him to return to Basildon to comfort me, the officers left. They had assured me that Wayne wouldn't be long, but he was delayed from leaving work by two hours because a replacement driver had to be found for his train. Alone in my home, I was unable to cry; it didn't seem real. I kept telling myself that the police must have made some sort of terrible mistake.

'When Wayne eventually did arrive, he told me that he had seen a headline about a gangland execution taking place in Essex on the newspaper billboards in London, but he had no inclination whatsoever that it had anything to do with his brother. We began asking each other the same questions – who had done this and why? – but neither of us had the answers.

'I didn't wish to remain alone in the house and so that day I collected all of my personal belongings and moved into Wayne's home. A day or two later, the police contacted me again. They said that they wanted me to go to Southend hospital with them to identify Dean's body. They said that they had already identified it and confirmed that the body was Dean's by using his fingerprints; however, they still needed a family member to formally identify him.

'Wayne and I were taken to the hospital mortuary in an unmarked police car by two detectives. I noticed as we walked into the reception area that there was a small room with tea and coffee making facilities, a door leading to a toilet and another, facing us, which I assumed led to the room where Dean's body lay. I had only ever seen one dead person in my life. I had paid my respects to my late stepfather in a chapel of rest, but that experience had been totally unlike this. I was in a place that was cold and clinical; I tried to blank everything out by staring straight ahead and focusing my thoughts on Dean.

'I heard footsteps. The door opened and a man dressed in surgical clothing entered the room. He looked at the detectives and asked if everybody was ready. Wayne looked at me; I could see in his face the pain that he was feeling. He told me that he couldn't go through with it. He said it would be too upsetting. One detective remained with Wayne and I was escorted into the room with the other.

'I entered a dreadful place. My son was lying on his back on a table in the centre of the room. A white sheet stretched from his feet to his shoulders, covering his body. I could tell by the indents and bulges that Dean was naked beneath it. Bandages were wrapped around the back of his head, presumably to hide the gunshot wounds that had extinguished his life. The walls of the room were bare and the sound of pathologists or morticians working beyond them could clearly be heard.

'An electrical saw buzzing and men talking, not loud but audible, filled my head and made my blood run cold. It was obvious from what they were saying that an autopsy was in progress. The very thought of such a macabre procedure taking place so close to my son and me was horrifying. Thoughts of what these people and my son's killer had done to him filled my head. I was no longer sure that I could go through with identifying him.

'Before taking another step towards Dean's body, I asked the detective if he had sustained any facial injuries. To my relief, he said that he had not, but when I looked down upon my son I saw that he had big red blotches all over his face. "What are those red marks?" I asked.

'"We don't know yet," the detective replied. I later learned that Dean's killer, or an accomplice, had squirted ammonia in his face before shooting him. The ammonia had irritated the skin, causing the blemishes.

'I found myself staring at the bandages around his head, trying to imagine what grotesque injuries they were hiding. I felt an urge to remove them so that I could see for myself if Dean had really been shot. It was hard for me to believe because he looked so peaceful, as if he were asleep. The longer I spent with Dean, the less certain I became that it was, in fact, him.

'The last time I had seen my son he was far from muscular, as this person was, and he wasn't as full in the face either. Unbeknown to me at that time, Dean had begun weight training and using muscle-enhancing products.

'"I can't be sure that this is my son," I eventually said to the detective.

'He assured me that the body was Dean's, but my heart refused to be convinced of the awful truth. "We will of course check and double-check," he said, before leading me out of the room.

'A part of my heart remained in that hospital with Dean as we drove off towards home. It has remained with him ever since. I know, because I felt it breaking in two whilst I was there. I don't believe that it will ever heal because the indescribable pain I felt that day has failed to diminish.

'The following morning I contacted the police and asked them if it would be possible to look at a tattoo on Dean's arm, as it might have helped me to positively identify him. A few years earlier, he had been tattooed with a pouncing puma that he had designed himself. I told the police that if I could see this unique tattoo, then I would know in my heart that the body in the morgue was my son's.

'If I am being totally honest, I was misleading the police. I knew it was Dean in that godforsaken place, but I was finding it hard to come to terms with it. I needed to go back to my boy, to be with him for myself, not for any horrible identification formality. The police were very understanding and of course keen for me to give them a positive identification.

'Going back was in many ways harder than my initial visit. The vague possibility that this had been some sort of unthinkable mistake had been snatched from me. All hope of Dean being alive was now gone. I was being forced to accept that my youngest son, the baby of my family, had been brutally murdered.

'Being with Dean on this occasion brought me a lot of comfort. It felt as if it was only me and him in that cold room, which, for a fleeting moment, felt warm with his presence. I looked at the tattoo on Dean's arm and confirmed to the detective that this body was indeed my son's. I have since had an exact copy of the pouncing puma tattooed on my shoulder blade. I hadn't previously dreamed of ever getting one, but this has made me feel as if a part of Dean is with me at all times.

'I have a lot of regrets regarding Dean. The benefits of hindsight are, in my case, proving to be non-existent, only cruel. It's never easy bringing up children, but I keep telling myself that I could have done better. I guess every parent says that at some stage. We do what we think is best at the time, but a parent's input is often over-ridden by outside influences. We live in the fifth-richest country in the world and our children are butchering each other in the streets. Why? It's not as if there are no opportunities or things for kids to do in this country. Basildon, where Dean grew up, has estates with high unemployment, where kids who were bottom of the class can earn thousands of pounds per week dealing drugs. They lie in bed during the day playing computer games in which they can shoot people 50 times on screen and watch them get up again. Then they go out onto the streets at night, dripping in jewellery, brandishing knives and guns. Their role models are musicians whose message is "get rich or die trying". It's a sickness that is prevalent throughout society and it really needs to be cured.

'I did ask the police if I could visit my son for a third and final time. I told them that I needed to say goodbye to him, and thankfully they agreed. I was not allowed to visit without police officers being present for evidential reasons and we had to give the mortuary several hours' notice before we arrived. When I asked why, I was told this was because my son was being kept in a freezer and it would take a few hours for his body to defrost enough for me to view it. These words, spoken honest and true by the officers in reply to my questions, felt like a knife being plunged into my chest.

'I cried and prayed I could travel back to the last occasion that I had seen Dean alive. I could then embrace my boy and ensure that he never left the safety of my home. My prayers never were answered.

'When the door leading into the mortuary was opened, I saw that Dean's entire body was covered with a sheet. Nobody had warned me that this visit would be any different to the previous visits I had made. I was unable to see Dean's face, and when I asked why, I was told that the bandages covering his wounds had now been removed and seeing him would be too distressing for me.

'How does a mother say a final goodbye to her young son? What words do you express to a bullet-riddled body hidden underneath a white sheet?

'May God never find it in his heart to forgive the bastards who did this to my Dean.'

• • •

I first contacted Beverley Boshell by telephone shortly after the conclusion of her son's murder trial. I was surprised to learn that she lived fewer than a hundred yards from my former home in Basildon. I had moved from there in 1995, following the execution of my three former associates in the Range Rover at Rettendon. For nearly a decade, the Essex Boys firm, as we had become known, controlled the doors of pubs and nightclubs throughout Essex, London and the south-east. The security we provided for these venues was little more than a front for the drugs the firm imported from Europe and distributed to revellers using local dealers. Greed, paranoia and illusions by some that we were invincible resulted in mayhem, murder and our eventual demise. On the day I had arranged to meet Beverley, I left my home in Birmingham early to ensure that I wouldn't be late. Motorways these days are fine if you want to spend the best part of a day sitting alongside thousands of other stationary motorists, but they are rarely much use if you want to get from one place to another without delay. Arriving in Basildon an hour or two before I was due to meet Beverley, I decided to kill time visiting some of my old haunts.

I drove to the house my late wife Emma had lived in as a child. I walked around the snooker hall that was once Raquels nightclub, the venue where I had worked as a doorman, and I sat reminiscing outside the house of my former business partner, Tony Tucker. Driving towards Beverley's home, I passed a public telephone box that I had regularly used to call my associates to discuss our illegal business ventures and violent misadventures. At the time, we believed that using public telephones would circumvent attempts by the police to trace calls between gang members. We were, of course, wrong: the police knew about most, if not all, of our activities. Being a gangster and not being able to tell all and sundry about it was too much to bear for some of my colleagues.

I passed the garages at the back of my old home, where I used to play football with my son, Vinney. The same garages had once been raided by police and an arsenal of the firm's weapons found. Naturally, everybody questioned suffered bouts of amnesia and couldn't remember anything that might have assisted the police with their inquiries.

It was, to say the least, a thought-provoking journey to Beverley's modest home. It made me realise that my mother could easily have been in Beverley Boshell's shoes and I could have been buried alongside Dean, Tucker, Tate or Rolfe. Gangsters? What a joke! They are only good for keeping florists, undertakers, police and prison officers in employment.

I parked my car in the quiet cul-de-sac where Beverley lives. Opening her wooden gate, I made my way along a path, through her well-kept garden. Before I could knock on the front door, Beverley opened it and invited me inside. Entering the lounge, I noticed three photographs of Dean – one on top of the television, one in a cabinet and one on the wall of him as a child. A greenfinch chirped and whistled as it flapped about in a cage near the door. Scattered all around the room were toy or ornamental polar bears. Beverley noticed me looking at them and said that she had been collecting them for years.

For the next five minutes, she talked non-stop about the polar bears, the greenfinch, any subject other than her son. I could tell that she was dreading discussing a subject that had already caused her so much anguish and pain. When she did eventually pause to take a breath, I asked her if she was up to talking about Dean.

'This jumper that I am wearing was Dean's,' she replied. 'I wear it now and again, to feel close to him.' There was nothing I could say in response to such a statement and for a few moments we sat together in an uneasy silence.

Beverley kept looking up at a photograph of her son, as if she were seeking some sort of reassurance from him. Her hands opened and closed continuously, as she nervously turned and pulled at the numerous rings on her fingers. After clasping her hands tightly together, she inhaled deeply and began to talk.

'The first thing I want to say is that the police have advised me not to assist you with the book you are writing. Why they said this to me, I don't know. Perhaps the truth about my son's murder is more terrible than I have been led to believe. I am in no doubt whatsoever that the whole truth about his death has never been told. There are too many loose ends and unanswered questions. I really hope that your book will help to answer them all.'

I agreed with Beverley's sentiment and promised to do all I could to help her learn the truth in the hope that she could have some sort of closure. I explained that in order to do so I would need her to tell me everything she could remember about Dean's life and the events that followed his death.

'OK,' Beverley replied, 'I suppose the best place to start is at the beginning.

'On Valentine's Day, in 1975, I married Dean's father, Fergus Paul Boshell. I still wonder why I went through with the marriage. We were far from compatible. Fergus was a drinker and would turn violent after consuming as little as a pint of cider. When I was seven months' pregnant with Dean, Fergus got drunk and decided to use me as a punch bag. After hearing my screams for help, my brother telephoned the police. When they eventually arrived, they wrote down everything I said had happened and promised that it would be acted upon in the future if there was any further violence. I wasn't impressed. The next assault could have resulted in the death of my unborn baby, or mine, or both of ours. I wanted them to take action that day, but they refused to do so.

'On 13 April 1976, my son Dean Fergus Boshell was born in Basildon hospital. Life didn't start off too well for him. I was discharged from hospital just six hours after his birth. It was a cold, foggy day, but his drunken father insisted on taking him out in a pram to visit relatives. When he eventually staggered home, I had to call the midwife out because Dean was having difficulty breathing.

'I already had a son from a previous relationship named Wayne. Certain family members, whom I don't wish to name, treated Dean's arrival into the world with open hostility. I don't know why, but Dean was never given the love and affection that was bestowed upon his brother by these individuals.

'Fergus continued to drink and I grew increasingly fearful for not only my own safety but also the children's and so I instigated divorce proceedings. As well as granting me a divorce, the court put a restraining order on Fergus, which meant that he couldn't have any contact whatsoever with me or the children.

'It's hard to describe what Dean was like growing up. He used to get a buzz out of causing trouble, but he was also an extremely nervous person. There was no way that he would upset anybody unless he had a good head start and plenty of places to run and hide. I have known Dean fall out with people in our street and become so scared he wouldn't answer the door for days. If I went out of the house for more than ten minutes, Dean would go mad at me for leaving him alone.

'Whatever he did to people or whoever he upset, Dean had no sense of guilt whatsoever. If he got caught doing anything wrong, he would deny it regardless and act as if nothing had happened.

'Despite his numerous faults, Dean was very loving towards me and would do anything I asked of him. Wherever he was, he would always keep in touch and never forget my birthday or other special occasions.

'Unfortunately, Dean did like to be associated with "hard men" and "faces", but he was certainly not one himself. I suppose he liked the idea of people looking up to him, and he felt safe and secure in the company of so-called tough guys. I used to joke with him by saying that he was a whinger and not a ninja.

'His problems began when he started at Nicholas School in Laindon, Basildon. Dean got involved with the wrong crowd and ended up falling out with them because they tended to bully him. Dean harboured an immense feeling of injustice following one particular incident at school and that remained with him. Somebody had deliberately loosened the nuts that held on the front wheel of a boy's bicycle and, riding home, the boy was thrown in front of a vehicle when the wheel came off. Fortunately, he was not seriously injured. The police called at our house and initially blamed Dean, saying that he could be facing an attempted murder charge. They really did intimidate and scare Dean; he was sick with worry for days. A week later, the police were told that another boy was responsible, but they didn't take the time to come and apologise to Dean. It may not seem like a big deal when you compare it to what goes on in the world these days, but it troubled Dean for as long as I can recall.

'When Dean was growing up, he was always up to mischief. I can remember him as a young kid cooking chips for himself. He wouldn't fry them in the chip pan; he used to put them in a saucepan with a whole tub of butter. When he had finished his culinary masterpiece, he would pour the whole pan of melted butter down the sink and I would spend the rest of the day trying to unblock it.

'Dean absolutely loved the film *Grease* and would watch a video of the film he had over and over again. He would sing along with Olivia Newton John and John Travolta whilst prancing around the living room. If the film or any of the songs come on the television now, I have to switch it off. It really upsets me.

'Dean's greatest love – apart from pretty girls, that is – was always cars. When he was a young boy, I used to take him to the banger racing at Essex Arena. He used to get really excited watching the cars flash past and then crash into one another.

'At the age of 14, Dean appeared in court for the first time after he had been caught attempting to steal a car which he had been intent on racing. The magistrate lectured Dean about the effect of his criminality on not only himself but also the long-suffering local community. He was conditionally discharged and given a £20 fine. Dean didn't take any notice of the magistrate, his lecture or the plight of the wider community and continued to live his life as before.

'I contacted social services because I had become increasingly concerned about Dean's involvement in petty crime. As a result of me doing this, he was put into care for two months. I thought this course of action would succeed where the magistrate had previously failed and make him see the error of his ways. I couldn't have been more wrong. When Dean returned home, he continued to commit crime as before and he ignored my pleas for him to behave.

'After two further court appearances for burglary and theft, for which he was given supervision orders, Dean announced that he wanted to move out of the Basildon area and start his young life anew. I soon found out that this almost miraculous change of heart was not as a result of Dean seeing the light. To my dismay, I learned that I was not the only one who was tiring of my son's disruptive and antisocial behaviour. Local teenagers had been beating him up and bullying him and he soon became too scared to leave home.

'A local couple I had befriended told me that they too were fed up of life in Basildon and were moving to Leeds to run a pub. They were aware of the problems that my son had created for himself and suggested that Dean could, if he wished, move to Leeds with them. They offered to teach Dean the pub trade and said that when he was old enough they would employ him. Dean feared that some or all of the many people that he had upset in Basildon would soon catch up with him, so he jumped at the chance and almost pleaded to go. It was blatantly obvious that Dean had no future in Essex and so, reluctantly, I agreed to let him leave home.

'Within a fortnight of moving, Dean was assaulted by my friend's husband. The couple had been quarrelling and Dean had become distressed and tried to step in to calm things down. In a rage, the husband had then attacked and strangled Dean, who was later taken to a child-protection unit by police. The following morning I was contacted by social services, who told me what had happened. I wanted Dean to return home, but they said that he had indicated that he wished to remain in Leeds. Approximately one week later, I was informed that Dean had been placed in a foster home. I was told that the man who Dean had gone to live with had a son of his own and was deeply religious. After all that had happened to Dean, I wanted to know that he was happy and safe, so I travelled to Yorkshire and stayed with him for two weeks.

'Free from any threat of violence, Dean appeared to be really happy. He told me that despite initial concerns about his foster parent being a devout Christian he had turned out to be really OK. He said that the man didn't preach religion to him and generally treated him well. I asked Dean to return to Essex with me, but he was adamant that he wished to remain in Yorkshire. Once a month, Dean would travel down to Basildon to visit me.

A MOTHER'S TALE: BEVERLEY BOSHELL

'Occasionally, he would be alone, but more often than not he would have other lads or a female "friend" in tow. One time, he arrived with a young girl named Sam, who was heavily pregnant. Dean told me that he was the father and the girl was too scared of her parents to return home. He begged me to let her stay until he had sorted out accommodation for his new family. Thinking this was my future daughter-in-law and grandchild, I was more than happy to welcome her into my home. As soon as the girl had unpacked her bag, Dean disappeared back to Leeds to "sort things out". Within a few days, the girl, who was very timid, told me that Dean wasn't, in fact, the father, but he had promised to help her. I was naturally shocked and annoyed, but I soon mellowed. That was Dean all over; he had agreed to help the girl after hearing about her situation, even though it really wasn't his problem. Sam remained at my home until she gave birth to a son and then she returned to live in Leeds.

'Dean moved from one address and from one female to another whilst in Yorkshire. His unquestionable good nature was only tarnished by his inability to keep out of trouble, most of which was motor-vehicle related. By the time he was 18, Dean had accumulated no less than 22 criminal convictions and inevitably was sent to jail.

'He was sentenced to serve 15 months in a young offenders' institute, but like all previous punishments, it failed to have the desired effect.

'I wasn't aware that Dean had been imprisoned; he would never talk to me about any trouble that he was in because he said he didn't want to worry me. I would learn about his exploits second-hand, or by the appearance of police officers on my doorstep who were trying to trace him. As soon as Dean was released from custody he returned to his old ways, using other people's cars as taxis and committing the occasional burglary when he ran short of money. Like a lot of young boys, I guess he thought he was being clever, or a bit of a Jack the Lad. He came to visit me in a stolen car on one occasion. As he climbed back into it to leave with his three friends, a police car turned into the road where I live. Thinking the police were in pursuit of him, Dean jumped out of the car and ran, followed closely by his friends. The police officers realised something was not quite right, radioed for assistance and quickly rounded up all four of them. Dean was put into the back of the police car, so I went out to speak to him. It was snowing heavily, and I had no shoes or socks on, but I was desperate to check that he was OK. A female friend of Dean's, who had also been arrested, was in the car with him and she was protesting loudly about her treatment. She told the officers that they had no right to arrest her as she had not been driving and she had left her baby alone at her home in Leeds. One of the officers turned to me and said, "You're the grandmother – get yourself on a train up to Leeds and sort her baby out now!" I laughed and told him that, as far as I knew, I wasn't anybody's grandmother! I had enough problems of my own without adopting the waifs and strays of Leeds.

'I offered to go down to the police station to make sure Dean was OK, but he insisted I should remain at home, adding, "I will sort things myself, Mum, and let you know the outcome."

'I didn't see or hear from Dean for approximately two months. I assumed he had either been imprisoned or had returned to Leeds with his friends. Then one day, out of the blue, Dean knocked on my front door, said that he had left Leeds for good and wanted to move back in with me. Things between us were OK at first, but we fell out when Dean stole a brand-new stack-system stereo from my home. I had only just purchased it; in fact, it was still in the box. I put it in my lounge, popped out to the shops and when I returned it had gone.

'A neighbour told me that she had seen Dean carrying boxes from my home to an address around the corner on three separate occasions. I went around to the house and demanded that they return my stereo, but the occupants denied having it or even having seen Dean that day. I was absolutely devastated by what Dean had done. I told him I wanted my property back or I would call the police, but he refused to return it.

'With a heavy heart, I did inform the police and Dean was arrested. When questioned, he admitted that he had taken my stereo, but he refused to say what he had done with it. When he appeared at Basildon Crown Court, he was given a meagre financial penalty. Sending Dean to prison was, the wise and learned judge decreed, a waste of time. Whenever Dean was imprisoned, he used to write to me and say that life inside was like being on a holiday camp. Some of the establishments that Dean had spent "vacations" in were equipped with swimming pools, tennis courts and gymnasiums. In his cell, Dean claimed, he had a television, a variety of computer games and a PlayStation. If they had made prison a little tougher, he and others like him might not have been so keen to return.

'Dean never valued anything material. If I bought him jewellery, he would either sell it or give it away, and if there was a television or PlayStation around he would unscrew it and fiddle about with all the bits. Rarely was he able to put them back together again, so he would just bin the components.

A MOTHER'S TALE: BEVERLEY BOSHELL

'The last letter I ever received from Dean was sent in 1999. He was in HMP Chelmsford at the time, where I believe he met Damon Alvin, the drug dealer who drove Dean to the place where he was murdered. The letter is filled with regret about his relationship with me, his love for others and, sadly, his hope for a decent future.'

> Dear Mum,
>
> Well, how are you? As for me, I am OK. Well, we ain't spoken now for six years. I said I am sorry for what happened. I don't want nothing off you, but I would like my daughter, Lauren, to know her nan. Well, she is four now, she had her birthday party last month. We hired a bouncy castle for the day.
>
> She was born on 18 September. She is still at playschool. If she was born two weeks earlier, she would be at infant's. She looks a lot like me when I was a kid, but she won't end up like me. She is the most loveliest kid, apart from she still has a stammer all the time.
>
> Well, if you would like any photos of her, let me know, but please get in touch. It's been six years now and a lot has happened since then.
>
> Love,
>
> Dean

'I did reply to Dean, because I thought that at last he was turning his life around, but by the time my letter arrived at the prison he had been released.

'My hope that Dean had finally fallen in love and settled down with a girl was dashed within weeks. Dean came to see me in a really flash car, which I now know was owned by Damon Alvin. He was with a pretty girl with dark hair. Dean told me that he was living near Southend seafront, a place he had always loved. We didn't get to speak alone that day, which I will regret until my dying day. There was so much I wanted to ask him about his daughter and the new life he had talked about in his letter. Unfortunately, that same day Dean stole £400 from his brother Wayne by forging his signature on a cheque and withdrawing the cash from his bank account. The next time I saw Dean we had a terrible argument over this and he walked away from me. Two weeks later, he turned up at my home as though nothing had happened.

'Dean's couldn't-care-less attitude enraged me. I shouted at him for what he had done and uttered the last words that I was ever to say to him: "Piss off, Dean. I want nothing more to do with you and, as far as I am concerned, you are not my son."

'I torture myself with the thought that maybe, if I had held my tongue, my son would still be here now. I cannot put into words the pain those words cause me today. We all say things we don't mean to those we love, but the person we say them to doesn't usually get murdered before we can make amends. Dean did come to my home a few times after that, but he never knocked on my door. He would pull up outside the house in a car so that I could see him through the kitchen window. As soon as he knew that I had caught sight of him, he would drive off. I think it was his way of saying, "Look, Mum, I am OK, don't worry."

'Any mother knows just what a foolish sentiment "don't worry" is. I worried about Dean every time he left my sight. I still worry about the circumstances in which he died. I was told that he did not die instantly. What haunts me, what worries me sick, is wondering what his final thoughts were, as some bastard was murdering him. I wonder what he was feeling and whether he was thinking of me. I hope he was; I want his last thoughts to have been of those who loved him, because we will never stop thinking of him.

'On the day that I heard Dean had been murdered, the police appointed a family liaison officer to keep me informed of any progress in their investigation. Unfortunately, they never did seem to have much, if any, information to pass on to me. I was told that it was likely Dean's killers would be at his funeral because more often than not people who commit murder do attend their victim's service. When it was over, I asked if any of the suspects had attended, but I was told that they had not.

'The police said that they knew in their own minds who had shot Dean, but they also said they could not do anything about it because they had no proof. No names of suspects were ever given to me. I still feel let down and frustrated by the lack of information I received from the police during their investigation. I know and accept that some material that might have been of evidential value could not be disclosed, but I was left feeling confused, isolated and unimportant.

'The police didn't seem to make any significant progress with their inquiries for the two years following the murder. There had been several arrests, but the people concerned had all been released without charge shortly afterwards. I only found out about these occasional developments through reading the local newspaper or from journalists ringing me for my reaction to the latest news. But then three long years after Dean's death, a £5,000 reward was offered by police to members of the public for information about the murder. Shortly afterwards, four people were arrested. The police wouldn't give me the names of those they had in custody, but they did say they were positive that they had the right *people* – not person. Two were being questioned about a conspiracy to pervert the course of justice and a third was being held for murdering Dean. They wouldn't say what the fourth person had been arrested for, but I formed the impression that it was to do with the murder rather than the conspiracy.

'I only heard that Dean's old prison cellmate Damon Alvin was the one who had been charged with Dean's murder a few months before his trial began. I felt a strange need to see him. I wanted to know what a cold-blooded killer would look like. I wanted to see the bastard who had taken my Dean's life. You think to yourself that somebody accused of something so evil is going to look really sinister or give off some sort of bad vibe to show that he is not a normal person. I suppose I had prepared myself to be confronted by some sort of monster. I was therefore surprised when Alvin was identified to me and I saw that he was just a normal-looking young man. I have to admit that I felt disappointed and somewhat confused. My rising anger collapsed into an avalanche of questions. Why would he do this? How did he do it? Did he mean to do it?

'For the first week of his trial, the barristers were locked in a fierce debate about evidence the prosecution wished to introduce into the case but which the defence objected to. Ironically, this evidence turned out to have been generated by Dean. I was shocked to learn that he had been a registered police informant and over a couple of years had been giving information to the police about Alvin, and that this may have been the motive for his murder. Eventually the judge ruled that the evidence could be presented to the jury. The defence barristers looked devastated by the ruling. The case was adjourned and nothing happened for six to eight weeks. Then I was informed by police that Damon Alvin had decided to become a supergrass.

'The prosecution had taken a witness statement from Alvin, dropped the murder charge against him and then charged his friend Ricky Percival with killing Dean instead. Alvin, the sinner had become Alvin, the saint – and the main prosecution witness – overnight. The police seemed delighted; they told me that they had now got what they had been hoping for. Despite the fact that they had originally charged Alvin with Dean's murder, they said that they had known all along that it had not been him. It was Percival who had pulled the trigger and murdered Dean, they said. It was explained to me that the police had been hoping that if Alvin thought that he was going to get a life sentence he would inform on Percival to save his own skin. They said that they had no evidence against Percival for the murder without Alvin's help, and so thankfully it had worked out the way they had planned.

'To be totally honest, I found this explanation and the tactics employed very worrying and began to wonder if Alvin might have been guilty and had turned supergrass just to escape a life sentence. If they knew for a fact that it was Percival who had murdered Dean, they must have had evidence in order to form that opinion. It follows that if the evidence against Percival did exist, why hadn't they charged him? Without the evidence, I couldn't understand how they could claim to know anything for certain. Any person facing a life sentence that has been given the identity of the alleged guilty party and who is then asked to name that party in return for freedom is eventually bound to repeat the name to save himself. I am not comfortable with a judicial system that operates by putting guns to people's heads to extract confessions.

'Once Percival's trial had begun and Alvin had testified against him, I did wonder, what if Percival did more or less the same as Alvin, and blamed him for the murder? Surely, the case against Percival would collapse? I would be back at square one and nobody would be convicted. It was such an unusual scenario, supported by nothing other than Alvin's word. I began to think that Alvin and Percival might have even planned the whole thing so both would escape prosecution.

'Regardless of who was actually guilty of murdering Dean, the police were unable to give me a clear motive for his death. I have repeatedly asked the detectives who were working on the case why it happened, but they told me that they didn't know why my son was killed. At Alvin's trial, it was suggested that Dean had been murdered because he was a registered police informant. When Percival was on trial, they said that Dean had met his death simply because Percival had lost his temper that night over a gun he couldn't find. The third motive, which was given to me by a police officer "off the record", suggested that Percival had been losing face amongst his criminal associates at that particular time and he had done it simply to show that he was still a man to be feared. All three theories raise more questions in my mind than they answer.

'Before Percival's trial got under way, I asked the police if any distressing images of my son would be shown in court, as I didn't wish to have anything upsetting sprung on me. I was assured that although images did exist of Dean in death, and that they would form part of the evidence, there was no way I would be able to see them from the public gallery. My only experience of murder trials had been gleaned from Hollywood movies and television programmes like *The Bill* and so I wasn't sure what to expect. During the first week of the trial, as one of the barristers stood up to address the jury, he began turning over photographs of the crime scene in an evidence book.

'I gasped in horror as I saw images of my son's blood-soaked body staring straight at me. Photographs of him lying in the mud, bathed in his own blood, and of him being butchered on a mortuary slab, were for ever etched in my mind. I couldn't get up and walk out of the court, as I didn't dare interrupt the proceedings, and so I just sat there, trying to avert my gaze. By the time the court stopped for a break that day, it was too late to move seats; all of the images had been exhibited. I hope and pray that no mother will ever have to sit through what I endured that day, but I fear in this day and age many more will.

'At the end of the trial, Ricky Percival was convicted of murdering Dean and was sentenced to life imprisonment. His friend, Kevin Walsh, was convicted of conspiring to pervert the course of justice because he gave him a false alibi. Walsh was sentenced to three years' imprisonment. His ex-girlfriend, Kate Griffiths, was found not guilty of the same charge. Damon Alvin was given a pat on the back and offered all of the help available to assist him in walking away and starting a new life for himself and his family. I have no thoughts on Kevin Walsh. As for Percival, I thought he sat through the entire trial as if he didn't give a damn about what might happen. I thought that he would be terrified, but he didn't take the proceedings seriously at all. I got the impression that he thought the trial was a load of crap that didn't involve him. I believe he really thought he was going home, not to prison. When he was found guilty, I expected him to lose his temper after all I had heard about him, but he stood motionless, cool as a cucumber, as though what was happening wasn't real. I didn't think he would be convicted because there were a lot of unanswered questions, and a lot of answers that should have been challenged but were not. I don't think Alvin's evidence was explored in depth because the prosecution did not want to really test his story.

'You cannot publish what I really think of Damon Alvin. Because he had been charged with the murder and spent a year on remand awaiting trial he had an intimate knowledge of the case from reading all of the paperwork. It was too easy for him to make up a convincing story to fit the available evidence without implicating himself. Plain and simple, Alvin has got away with murder and he is laughing at us all.

'He admits that he had involvement in my son's death; he knew what was going on that night, yet the police have treated him like Lord Muck. After watching my son being executed, Alvin says that he left the scene, went home, ate a Chinese meal and went to bed, where he enjoyed a good night's sleep. What sort of callous animal could do that? The trial left me more confused than I had been before it started.

'I want answers about the night my son died and the events that led up to it. It's hard to move forward when your mind and soul are imprisoned in the past.'

• • •

Throughout her long and detailed story, Beverley broke down many times. I cannot help but feel sorry for her and the pain she continues to endure. The courts have convicted Percival, but, as you will read, it's more than likely that conviction will be overturned and the case will remain unsolved. For that reason, I too hope that this book will help to answer the questions Beverley has about her son, because I do not believe she will hear the truth elsewhere.

Beverley Boshell is a fine lady who accepts she has made mistakes. None of us goes through life blameless and we all have to live with the burden of regret. The mistakes Beverley made can never be rectified and the regret that eats away at her intensifies with time rather than diminishes.

Dean, the end product of many of Beverley's mistakes, paid a terrible price for the lifestyle he chose. His troubles are now over. However, Beverley, like all mothers whose sons immerse themselves in the world of drugs and guns, continues to pay the price for his foolishness on a daily basis. Please don't judge her too harshly.

2

A MOTHER'S TALE: SANDY PERCIVAL

Friday, 24 August 2007 I am in Leigh-on-Sea to talk to Sandy Percival, whose son Ricky has been convicted of the murder of Dean Boshell, among other matters. Having arrived in the village with two hours to spare, I decide to take a walk along the seafront to kill time.

Leigh-on-Sea stands on the north shore of the Thames River, just 30 miles from London, in the borough of Southend. Voted in 2006 by the readers of the London *Evening Standard* as the best place to live in the south-east of England, Leigh-on-Sea, for most of its long history, has been primarily a fishing village. It is a pretty, unspoilt middle-class area – hardly the setting for a story about drug dealing, armed robbery, maiming and murder.

A narrow, cobbled footpath leads me from the main street down to the sea. The tide is out and small boats lie stranded on their sides in the mud. An abundance of cockle sheds, small market-like stalls and two public houses are receiving deliveries for the tide of day-trippers that will soon arrive. I walk to St Clement's Church; for more than 100 years, it has stood on the cliffs that overlook the Thames Estuary. A brief stroll around the cemetery in search of old friends reveals that one local resident had lived in the village until the ripe old age of 119. 'Here lies the body of Mary Ellis,' her tombstone reads. 'She was a virgin of virtuous courage and very promising hope, and died on the 3rd of June 1609.'

If correct, this would make Mary Ellis one of the few virgins in Essex and the oldest person in UK history, her closest rival for the title being Charlotte Hughes, who died at the tender age of 115 years old. Perhaps it was the sea air that kept virtuous Mary going, or more likely the laid-back atmosphere that engulfs the village and its inhabitants.

On the High Street, I notice that the shops tend to be owned and run by traditional local traders. It really was refreshing to see a row of shops with character rather than the usual brand-name clones that sell the same items in every one of their stores.

Sitting in the Terracotta Tearooms on Leigh Broadway, enjoying a much-needed break, it feels as if I have been transported back to some bygone age. The middle-class clientele, a mixture of guys who look like lawyers and sweetly scented females who are doing their best to mimic footballers' wives, chat amongst themselves about the weather, their plans for the forthcoming weekend and their numerous purchases from the nearby boutiques and stores. Pleasant, that's what I keep thinking, as I sit sipping my morning tea. This place is really fucking pleasant.

Picking up the local newspaper, I read that a campaign has been launched to save the local shops because high rents and rates are threatening to close many of them down, the fear being that they will be replaced by the high-street giants or, worse still, an out-of-town superstore. One disgruntled resident supporting the 'save our Leigh-on-Sea' campaign had written to the editor claiming that he would not use one of the larger nearby town's shopping centres because they were full of 'lowlifes', 'benefit scroungers', 'dirty alcoholics, lying on the footpaths' and 'groups of students, sitting in places, spending nothing and taking up all of the seating'. Clearly outraged by the very thought of Leigh-on-Sea losing its old-world charm, the author of the letter went on to suggest that councillors intent on spoiling the atmosphere of the village should be shot.

In another section of the newspaper I read that the residents were equally outraged by an influx of sexual thrill-seekers who were using an area just behind the railway station to meet like-minded deviants in an activity that has come to be known as dogging. Complete strangers meet in public places and fornicate with one another's wives and girlfriends, or watch as others do so. This particular group of people had been spared the suggestion of being shot by the readership of the newspaper, but the method suggested to bring about their demise was equally unpleasant.

I begin to wonder if Leigh-on-Sea is such a friendly place after all. I settle my bill and then check the street outside for scantily clad couples in cars and gun-toting 'not-so-happy' shoppers before making my way to my vehicle.

A MOTHER'S TALE: SANDY PERCIVAL

The Percival home is just a short drive from Leigh Broadway. En route, I pass the first purpose-built police station in the Chelmsford area. I cross the busy A13 London road with caution and drive past the allotments where Dean Boshell met his death. Less than 100 yards away, I turn into a very respectable-looking road that is lined with neat houses and well-kept gardens. Halfway along that road I park my car and walk towards the Percival home. Before I can reach the door to knock, Sandy Percival opens it and invites me into the kitchen, where husband David, eldest son Danny and friend Kevin Walsh are sitting.

Today has been a particularly emotional day for Sandy. Kevin, the man who stood alongside her son Ricky in the dock, is on home leave from prison. He was sentenced to three and a half years for conspiring to pervert the course of justice. Despite his denials, he was convicted of giving Sandy's son a false alibi on the night Dean died. Seeing Kevin sitting in her home without Ricky is clearly difficult for Sandy. She cries every time her son is mentioned. After Kevin announces that he is leaving with Danny and his father, there are more tears from her.

When Sandy and I eventually sit down to talk at a large family-sized table in the kitchen, I become acutely aware of just how empty such a once-vibrant house must feel for her without her son. 'Ricky was in and out throughout the day,' Sandy tells me. 'He would be running around with the dog, who he loved, or laughing and joking with friends in his room. He didn't drink or smoke because he enjoyed going to the gym and keeping fit, but that didn't stop him having fun. He loved being around his family and friends; material things meant little or nothing to him, it was all about family for Ricky.'

An aura of sadness surrounds Sandy Percival. She tries hard to be upbeat, positive and occasionally jovial, but her eyes betray her. Welling up every few minutes, Sandy is clearly finding it hard to come to terms with the events of the last six or seven years. 'Do you want another cup of tea, Bernie?' is a question she asks often. It's not that I appear thirsty or have ever claimed to have particularly enjoyed her tea, although I must say it isn't bad. Sandy asks the question often, I assume, because it allows her time to compose herself, turn away from me towards the sink and wipe the tears from her eyes.

Any young man who thinks that crime is glamorous need only spend time with Beverley Boshell or Sandy Percival. They are living proof that neither the guilty nor the innocent, the victim nor the criminal, ever wins. Young, impressionable fools punch, kick, stab and shoot their way to the top of the gangland heap before the courts send them to prison or a bullet sends them to an early grave. The lifestyle chosen by all the young men in this story has only spawned one thing: losers.

The only time that Sandy appears to be happy is when she is talking about her distant past. Times when David, Danny and Ricky were home and their only troubles were the type that all families face in life.

'I met my husband David 40 years ago in the East End of London,' she says. 'David was bringing home £9 a week when we first married, which doesn't seem like a lot now, but it kept a roof over our heads at the time.

'We were from Upton Park, near the West Ham United Football Club ground, but we eventually moved to nearby Manor Park in the London borough of Newham, which sounds a lot grander than it actually is, but David and I were really happy there. After we had married and set up home together, we had our first son, who we named Danny. Six years later, our second son, Ricky, was born. David and I worked hard to provide for our children. We had our ups and downs, as everybody does in life, but we loved one another dearly throughout and faced whatever difficulties life threw at us as one. Growing up in the East End, you have a natural resistance to hardship instilled into you. The people who live in that part of London are so down to earth. In times of trouble, they will tell you that there is always somebody worse off than yourself and tomorrow things will be much better. It's not very often that advice is proven to be wrong.

'Danny fitted in well when he started school, but Ricky had problems, which we found out stemmed from him being dyslexic. This is a very frustrating condition that few people know much about. The most common view held about dyslexics is that they are thick. The truth is that dyslexia has nothing whatsoever to do with mental ability, or lack of it. It occurs at all levels of intelligence – average, above average and highly gifted.

'When Ricky started school, he struggled with the positioning of letters. He couldn't distinguish a "p" from a "d", or a "d" from a "b". "Was" became "saw", "pet" was read as "bet". Even in senior school, he was reading things like "nuclear" as "unclear". School became a nightmare of frustration for Ricky.

'Teachers who failed to recognise his problem thought that he was lazy, slow or not trying hard enough. This led to him being punished, which understandably made him resent everything about school. I am not blaming the school or the teachers for Ricky's problems, because dyslexia was not really recognised back then.

'When Ricky was eight years old, we took the agonising decision to leave London and move to Leigh-on-Sea. The influx of foreign nationals into his school in London meant that teachers were trying to cope with non-English-speaking pupils, and so Ricky's dyslexia was almost ignored. The teachers did their best to assist everybody, but they simply didn't have enough time. We found a school in Leigh-on-Sea that was prepared to offer him some assistance, providing one-hour sessions of one-to-one tuition in an effort to try and help him.

'The teacher who worked with Ricky regularly described him as being the perfect pupil and a well-behaved boy. Unfortunately, all of the other time he spent in school was in a normal classroom environment and this led to him becoming frustrated, understandably bored and, as a consequence of that, disruptive. Ricky has always been one to voice his opinion and the constant disputes he was having with staff at his school resulted in a complete breakdown of communication between him and them. When Ricky was 15, it was agreed by all parties that it would be better if he sought employment rather than continue at school.

'Ricky started work at a local fresh-fish shop, which involved him getting up in the early hours of the morning and working for long hours in extremely cold and damp conditions. I didn't like him having to do the work he was asked to do, but he thought anything was preferable to school. My husband had always kept himself in shape training and, as the boys were growing up, he taught them to do the same.

'Aged eight, Danny began to attend kick-boxing and martial arts lessons. He was, by all accounts, very good at both. So much so, Danny was billed to appear at York Hall in Bethnal Green in one of the preliminary fights before the main event: a Thai kick-boxing bout for the British championship title. The reigning champion's opponent didn't turn up that night for some reason and, rather than disappoint the crowd, Danny was chosen to stand in for him. Despite being knocked down twice, Danny gave a good account of himself, and lost on a disputed points decision. Everybody was saying that he was good enough to become a professional and Danny went on to prove them right.

'Like most boys, Ricky looked up to his elder brother and wanted to be just like him. With his father's encouragement, Ricky too began training. He was careful about what he ate and religiously attended the gym. When he wasn't working out, he was doing what all kids do – playing out in the street or running around in the park. He did get into mischief and this attracted the attention of the police.

'Respect isn't given, it's earned, and respect has always been high on Ricky's list of priorities. If people were well mannered and polite in his company, he would be absolutely charming and hospitable in return. If people chose to be rude and ignorant, he would treat them with the contempt he felt they deserved. The police, unfortunately, were often sarcastic, rude and abusive when dealing with Ricky and this caused quite a lot of ill feeling between them and him.

'I remember two officers calling at our home to speak to Ricky about him handling stolen goods. When they knocked on the door, Ricky answered and invited them both inside. The officers questioned Ricky about some cheap stolen goods that he had sold to a man and he readily admitted that he was responsible. Looking at Ricky in disbelief, one of the officers said, "I really am surprised by the reception you have given us, Ricky. Everybody told us that we would get nothing but grief off you." Ricky looked a bit confused and replied, "Why would I want to be rude to you when you have been nothing but polite to me?" It really was that simple with Ricky; he couldn't understand why people chose to be rude and, if they were, he would not tolerate it.

'The turning point in Ricky's life, for many reasons, was the murder of Kevin Walsh's older brother, Malcolm. Ricky was only a teenager at the time and he had never experienced somebody close to him dying. He had become friendly with Malcolm, who was much older than him, because they used to attend the same gym and knew the same people. When Ricky bumped into the family of the man who had killed Malcolm, he shouted and swore at them. It was nothing serious, even the police said it was just anguish and frustration. A year after Malcolm's death, three people connected to his killer were shot and Ricky was arrested. My son wasn't involved, but the general consensus around Southend was that there was no such thing as smoke without fire. A lot of people genuinely believed that Ricky had shot those people simply because he had been arrested for it.

'He wasn't charged with anything, but his relationship with the police deteriorated further because of this and younger people started talking about Ricky as if he was some sort of gangster. Years later, when he was charged with murdering Dean Boshell, this ridiculous, unwelcome and undeserved reputation that he had been given over the shootings helped to get him convicted. I have honestly never met, seen or spoken to Dean Boshell, so I fail to see how he could have been any sort of real friend of Ricky's.

'I felt sad, like everybody else did around here, when his body was found just down the road on the allotments. I never suspected for one moment that my son could have been involved; he certainly never spoke or seemed concerned about the murder in the weeks and months after it had happened. Mothers know if something is troubling their children and I know that around that time Ricky was not acting out of the ordinary or in any other way suspicious. To this day, I refuse to believe that my son took that boy's life and if I did find out that he had I would not stand by him. I couldn't.

'This may sound callous, but when the police first asked Ricky and everybody else who knew Dean Boshell to make a statement about their knowledge of him, Ricky didn't seem one bit bothered. If he had been involved in the murder, I know that he would have been sick with worry. What human being wouldn't be?

'The morning the police came to arrest Ricky for the murder was one of the worst of my life. Both my husband and I had guns put to our heads. Danny, who hadn't been home long after a work's party in London, was dragged from his bed naked. Five officers armed with machine guns stood outside the front of the house; thirty officers conducted a fingertip search of our garden and neighbours' gardens and another twenty officers searched the house. They even drilled holes in our floorboards and put remote-controlled cameras down them, so they could see what was underneath. It really was ridiculous, considering Ricky wasn't even home and the murder had taken place years earlier.

'The general behaviour of the police that day was so over the top that one of our neighbours wrote to police headquarters and complained. They did not complain about Ricky or anybody else in our family; they were annoyed about the way the police had conducted themselves. The people in our street won't have a bad word said about Ricky; they know that he has been wrongfully convicted of these crimes.

'When Ricky heard that the police were looking for him, he didn't run away because he had nothing to hide. He telephoned the police station and asked for a convenient time for the officers involved in the case to meet him. When an appointment had been arranged, he walked into the police station with his brother Danny and was promptly arrested.

'I think that storming our home like that was both pointless and vindictive. After Ricky's former friend, Damon Alvin, blamed him for the murder that he had been initially charged with, I sat through the trial that followed in total disbelief. The man the prosecution were talking about was not my son. It was lie after lie after lie: the facts were twisted and countless stories were invented to paint the required picture. At one of the first hearings, the facts became so distorted that a member of the defence team got to her feet, threw her hands in the air in despair and asked out loud if she was in a court of law. That isn't a common event and so I know that it wasn't just me wondering what the hell was going on. I won't deny there were things I heard about my son that I didn't like and wasn't happy about, but there was absolutely no evidence whatsoever produced to link my son to the murder of Dean Boshell and the other matters he was charged with. Everything hinged on the word of Damon, who had been given access to all of the case papers and who had a year in which to come up with his story. Damon is an intelligent man and so I'm sure it wasn't hard for him to think up a plausible case against Ricky that fitted the available evidence. I wasn't in court to hear the verdict. I couldn't go: the very thought of Ricky going to prison for life was breaking my heart.

'It was Kevin Walsh's sister, Michelle, who telephoned me and gave me the news. Don't ask me what I said or what I did when she said Ricky's been found guilty because the weeks that followed are a fog of tears and uncontrollable grief. I fell apart. I can't describe it any other way. So much evidence had been "lost" or proven to be false or non-existent in court that I was convinced that there was no way on earth that Ricky could be convicted of anything. I think the total lack of evidence makes it that much harder to deal with. How could the jury not see what everybody else in that room could see and hear? There was something just not right about the whole process.

'Looking back on the case, even if somebody else had admitted that they had committed the crimes I don't think Ricky could have been found not guilty. Even after Ricky was convicted things appeared to have been rehearsed. There was no adjournment to consider what sentence he would be given; it was just read out there and then. People in court said it seemed as if the judge was reading from a prepared statement, but that would mean that he knew the verdict before the jury had given it. I'm sure there's absolutely no way that could happen in this country.

'Going to visit Ricky in prison is soul destroying. We try to put on a brave face for each other, but neither of us can hide our pain when it's time to say goodbye. Going home isn't even like going home any more, if that makes sense. The police had listened in to our private phone calls for months before Ricky was arrested; I still think that our home is bugged now. I loved this house, but, after what the police have done here, it doesn't feel like ours any more.

'My thoughts about our future are moulded by our past. We have decided that we are going to move and start anew when Ricky comes home.

'I have used those words again: "the past". They are the two words that dominate my day, my thoughts and my dreams. The past is all I long for. It's a time when this nightmare didn't exist and I was surrounded by my family. Dare I think about the future?

'I will when Ricky's appeal is granted and the vast amount of new evidence that has been uncovered is presented to the court to secure his release. Because of the fresh evidence that this book has unearthed that day might not be too far away, and that thought alone gives me hope and the strength to keep going.

'The police held a press conference after the trial and said that they were pleased the case was over. I want everybody involved in wrongly convicting my son to know that this case is far from over: in fact, it's just beginning. This case will only be closed when the truth about the matters my son has been convicted of have been laid bare, and Ricky walks back through my front door.'

3

CLOWNS AND ACID TRIPS

Southend seafront's neon-lit landscape is somewhere between hell and a down-at-heel Las Vegas. Like its vastly superior and more glamorous American equivalent, Southend has for many years been the haunt of delinquents, the deranged and anybody else trying to make a name for themselves in the thriving Essex underworld, where life is all about the paper chase. That is: hard cash.

During the 1980s and 1990s, gangs led by men such as Tony Tucker, Mickey Roman and Malcolm Walsh would spend their ill-gotten gains in the numerous bars and nightclubs that litter the area that once adjoined Southend Pier. Tucker and Walsh have since been murdered, Roman blew his own brains out with a handgun, and Southend Pier, once the world's largest, sank beneath the waves after being destroyed by fire in October 2005. These days the gangs, mainly Burberry-clad chavs, loiter with intent around the Adventure Island theme park, revelling in the fact that their town, their county, is considered by many to be the baddest of Britain's most notorious badlands. If you dare to ask these snarling morons what it's like to be an Essex boy, they will proudly boast that, according to legend, Essex is such a magnificent place to be born it was originally chosen by God to be the birthplace of Jesus. Unfortunately, due to its lack of virgins and wise men, God was forced to abandon his dream of bestowing such a coveted title upon his only son and ended up making last-minute arrangements for his debut appearance in Bethlehem. Into this make-believe environment, where visions of grandiose and false hope are the norm, emerged the ultimate wannabe: Damon Alvin.

At the tender age of ten, he was already out of control and had been arrested by the police for arson. Aged 14, he had put away his matches and progressed to committing commercial burglaries, a trade he excelled in. When Alvin left school at the age of 15, he also left home, because he 'was bored'. The sparkle that lit up his dreary life of crime came in the form of a man several years his senior named Malcolm Walsh.

Alvin had got to know Walsh through Malcolm's younger brother, Kevin. They both attended Our Lady of Lourdes Catholic School on Manchester Drive, Leigh-on-Sea. Alvin would often visit Kevin's home after school and it was during these visits that Alvin met and became acquainted with Malcolm. Despite the fact that Alvin was just eleven years of age and Malcolm was seven years his senior, members of the Walsh family have described the pair as inseparable.

Having left school with no job and few prospects, Alvin moved into Malcolm and his wife Bernadette's flat in Southend. The product of Irish parents, Malcolm was by no means perfect; he was well known to the police and rumoured to be one of Southend's major drug barons. For many years, Malcolm had been involved in committing burglaries, and during the hours of darkness he taught Alvin everything he knew about his unscrupulous trade.

One night Alvin and Walsh broke into a chemist's shop on Hamlet Court Road, Westcliff-on-Sea. They gained entry to the premises by climbing the fire-exit stairs to the roof and hacking through a fire door with an axe. Once inside, they began to fill two large rubbish bags with Walkman CD players, perfume and anything else they thought they might be able to sell. Whilst they were in the process of filling the bags, a police car pulled up outside and two officers got out. Walsh and Alvin, fearing they would be apprehended, ran towards the rear of the premises and up the stairs.

Walsh went back out onto the roof, but Alvin dived straight through a ten-foot-wide plate-glass window. When he hit the ground, he saw that he had landed in an alleyway. Shaking shards of glass and debris from his clothing, he looked up to see a very bewildered police officer standing over him.

'You're under arrest, son,' the officer said, as he bent down to grab Alvin.

'Not unless you can catch me,' Alvin replied, before jumping to his feet and fleeing. The officer gave chase, but he had no chance of catching the terrified teenager.

Once Alvin was satisfied that the policeman had stopped pursuing him, he walked to the nearby car park where he and Walsh had left their getaway car. The lights on the battered old Capri had been left on and the engine was still running.

'There were a number of officers in the car park when I got into the vehicle,' Alvin later recalled. 'They came rushing towards me when they saw me jump into the car, but I accelerated away before they could reach me. I drove out onto the main road, but they had blocked my escape route with a police car. Fortunately, the officer sitting in the vehicle must have thought I was an innocent member of the public because he reversed out of my way. He obviously hadn't been contacted by his colleagues to look out for me or the Capri.'

Walsh, meanwhile, remained trapped on the roof. Rather than face arrest, he brandished the axe he had used to breach the door and charged the police. Immediately recognising the difference between stupidity and bravery, the officers stepped aside and watched as Walsh disappeared into the night, waving the axe above his head and howling.

The following day Walsh and Alvin scoured the local paper for news of their near capture and were surprised to read that the police were claiming that a 'number of bottles of perfume' had been stolen.

'We didn't have any perfume,' Alvin said. 'I suppose somebody could have just been walking through the car park, accidentally climbed the fire escape and found the two bags of perfume, but it's unlikely. I'm certainly not saying the police would have taken the perfume for themselves. There's no way they'd do that, is there?'

When Alvin wasn't sleeping, drinking, fornicating or thieving, he was terrorising those who displeased him in the area where he lived. On one occasion, Alvin, Kevin Walsh and another man were walking down London Road in Leigh-on-Sea when a taxi slowed down alongside them in traffic. Alvin was wearing a West Ham United hat and scarf and when the four men in the taxi noticed this they began shouting out obscenities and making offensive hand gestures at him. Having supported a mediocre football team for most of his life, Alvin should have been accustomed to this kind of reaction from strangers, but for reasons known only to himself he got annoyed. Gesticulating with his hands and issuing threats, Alvin approached the taxi, but, before he could reach it, the traffic eased and it continued on its journey. After just a few yards, the taxi suddenly slewed across the road and its four passengers leapt out. Realising that a confrontation was inevitable, the man with Walsh and Alvin ran away. The men who had got out of the taxi began shouting abuse again and threatening Walsh and Alvin, who, although outnumbered, responded in kind. Both sides advanced towards each other, and when Alvin was within striking range one of the men punched him hard in the face. Dazed, but remaining on his feet, Alvin began trading punches with his assailant. Walsh, too, began to fight, and for a while it looked as if he and Alvin were going to be overwhelmed. The man who had punched Alvin had got in close enough to grip him in a headlock and had begun to rain blows down into his face and head.

Alvin claimed that as he was ducking down to protect his face from the onslaught, he 'noticed that there was a knife on the ground'. When discussing this incident with police many years later, Alvin said, 'It seemed like a miracle, to be honest.' Alvin being assisted in a brawl by an act of God may have been believed by Essex police, but I remain rather sceptical about the alleged divine intervention. Perhaps the endless prayers Alvin would undoubtedly have been made to recite at Our Lady of Lourdes Catholic School were finally being answered.

Regardless of its origins, the knife, which happened to be a mere eleven-inches long, was plunged into the top of Alvin's opponent's leg – not once, not twice, but three times.

'I think he fell, because he let go of me, and I backed away from him,' Alvin said. 'I don't remember him saying anything; it sort of went silent after that.'

That silence was broken not by a heavenly choir singing 'Hallelujah' but by the injured man's friends shouting for help. As they carried their wounded comrade to a nearby taxi rank, Alvin disposed of the knife over a garden wall and ran from the scene with Walsh. The police arrived shortly afterwards and began patrolling the area, looking for the pair. Taxi drivers at a nearby rank were so incensed by Alvin's cowardly act that they assisted the police in their search.

Fearing capture, Alvin and Walsh made their way home using the network of alleyways that link the roads in that area. The following morning Walsh, Alvin and their friend met up to discuss the incident. Alvin had a black eye and fat lips, and his face was swollen. Still feeling sorry for himself and trying to justify his despicable behaviour, he later recalled, 'I wasn't laughing and joking about it, I was hurting. I don't go around stabbing everyone I meet in the leg.'

After the three had finished discussing the incident, Alvin returned to the garden to retrieve the knife. A cynic might take the view that he was depriving future combatants of miraculously finding an 11-inch-long knife midway through a fight, but Alvin was no doubt acting with only good intentions. The extent of the stabbed man's injuries is not known.

As he grew older, Alvin's violent response to anybody who insulted, upset or generally displeased him became part and parcel of his everyday persona.

Living on the same street as Alvin was the Percival family. Alvin and Danny Percival had become firm friends; they were the same age and mixed with the same crowd. Danny's younger brother, Ricky, had his own circle of friends. For reasons known only to Alvin, he would often try to intimidate or bully this younger group of boys and in particular Ricky. Alvin would twist his arm, push or shove him for no apparent reason and on one occasion he used a set of handcuffs to tether Ricky to a bridge. Danny confronted Alvin after this incident, and when he too was threatened he floored Alvin with a head-butt to ensure he was in no doubt that his bullying would not be tolerated.

Nobody who knew Alvin would suggest that he was some sort of violent Neanderthal man, who dragged his knuckles around the streets of Southend, beating everybody who had the misfortune to cross his path. On the contrary, Alvin was known to be a very shrewd and cunning individual. He selected weak or defenceless people to use violence against simply because he wanted others to think that he was a force to be reckoned with. Alvin was sitting in a café with his friends, reading a copy of my best-selling book, *Essex Boys*, when a friend of mine, Gavin Spicer, first met him.

'This O'Mahoney is a fucking mug,' Alvin said to Gavin, whilst prodding the cover of the book with his finger.

'That fucking mug is my mate,' Gavin replied. 'Do you have a problem with that?'

Unlike Gavin, Alvin was all mouth and no genuine muscle, so he laughed off his own comment as a joke and buried his head back into the book.

This incident highlights the sad truth about Alvin: despite being a very violent and dangerous individual to some, behind the facade he was no more than a coward.

One evening, Alvin was perched on an elderly man's garden wall, having an argument with his then girlfriend, Clair Sanders, who many years later would become his wife. Clair handed Alvin a letter, which he screwed up without reading and threw into the well-kept garden.

Upon seeing this, the owner of the house came out and complained bitterly about the litter that had been deposited in his garden. He asked Alvin to get off his wall and leave, but he refused to do so.

Irate, and perhaps rather foolishly, the elderly man tried to physically remove Alvin, who responded by giving him a mouthful of abuse before walking off. Later that night, Alvin returned to the house with another man. He knocked on the door and when the unsuspecting occupant opened it, Alvin struck him hard in the face. The force of the blow threw the man back into his doorway. He staggered forward in an effort to regain his balance and fell head first into the garden.

Feeling satisfied with his handiwork, Alvin bowled down the street with his friend, leaving his victim dazed. The man suffered a broken ankle and told police that Alvin had assaulted him with a pickaxe handle, but unsurprisingly, when Alvin was arrested, he denied using any weapon.

Regardless of how the man sustained his injury, Alvin was charged with grievous bodily harm and remanded in custody to await trial. This was his first experience of prison life and he promised the judge, whom he eventually appeared in front of for sentencing, that it would be his last. Believing Alvin would never wish to return to prison after his experience on remand, the judge sentenced him to a two-year period of probation.

The following year Alvin and four others were arrested after two men were found, one having been punched, kicked and beaten with sticks as he lay on the ground and the other stabbed. Alvin was charged with violent disorder and inflicting grievous bodily harm, but the case was discharged after the witnesses and victims failed to appear at court. It's unclear why the victims changed their minds about testifying against Alvin as they have refused to answer any questions about the matter since. Perhaps they had a genuine change of heart, or God once more intervened on Alvin's behalf. Whatever the reason, Alvin was freed. One person Alvin couldn't convince to come round to his way of thinking was Clair Sanders. She had grown tired of Alvin's constant brushes with the law and, after failing to honour numerous promises to mend his ways, ended their relationship. Distraught and disillusioned, 18-year-old Alvin left Essex in the hope of turning his life around. He washed up on the Aylesbury estate in Walworth, south-east London, where he set up home with Barbara Russell, who was several years his senior.

The Aylesbury estate, known locally as 'the Bronx', is made up in the main of high-rise flats and is often used by politicians as a typical example of urban decline. A contradiction of style and sorrow, it is considered to be an area of extreme social disadvantage. Alvin, a Jack-the-Lad Essex Boy, didn't quite command the same level of respect on the estate as he had enjoyed in sleepy Leigh-on-Sea.

His wafer-thin hopes of starting a new trouble-free life also failed him. Travelling home through the Rotherhithe tunnel one evening, with his brother Darren at the wheel, Alvin's car was stopped by police, who suspected that it might have been stolen. When the officers searched the vehicle, they found a stun gun in Alvin's sports bag. When asked what he was doing in possession of a prohibited weapon, Alvin said that it was not for his personal use and that he had merely purchased it for his partner, Barbara, because they lived in the Bronx.

With the very real possibility of a return to prison hanging over his head, Alvin abandoned his quest for salvation and returned to Essex. When Alvin appeared in court, he was given a conditional discharge and the weapon was confiscated. The news that welcomed Alvin upon his return to Essex did not please him. Malcolm, the man he idolised, was having an affair with his ex-girlfriend, Clair.

Those who knew Alvin at that time say that he tried to put on a brave face and laugh about it, but deep down he was a cauldron of boiling anger and jealousy.

By all accounts, Barbara is a thoroughly decent woman, who did all she could to make things work with him. Unfortunately, her hopes for happiness were dashed by Alvin's overwhelming desire to become a 'somebody'. The life he chose to lead brought the same sort of trouble to her door as Clair had endured. Trouble had also arrived at Malcolm's door when his long-suffering wife, Bernadette, found out about his extra-marital affair with Clair and she kicked him out of her home. Due to circumstance rather than choice, Malcolm moved into a flat and was soon joined by his mistress. When Alvin learned that Malcolm and Clair had become an item, he resigned himself to the fact that he had lost his teenage sweetheart and did his sorry best to make his relationship with Barbara work.

His habitual offending, however, continued to be a constant source of disagreement between the couple. Barbara realised that it would only be a matter of time before Alvin was imprisoned, but, despite her protests, he didn't seem to care.

Aged 20, Alvin was convicted of burglary, having robbed a clothes shop, and aged 24, he was charged with burglary at an MOT station. Like Barbara, the judge sentencing him realised that the threat of prison held no fear for Alvin and so he decided that a reminder of what life inside was like might help him to see the error of his ways. Alvin was sentenced to a term of nine months' imprisonment.

Prison, as has been proved time and time again, is looked upon as an occupational hazard rather than a deterrent to young men like Alvin. As soon as he was released, he was back committing crime with his mentor Malcolm Walsh.

Like Alvin, Ricky Percival had been forging a contrasting but equally criminal lifestyle for himself. He had tried to follow in his brother's footsteps, training hard at the gym, but his desire to look and feel good about himself was hampered by his lack of finances. The menial jobs his dyslexia attracted were never going to pay for the lifestyle he craved and so, like many foolish adolescents, he began to sell drugs to boost his income. Unlike Alvin, Percival's warm and friendly personality made him easy to deal with and he had no shortage of customers who were prepared to buy from him. In the gyms where nightclub bouncers and their ilk go to train, Percival soon met and befriended many 'useful' individuals in the drug world. These people, who had extremely valuable contacts in the pubs and clubs where drugs were sold around Southend, soon helped Percival's illegal business to prosper. Before he was 20 years of age, the boy who teachers had said would never do well for himself was wearing designer clothes, enjoying foreign holidays and driving top-of-the-range cars.

Whilst Percival was supplying the local community with drugs, Alvin and Malcolm Walsh continued to break into businesses and strip them of their hard-earned assets. Rather than invest the fruits of their criminality into material things, as Percival was doing, Alvin and Walsh preferred to spend them on regular suicidal drinking binges.

Staggering home from a particularly heavy drinking session one night, Malcolm encountered a gang of feral youths hanging around a street corner. 'Are you all right, mate?' one of them asked.

As Malcolm turned to face the gang, the thick gold chain that he was wearing could clearly be seen hanging outside his T-shirt. 'What the fuck has it got to do with you,' he snarled, before lurching through the door of a fast-food restaurant.

Not knowing Malcolm and assuming, rather unwisely, that he would offer little or no resistance, the gang decided to mug him as he walked out of the restaurant. Five minutes later, clutching a kebab in one hand and a bottle of soft drink in the other, Malcolm stumbled out of the shop.

When the first punch landed on the right side of his face, Malcolm instinctively looked down at his kebab to see if it had been knocked from his grasp. As the second, third and fourth blows hit Malcolm, he realised that these people were not going to allow him to dine in peace. Malcolm grabbed the nearest man to him by the hair and butted him full in the face. More annoyed about having to abandon his kebab than being assaulted by fools, he began tossing his assailants around the street like rag dolls. Those who failed to run at the earliest opportunity were left lying amongst the remains of Malcolm's late-night meal in the gutter.

Outraged by the audacity of his attackers, Malcolm spent the following day trying to identify them. One name that continually cropped up during Malcolm's enquiries was that of Russell Jones. In the Southend area, Jones was considered to be a hard man who feared nobody.

Although Jones was not personally involved in the attack, Malcolm soon established that it had been members of his gang who were. Having punished his attackers on the night, Malcolm reasoned – in his own unreasonable way – that he would teach Jones, the man this gang looked up to, a lesson in manners that they and others would all learn from.

Malcolm let it be known that he was looking for Jones and that he was not a happy man. When news of Malcolm's threats reached Jones, he laughed them off and said that he was looking forward to meeting Malcolm. Soon everybody in the pubs and clubs around Southend were talking about the likely outcome of what undoubtedly would be a bloody encounter. Associates of Malcolm vowed to stand by him and Jones's gang swore to damage anybody who dared to take them or 'their man' on. It was only a matter of time before the threats would end and the blood would begin to flow.

Late one afternoon, a friend of Malcolm's at the time was attending the offices of the Inland Revenue in Southend. He didn't notice anything untoward when he entered the building, but two hours later, as he stepped outside, he saw one of the men who had attacked Malcolm standing in front of him. Before he had a chance to speak, he felt a heavy blow to the back of his head, and fell to the ground. As he looked up, he saw the man bearing down on him with a sock that appeared to contain two or three snooker balls. Raising his arm to protect himself, he was struck a further two or three times before he managed to get to his feet. As soon as he did so, his attacker and an accomplice turned and ran.

When Malcolm heard about the liberty that Jones's gang had taken, he was livid. Rampaging around Southend, Malcolm apprehended one or two members of Jones's gang and beat them mercilessly. But the man Malcolm really wanted to punish – Russell Jones – was off the scene. He was embroiled in bigger problems of his own.

It had started as a fairly straightforward get-rich-quick scheme and ended with a handsome 28-year-old man being grotesquely disfigured and partially blinded. Darren Kerr, a characteristic Essex wide boy, was approached by a London-based fraudster named Michael Boparan, who wanted to know if he would be interested in getting involved with a bank scam, which he said was set to rake in millions.

Kerr contacted his friend, Russell Jones, and asked if he could help set the swindle up in return for a percentage of the profits. Jones agreed and had soon recruited friends who worked at a Southend bank to copy screen prints of credit cards. Once done, the screen-print copies were given to Kerr, who, in turn, passed them on to Boparan for use in cloning credit cards belonging to victims living as far away as New York City. Kerr was paid a percentage of the value of the credit cards, which was estimated by police to be as much as £100,000. It wasn't long before the fraud began to reward Boparan and Kerr handsomely, but not all the money Kerr received was, in fact, his.

The agreement had been that Kerr would pay Jones out of any monies that he received. The whole operation was simple, ingenious even, but it relied upon trust – a rare commodity amongst the criminal fraternity in Essex.

The fraud was discovered by accident when a police constable noticed an untaxed car outside Boparan's Regent's Park flat in London. Upon closer scrutiny, a large quantity of incriminating material could be seen inside the vehicle and items were subsequently found in Boparan's flat, including a credit-card imprinter, a number of blank plastic cards and confidential bank print-outs.

The police raids that followed terminated the operation before Jones had been paid a single penny. Pissed off might be an understatement when describing how Jones must have felt. His mood deteriorated even further when he read in a local newspaper that the bank claimed to have lost £200,000 in the fraud. When he asked about this figure, Kerr claimed that it was rubbish and said that he had not been paid any money either. In truth, Kerr had actually done very well out of the scam. The cash he had received had helped finance a new Range Rover and a top-of-the-range stereo.

CLOWNS AND ACID TRIPS

As the police investigation gathered momentum, Jones was arrested and held on remand in Brixton prison. There, fate played a hand. Jones met Boparan, who revealed that he had, in fact, paid Kerr a total of £8,000. Jones contacted Kerr and gave him ample opportunity to pay what was due, but every request made was met with a denial. Jones decided that he wasn't going to beg or plead for his money; instead, he would discuss the matter personally with Kerr as soon as he was released. Jones's first port of call when that day arrived was the home of Kerr's girlfriend. Her father answered the door to Jones's insistent knocking and was told to tell Kerr that he had four days to pay up – or else.

Determined not to share his ill-gotten gains, Kerr ignored the numerous telephone calls he received and did all he could to avoid meeting Jones. This blatant snub infuriated Jones. He told everybody who associated with Kerr that if he didn't pay him what was due he was either going to cut him up or grass him to the police for the bank fraud.

One Monday morning, Kerr was on his way to London when he decided to make a call from a public telephone near the Circus Tavern in Purfleet, Essex. As Kerr walked from his car to the kiosk, he had no inkling of the horror that was about to visit him. It was broad daylight and the phone box was adjacent to a busy main road, so Kerr thought nothing of the Mercedes containing two men that pulled up alongside him.

Suddenly, the telephone-box door was flung open and, as Kerr turned, he was sprayed in the face with acid. Dropping the handset, he raised his hands to his face and began to scream in agony, as the corrosive fluid burned through his skin and eyes and filled his lungs with noxious fumes. Moments later, his attackers – Russell Jones and friend Tommy Watkins – manhandled Kerr to their car and sped away from the scene.

Kerr pleaded with his kidnappers to let him wash his melting face with water, but they refused. They told Kerr that they intended to drive him around until the acid had eaten deep into his flesh. As Kerr screamed in fear and agony, the men demanded payment of £10,000, which they claimed was owed to Jones for the bank scam. Kerr repeatedly denied owing Jones anything, which only infuriated the men further. 'Tommy has got a gun on you,' Jones hissed, 'and you're fucking lucky you haven't been shot.'

Terrified for his life and in excruciating pain, Kerr managed to open the rear door of the car as it pulled up at a set of traffic lights and throw himself out onto the road. As other motorists went to Kerr's aid, the Mercedes sped away. The vehicle was later found abandoned, having been stolen earlier that day.

Kerr remained on the ground for several minutes, writhing in agony, before being led to a nearby garage where his face was doused with water. An ambulance was called and Kerr was rushed to Billericay hospital, which is equipped with a specialist burns unit.

Describing the attack, Kerr said, 'Even amongst the criminal fraternity there are certain rules. What happened to me broke every one of them. Throwing acid into my face was a horrible, evil thing to do. Every time I look in the mirror, there is a reminder of what was done to me. How can I forget or forgive? I would never have believed that the body could feel so much pain. And then there is the mental pain as well. My face has been marked, and so has my life.'

One side of Kerr's face was reduced to a mass of angry red scars. He was blinded in his left eye and doctors explained that he faced years of painful surgery to reconstruct his features. Despite the severity of the attack, Kerr refused to assist the police because he feared that Jones would seek even more violent retribution if he did so.

'I want to survive,' he said. 'I want to retain my dignity. What happened was awful. But I am still alive.'

Brave words indeed, but Kerr's ordeal was far from over. Five weeks after the acid attack, he was lying in his hospital bed when he heard a nurse laughing in the corridor outside his ward. Instinctively, he looked towards the door and saw a man carrying a large bunch of plastic flowers walking towards him. The man was dressed in a clown suit and wore a grinning mask, Dracula fangs and a ginger wig. As he approached Kerr's bed, he looked straight into his eyes before producing a sawn-off shotgun from the inside of his jacket. Nobody was laughing.

'He was aiming for my head,' Kerr later told police. 'It was an instinctive reaction to twist away and that is what saved my life. The man was a professional. It was not the man who had thrown acid in my face. And I am sure that this was not the first hit he had carried out. I actually managed to stagger out of bed after I had been shot. I saw him walk out; he did not run, he walked out. I am very lucky to be alive.'

Kerr underwent emergency surgery to save his life. The hole that had been blasted through his shoulder was so large doctors said it could have been made by an artillery shell.

Despite being subjected to two horrific attacks in just five weeks, Kerr still refused to assist the police. Amongst the police and criminal fraternity in Essex, speculation about who had carried out the attacks was rife.

Many blamed the Essex Boys firm and, in particular, their leading henchman, Patrick Tate. There was nothing of substance to support this allegation; the Hulk, as he was known, was safely behind bars at HMP Whitemoor in Cambridgeshire at the time. People just assumed that members of the firm were the only people in the area capable of committing such an atrocity.

Without Kerr's assistance, the police investigation into the attacks was destined to fail. In the weeks and months that followed, Kerr himself came under intense police scrutiny. Unable to get to Kerr to carry out a follow-up attack, Jones and his associates began to leak information, much of it false, to the police about his business activities. As a result of this, Kerr's home was searched and his associates were questioned, though nothing of evidential value was found. Outraged by the double standards of his rivals, Kerr later said, 'They were expecting me to abide by the criminal code not to grass, but they were bending the rules to suit themselves. A constant stream of information was being passed about me to the police. Allegations were being made about my business affairs. These turned out to be entirely false; the police found no evidence of wrongdoing against me. I did not make a statement to the police even after the shooting. I was still abiding by the code. But when my home was raided, It was obvious that the information that had led to the search had been supplied by the other side. I knew then that there was no reason why I shouldn't make a statement about them to the police.'

When Kerr did eventually tell the police who had attacked him, he and his wife and their eight-month-old son were moved to a secret address and given round-the-clock armed police protection. Kerr's evidence, and fingerprints that were found on vehicles used in the crime, led police to arrest 28-year-old Russell Jones and 24-year-old Thomas Watkins. They were charged with grievous bodily harm with intent and kidnap.

When they stood trial at Basildon Crown Court, the proceedings were halted after it was revealed that one of the jurors had been offered a bribe to convict them. Prosecution witnesses were also threatened before the start of a second trial, which was then moved to the Old Bailey. When this trial did eventually get under way, the jury was placed under police protection. Both Jones and Watkins pleaded not guilty, but, after hearing three weeks of evidence, the jury found them guilty of all charges. Sentencing Jones and Watkins, Judge John Rogers QC said, 'This was a case of horrible vengeance. It was premeditated, it was vicious and it was inflicted on a man who has been your close friend for ten years. I've noticed not a flicker of emotion or remorse throughout the proceedings. You bragged about what you were capable of and he learnt about it in the most unpleasant way possible. Mr Kerr will be disfigured for the rest of his life, scarred both mentally and physically. The only way I can view it is as a deliberate act of calculated cruelty, aggravated by the fact that you delayed him going to hospital.'

Jones was sentenced to sixteen years' imprisonment for causing grievous bodily harm with intent and four years for false imprisonment. At an earlier hearing, he was sentenced to serve four years' imprisonment for his part in the bank fraud and for firearm offences. Watkins was jailed for five years for the attack on Kerr and two years for false imprisonment. Michael Boparan was sentenced to five years' imprisonment for his role in the fraud. It's hard to comprehend how such a trivial dispute can escalate into senseless carnage, but the use of excessive violence to settle petty disputes is hardly unusual amongst feuding criminals in the county of Essex.

4

THE OMEN COMETH

In the summer of 1998, Malcolm Walsh, a man who could not contemplate losing face for one moment, had himself become embroiled in a festering dispute. It was such a trivial matter that none of his former friends can even agree on its origins. According to Ricky Percival and several others, Malcolm was gunning for two brothers, Steven and Stuart Tretton, who he claimed owed him £200 for drugs. An alternative version given by Damon Alvin for the alleged bad blood is that the Tretton brothers had been dealing drugs to Percival's customers and Percival, who was serving a prison sentence for possessing a can of CS gas spray at the time, had solicited Malcolm to warn them off.

It is true that Malcolm and Percival had been good friends at this time, but their relationship centred on their mutual interest in keeping fit rather than drug dealing. They would train together almost daily, but away from the gym led separate lives. Percival earned a living selling drugs, and Malcolm was in partnership with Alvin committing burglaries.

Percival was no fool, but he was certainly no hardened drugs baron either. Still in his teens, he and a friend, who has asked me only to refer to him by his nickname, 'Meat Head', roamed the streets playing childish pranks, like many of the local kids of the same age. Meat Head and Percival had acquired a can of CS gas and had spent the evening travelling around Leigh-on-Sea, spraying it in the open air in the hope that they would cause a little mayhem. The gas is an irritant used by police forces throughout the world to subdue those resisting arrest or being otherwise violent. Although the effects can include a burning sensation in and around the eyes, symptoms do tend to completely wear off within minutes. For the gas to be effective, it generally has to be dispensed from close range and so spraying it in the street is a fairly pointless exercise. Feeling disappointed that their efforts were having no effect on potential victims, Percival and Meat Head decided to spray the gas in a local garage.

'We got caught doing it in the garage forecourt on very good quality CCTV: colour, smiling faces, the lot,' Meat Head told me. 'The old bill kicked my mum's door in the following morning and I got carted off to the police station. I didn't see Ricky when I arrived, but I knew he was already in the cells because his name had been written on the board above the sergeant's desk.

'When I was interviewed, I could hardly deny it was me smiling up at the camera, and the police already knew the other guy with me was Ricky. When we went to court, Ricky was convicted and sent to a detention centre, but I somehow managed to get found not guilty. The CCTV had recorded me, but my back had been to the camera when I sprayed the gas. Ricky always thought that I had grassed him, but I hadn't. The police were determined that Ricky should be convicted. It wasn't my doing.'

It was while serving this short sentence that Alvin claims Percival appointed Malcolm to collect his alleged drug debt. Alvin conceded that he had heard the story about the drug debt from a second-hand source 'down the pub' and it is certainly not supported by any first-hand knowledge or factual evidence. Alvin's explanation for the rift seems unlikely because Percival was good friends with Steven Tretton at the time, and even if he had needed somebody to 'talk to' the Trettons, his elder brother Danny would have been the obvious person to call upon.

From a very early age, Danny had been an awesome boxer. Initially trained in Thai boxing and martial arts, he progressed to the noble art of traditional boxing and fought for the famous West Ham Boxing Club in the East End of London. Aged 27, Danny thought his chance at the big-time had gone. Despite chalking up a decent record of ten wins in fourteen amateur fights, he was flitting from job to job to finance his training at Broad Street gym in London.

One night, whilst working as a bouncer at a nightclub in Dartford, Danny became involved in a brawl with a group of men who had been intent on causing trouble. As Danny employed his boxing skills to defend himself, he was unaware that he was being watched by none other than top boxing promoter Frank Maloney, who happened to live nearby. After Danny had dispatched the men, Maloney approached him and asked if he wanted to turn pro. Without hesitation Danny accepted the offer and began training under the watchful eye of Maloney. His boxing skills were dramatically improved and 'Danny the Doorman', as Maloney called him, won his first three professional bouts. If either of the Percival brothers had a problem, there was certainly no need for them to call upon others for assistance, as Alvin suggested.

Regardless of who is wrong and who is right about Malcolm's motivation for wanting to confront the Trettons, what isn't in dispute is the fact that Steven, 18, and Stuart, 20, were subjected to a catalogue of abuse and numerous threats of violence over a number of months. Eventually, their mother, Lydia Watkins, became involved.

Not the type of lady to mince her words, Lydia confronted Malcolm, calling him a scumbag and a lowlife. Thereafter, the warring families exchanged abuse every time their paths crossed. This turned out to be on a regular basis because Malcolm often visited his ex-wife and their children, who happened to reside on Locksley Close, where Lydia and her sons lived.

In the spring of 1998, a mutual friend of Alvin and Malcolm named Richard Rice committed suicide. Rice was older than Alvin and Malcolm and enjoyed a reasonably affluent lifestyle; he lived on a farm, worked the land and dabbled in the car trade. As a sideline, anything that Malcolm and Alvin stole of value whilst out committing burglary Rice would usually buy and sell on at a profit. His income didn't match his lifestyle and so his debts began to mount. Facing financial ruin and the prospect of losing his home, Rice decided to take his own life.

On the morning of his funeral, Alvin drove to Malcolm's flat on Shannon Close, Leigh-on-Sea. As he pulled up alongside Malcolm's recently acquired 3-Series BMW, Alvin noticed that the back window had been smashed. The house brick used by the vandals had bounced across the roof and ended up on the bonnet, damaging all the paintwork that it had encountered along the way.

'What's happened to your car?' Alvin asked Malcolm when he opened his front door.

Initially, Malcolm thought that Alvin was joking, but, after searching his face for a hint of a smile and finding none, Malcolm pushed Alvin aside and ran into the street. 'Bastards! Bastards! Bastards!' he screamed when he saw his pride and joy. 'I'm going to kill those fucking Trettons!'

Leaping from side to side in a kind of deranged jig around his beloved car, Malcolm finally ran off, leaving a bewildered Alvin shaking his head in disbelief. When he eventually returned, Malcolm was still ranting and raving about the damage to his car and the damage he was going to inflict upon those he deemed responsible. He said that he had already visited the Trettons' grandmother's home, apprehended Steven on the stairs and beaten him up.

Throughout the funeral later that day and in the days thereafter, Malcolm constantly reminded everybody that the matter was far from over and both the Tretton brothers were going to pay. On 9 June 1998, Malcolm drove to Locksley Close to pick his children up. Several members of the Tretton family and their friends were in the street when he arrived. They glared at Malcolm and began to shout insults. Malcolm responded in kind, before collecting his children, getting back into his car and driving away. That night Lydia Watkins received several threatening and abusive telephone calls from Malcolm. He said that her house would be firebombed and her husband, Terry, would soon be a 'dead man'.

The following morning at 9 a.m., Malcolm returned to the close with Clair Sanders to drop off his children, but trouble flared again. Malcolm was subjected to a barrage of abuse by members of the Tretton family. As he advanced on them, they backed off towards their home, at which point Terry opened the door. Enraged by the threatening phone calls that he had been subjected to the night before, Terry was seen outside his home by several witnesses, holding a knife and shouting at Malcolm: 'Yes, you're going to get it!' Robert Findlay, a friend of Malcolm, went over to try to calm the situation but could only watch in disbelief as Terry confronted Malcolm. Findlay heard Malcolm asking Terry to drop the knife, but he just repeated, 'You're going to get it!' Terry then thrust the knife forwards in a stabbing motion.

Malcolm looked down at his clothing for blood, looked back at Terry and said, 'You want to get yourself a decent knife. It's blunt.' Then he staggered back and fell into Findlay's arms before collapsing, dying just yards from where his young children were standing. An ambulance was called to the scene, but the crew were unable to revive Malcolm and he was pronounced dead less than an hour after the incident.

Damon Alvin had been working at Shoeburyness that morning with his brother Darren. His partner, Barbara, telephoned him as soon as she heard about the stabbing. News of Malcolm's condition varied depending on whom she asked and so Barbara arranged to drive to Alvin's workplace and give him a lift to the hospital. Alvin assumed that his best friend, a survivor of numerous violent incidents, hadn't been badly injured; however, when Alvin spoke to several people on his mobile phone, they warned him that his friend might not survive. By the time Alvin and Barbara arrived at the accident and emergency department of Southend hospital, 32-year-old Malcolm Walsh had already been pronounced dead.

Kevin Walsh recalls Alvin being 'an emotional wreck' when he was given the news. 'Alvin became very withdrawn and very, very angry,' he said. 'He started talking about getting back at Terry, but I didn't take much notice. Everybody who knew Malcolm was upset about his death and so I just thought Alvin was doing and saying what others were doing and saying: "I'm going to kill this person or that family." I thought it was all just hot air brought about by grief. I never believed for one moment that Alvin or anybody else would actually do anything.

'Malcolm's funeral seemed to make Alvin even angrier. He helped to carry the coffin and was really, really distraught. I have to admit, I did become slightly concerned about some of the threats he was making that day and in the days that followed. He was talking about getting hold of grenades to attack Terry Watkins' house. Perhaps it was just the drink or drugs talking, I really couldn't say.'

When the police arrested Watkins for Malcolm Walsh's murder, he claimed that it was Malcolm who had brandished the knife. He said that Malcolm had somehow been stabbed with his own weapon after a confrontation and struggle on his doorstep.

'He came over in a right aggressive manner,' he told police. 'I wasn't going to be intimidated by him. He came round here tooled up. I saw the glint of a knife. I am very sorry he is dead, but it isn't down to me.'

Malcolm's death resulted in a barrage of threats and abuse being levelled at the Tretton brothers and their mother. Neighbours stopped talking to the family and they were receiving up to 50 nuisance calls per week, so it's safe to say that they were far from popular in the eyes of many in the local community.

Eighteen-year-old Ricky Percival was saddened by the loss of a friend and joined in with the name-calling and idle threats that many who knew Malcolm were making. These were not the actions of a homicidal maniac plotting bloody revenge; they were simply nuisance calls and immature insults being made by a young man trying to come to terms with a violent and unnecessary death.

Lydia Watkins accepted this at the time and told police that she had not felt threatened by the calls or insults at any time. The sheer number of calls, however, became impossible for Lydia to bear and so, in an effort to stop them, and the abuse, she asked her solicitor to write to not only Percival but two females who had also made calls and given her grief.

The solicitor's letter warned all three individuals that if their campaign of harassment did not stop, further action would be taken. As a result, Lydia did not receive another nuisance call and the abuse stopped forthwith. That was until Percival and Lydia came face to face at Chelmsford prison.

Percival had been visiting a friend and Lydia had been to see her husband. What was later described by police as a 'bit of a slagging match' took place between the pair and Percival was arrested under Section 5 of the Public Order Act, for which he was fined the princely sum of £90 and ordered to pay £150 in costs. The unusual decision to prosecute Percival for such a trivial matter was taken because Essex police said they were concerned about witness intimidation. Because the killing had taken place in such a close-knit community, they said they wanted to send out a clear message to everybody that this type of behaviour would not be tolerated.

Terry Watkins would later claim that the incident in Chelmsford prison had been more than a slagging match; he said that Percival had, in fact, threatened to shoot him and his family. 'My wife came to see me in prison just before my trial,' he said. 'She was upset because she had just seen Ricky Percival. He made threats that he was going to shoot my family, including my little girl, Laura, who was just four years of age.'

Watkins, of course, had not personally heard the threats and so his account of this incident cannot be given credence. Whether Lydia's claims are true or false, there was undeniably a growing feeling of intense hostility towards Terry and his family in the Southend area, but very little of it originated from Percival. Some of the threats were childish, others more sinister, but they were all treated as serious by the police.

On one occasion, Stuart Tretton nearly came to blows with a neighbour who had complained to him bitterly about loud music being played at unsociable hours. During the argument, the neighbour said to Stuart, 'You had better watch your back.' Unfortunately for the neighbour, even such a common phrase as this, used by many in similar altercations, was reported to the police as a death threat.

THE OMEN COMETH

Damon Alvin's feelings following the murder of his friend were mixed. After being dumped by his first love, Clair Sanders, Alvin had been heartbroken to learn that his childhood hero and so-called friend had started having an affair with her. The thought of any man being with her was upsetting enough, but the fact that it was his best friend, and that he had heard that Malcolm was beating Clair, made it particularly hard for Alvin to take.

A few months after Richard Rice's funeral, Alvin had been imprisoned for burglary. Shortly after his release, Alvin had visited Malcolm's ex-wife Bernadette. It was mid-morning and she had been kind enough to cook him breakfast. As he sat talking to Bernadette at the kitchen table, Malcolm had burst into the house and started ripping up carpets and destroying furniture. He tipped over the fridge-freezer, causing all the food to spill out onto the kitchen floor. Shouting and screaming abuse, he dragged the fridge outside and attacked it. When he had finished kicking it, Malcolm barged his way back into the house and told Bernadette that he was going to remove everything that he had paid for; to highlight this, he wrenched the toilet seat off and walked out of the door with it under his arm. Alvin claims that he just sat at the table throughout Malcolm's tirade without uttering a word, and that he didn't get involved or even acknowledge him because his feelings towards Malcolm were running so high.

Now that Malcolm was dead and Clair was alone, Alvin became desperate for them to be reunited. Alvin was aware that Clair was grieving for Malcolm and the last thing she would want to hear was her ex-boyfriend rubbishing her deceased lover's name, so, biting his tongue, Alvin became her rock. He volunteered to be a pall-bearer at Malcolm's funeral and remained at Clair's side, consoling her, night and day.

Everybody knew that somebody would have to pay for Malcolm's death; it was what he would have wanted. Nobody took liberties with him when he was alive, so why should anybody get away with it now that he was dead?

Word spread around many of the pubs and clubs around Southend that a member of Russell Jones's gang, whom I shall call 'Lee Harris', had stood over Malcolm's grave and urinated on it. Nobody bothered to ask if it was true or not; the very fact that Harris had had the audacity to even say such a thing meant he would have to suffer some form of terrible retribution.

Alvin, who confided in close friends that he resented Malcolm, was said by many casual associates to have appeared incensed by the rumour that somebody had desecrated his best friend's grave. In an act designed to prove to Clair that he was not only a decent man who was mourning his friend but also a worthy contender to fill his shoes and win her affections, Alvin decided to teach Harris a lesson. According to Alvin, he and five other men – whom he later named as Kevin Walsh, Trevor Adams, Danny Percival, Ricky Percival and Gavin Spicer – arranged to meet at Kevin Walsh's flat. Alvin said that Walsh had told those present that he didn't want anybody to carry a knife because he didn't want anybody to get seriously injured or hurt.

'I was given a balaclava, along with everybody else,' Alvin said. 'We all then left in Walsh's white Transit van. My impression was that it was going to be a fight and weapons would be used, like hammers and bats, but no firearms or knives. We were told that Harris lived in a three-storey building that had been converted into flats. I was aware that Walsh knew someone called Badger who lived there and he was going to let us in through the security door.

'When we arrived, we all got out of the van. Three of us went round one side of the building and three around the other. Danny Percival rang Badger's doorbell. There was no answer, but a minute or two later I saw that two people were approaching the flats. From everybody's reaction, I guessed that one of these people must have been Badger. Somebody said that the guy with Badger was Harris and everybody seemed to get really excited. When the two men reached Danny, I could see Badger motioning with his eyes towards Harris, as if to say, "That's him, that's him." Danny took a few steps forward, pulled out a washing-up bottle from his jacket and squirted a noxious fluid into Harris's face.'

According to Alvin, Harris's face and jacket began to melt. Screaming for help and clutching his face, Harris tried to run off back down the garden path.

'Danny began to wrestle with Harris in an effort to get him to the floor. I ran forward and began to hit Harris repeatedly around the legs with a hammer. He fell to the floor, but I continued to hit him around the leg area, as that was the clearest part of his body. I remember Danny pulling a hammer out of his jacket and him starting to beat Harris around the body because he had curled up into a ball on the floor. By this time, there were a few of us laying into him. I don't know how, but my hammer got knocked out of my hand. As I went to retrieve it, I can remember standing and watching some of the others punching and hitting Harris as he lay on the floor. I was also aware that the majority of our group were wearing knuckledusters.

Kevin Walsh's knuckleduster was a manufactured brass-type, with a blade protruding from the side, but all the others were handmade. I personally didn't have one.'

The assault, according to Alvin, ceased only when passing vehicles halted and their occupants began to shout and scream for the onslaught to stop. Instead of returning to the van and making good their escape, the gang ran towards the seafront and mingled with the crowds of holidaymakers. That is, of course, except for Alvin. He claimed that he had run back to his home and he met up with the other gang members later that evening.

'I found out that Ricky Percival had taken a knife with him,' he said. 'He told me that he had stabbed Harris. He said that he had stuck the knife in him up to the handle and the blade had snapped off. Percival told me that he had said, "This is for Malcolm," as he stabbed Harris.'

Alvin's apparent shock at discovering that Ricky Percival had defied Kevin Walsh's request not to carry knives is laughable when one considers Alvin's description of the weapon Walsh was alleged to have been carrying.

His claim that Walsh had requested that nobody should carry guns or knives to prevent the intended victim from being seriously injured or hurt is equally bizarre, considering the fact that Harris was squirted with a substance that melted his jacket and he was beaten with hammers and knuckledusters.

Gavin Spicer is one of my closest friends and has been for many years. Together we dealt with countless violent incidents as we stood on the door of Raquels nightclub in Basildon. Occasionally, weapons were used by all parties, but I have never known my friend to take part in or condone an attack on a defenceless man by a gang. I have read Alvin's account of the incident to Gavin and, when he had stopped laughing, he described it as 'total bollocks'.

'Alvin is an idiot,' Gavin said. 'He doesn't know where fact starts and fantasy ends. The guy is full of shit. He might have been there when this person was beaten up, but I certainly wasn't. I am quite sure that the police would have questioned me if I had been present, but nobody has ever spoken to me about it. Using that sort of mob-mentality cowardly violence just isn't my way of resolving matters. If somebody upsets me, I deal with it personally; I don't invite an audience. It sounds to me like Alvin has been spending time in fantasyland. I am aware that he is a regular visitor.'

Having carried out several gallant tasks, talked himself up and shed numerous tears, Alvin had made sure the required image was firmly implanted in the grieving widow's mind, and it wasn't long before Alvin and Clair had rekindled their teenage romance. They did not conduct their affair openly, but the Walsh family have told me that they are in no doubt whatsoever that they had been reunited before Malcolm had even been buried. Regardless of the exact timescale, Barbara had found out about Alvin's infidelity and asked him to leave her home within weeks of Malcolm's funeral. Rather than apologising for his bad behaviour and seeking reconciliation with Barbara, Alvin dutifully packed his belongings and moved into a flat with Clair.

The ill feeling generated by Malcolm's passing was not going unnoticed by Essex police. In an effort to calm the situation and reassure the Trettons and their relatives that they were safe, the police agreed to install personal panic alarms in their home. These alarms, when activated, would have an armed police-response unit racing to their location within minutes.

In March 1999, 54-year-old Terry Watkins appeared before Chelmsford Crown Court charged with the murder of Malcolm Walsh. He pleaded not guilty but, after a two-week trial, was convicted of an alternative charge of manslaughter and sentenced to life imprisonment. Manslaughter usually attracts a lighter sentence than murder, but in Terry's case the judge imposed life after hearing that Watkins had been jailed in 1986 by the same court for two counts of wounding with intent. Back then, he had forced his way into an ex-girlfriend's home, where he had stabbed her and the man she was then in a relationship with.

Dabbing her eyes, Clair Sanders told reporters outside the court: 'I would have liked the jury to have found that Malcolm was murdered, but as long as life means life then Watkins has been given the punishment that he deserves.'

The Walsh family also issued a statement: 'We know Malcolm was no angel, and we are not saying he was, but he would not have had anything to do with drugs. The court was told that he was high on cocaine that morning, yet the post-mortem examination found nothing. It isn't fair on those left behind to have to deal with what has been said. We want to put all of this behind us and remember Malcolm for what he was – a loveable rogue. Because of the tests on Malcolm's body we were not able to bury him until two months after he was killed. It was a really stressful time. We wanted to put him to rest, but we couldn't. It's almost a year later now and it is still not over.'

Unbeknown to the Walsh family and everybody else affected by Malcolm's premature death, their problems had only just begun and they would continue to impact on their lives for many years to come.

5

THE SOUND OF THE SUBURBS

A persistent criminal rather than a serious one, Dean Boshell was no more a successful human being than he was a villain. The many mistakes he had made in his short life were not all of his own making.

On 22 October 1998, he found himself incarcerated within the confines of HMP Chelmsford. There was little he could do about his situation after the police had caught him handling stolen goods and a judge had sentenced him to nine months' imprisonment; however, he could have, and should have, steered clear of the prisoner in the cell next to his own.

Boshell was impressed with the smooth-talking, flash wide boy who had become his neighbour. Damon Alvin appeared to be everything that Boshell had one day dreamed of being. Never one to miss an opportunity to exploit somebody, Alvin had cultivated his friendship with Boshell and effectively made him his errand boy. In return for the numerous trivial tasks Boshell carried out for his new friend, Alvin would fill out the occasional prison application form and help him with his reading.

Describing their first meeting, Alvin said, 'He was teased a lot because of his stutter and I felt rather sorry for him. He seemed a bit simple but pleasant enough. I sort of took him under my wing. I do not know whether he could read or write properly, but I used to read his mail for him and also write letters to his girlfriend on his behalf.'

Over the next few months, the pair were transported to and from court together to attend their respective hearings and these days out cemented their friendship further. Alvin had been remanded in custody for his part in a botched burglary on a furniture shop.

Together with his brother Darren and another man, Alvin had stolen a Luton van from a local hire company and driven it to John James furniture store on Southchurch Road, Southend. There was no need for the would-be burglars to clamber onto the roof or force windows and doors because Alvin had a key for the back door of the premises.

A few days earlier, he had been browsing in the store with his partner when he noticed that a key had been unwittingly left in the back door by a member of staff. Continuing to browse, he noticed an expensive cabinet that he fancied would look good in his recently acquired flat. Deciding to return to the shop with a van for some late-night shopping when the staff had gone home, Alvin took the key out of the back door and slipped it into his pocket. Stealing a Luton van to transport the stolen furniture home turned out to be as effortless as gaining access to the shop. Customers at a local van-hire company who returned vehicles after hours were required to drop the keys through a letterbox. Alvin simply fished out a set using a long piece of wire with an improvised hook on the end. He then read the registration number on the key fob, located the vehicle in the car park and drove it away.

After entering the furniture shop, the three men selected items of their choice and began to load the van, which was backed up to the open door. When it was completely full, they drove to one another's homes and unloaded the goods before returning the van to its rightful owner and dropping the keys back through the letterbox. Thinking they had committed the perfect crime, the men couldn't resist boasting to their friends about the ease with which they had stolen their new furniture and it wasn't long before this loose talk made the police aware of Alvin's involvement in the audacious crime. In an early morning raid, Alvin was arrested at his flat, charged with handling stolen goods and remanded in custody at Chelmsford prison.

Another resident at that establishment who befriended Boshell was 45-year-old Christopher Wheatley. On 8 August 1998, he had been sentenced to seven years' imprisonment after police raided his flat and found 30 grams of cocaine, 3 grams of amphetamine, 357 Ecstasy pills and £950 in cash. A further 170 grams of cocaine were discovered hidden under the seat of his car. The drugs had an estimated street value of between £10,000 and £17,000. Wheatley's solicitor told the court that he had become addicted to drugs after losing his job as a doorman.

Five years earlier, Wheatley had been a prominent member of the Essex Boys firm. His boss, Tony Tucker, had often introduced Wheatley to people as being 'like my brother'. It's a term I had heard Tucker use often. The true meaning of his words were, in fact, 'This is the latest man I am going to pretend to befriend, use and when exhausted of use, abandon.' And so it was with Christopher Wheatley. When a more 'useful' individual named Patrick Tate was released from prison in 1993, Tucker disposed of Wheatley and replaced him with Tate.

The drugs that Wheatley had once sold with ease and relative safety through his job as head bouncer at one of Tucker's clubs in Southend suddenly became a commodity he could only offload at great risk. The steady stream of punters knocking on Wheatley's door soon came to the attention of the police and, after a short period of surveillance, they raided his home and caught him red-handed.

Whilst in prison, Wheatley continued to deal in drugs and one of the men he employed to distribute them was Dean Boshell. An unlikely friendship developed between the two and Wheatley, a competent, powerful athlete, introduced Boshell to the world of bodybuilding, supplements and steroids. With his ever-expanding frame and ego, coupled with Wheatley and Alvin, his new gangster friends, Boshell really believed that he had finally fulfilled his dream and become one of the big boys. He told fellow inmates that when he was released he was going to set up a drug-dealing empire and live lavishly off his ill-gotten gains.

When Boshell did eventually walk out of prison in the spring of 1999, he left his friend Alvin behind, but he did promise the man he now referred to as 'brother' that he would not forget him. In an attempt to walk the walk and talk the talk, but not quite managing to master either, Boshell contacted Alvin's girlfriend, Barbara, and assured her that whilst his 'brother' remained in prison, he would look out for her.

'You have nothing to worry about,' he told her. 'I am out and I will be taking care of business for Damon from now on.'

• • •

In the weeks and months that followed, Barbara would give Boshell and his girlfriend Emma Moore a lift to the prison and the foursome would enjoy visiting time together. It was the first time in many years that Boshell had experienced any sort of stability in his life. In Alvin and Barbara, he had two new friends, and in Emma he had a girl he thought he loved – so much so that he had her name tattooed on his chest.

As the relationship went from strength to strength, Boshell and Emma decided to move into a flat together on London Road, Leigh-on-Sea. Instead of trying to set up the drug-dealing empire that he had dreamed of, or securing gainful employment, Boshell signed on the dole and topped up his state benefits with the proceeds of petty crime. In the main, this involved him stealing property from cars or occasionally supplying scrap-metal merchants with stolen vehicles to order.

Unlike her ne'er-do-well boyfriend, Emma made an honest living as a barmaid at a snooker club in Wickford, a small village on the outskirts of Basildon. Boshell used to visit Emma regularly at her workplace and was subsequently introduced to her work colleagues, one of whom was Carla Shipton. There was an instant attraction between Carla and Boshell, which in time flourished into much deeper feelings. The smiles and knowing looks between the two didn't escape the attention of Emma, who convinced herself that her boyfriend was being more than friendly with her workmate.

When Alvin was released from prison, he and his new sidekick Boshell immersed themselves in a criminal partnership. Everywhere Alvin went, Boshell would either be at his side or not too far behind. In the pubs and clubs around Southend, Alvin introduced Boshell as his mate, but Boshell would tell people that they were, in fact, brothers. It was around this time that Alvin first introduced Ricky Percival to Boshell.

Percival's memories of Boshell are hardly complimentary. 'He was a ponce who couldn't keep his dick in his trousers,' he recalls. 'He would never buy a drink and he would not hesitate to sleep with any female, so long as she had a purse and a pulse.' Apart from bumping into one another occasionally in Percival's local pub, the Woodcutters Arms, there was no other contact between Boshell and Percival during this period and nobody has ever come forward to dispute this. If Alvin hadn't taken Boshell to the Woodcutters Arms, it is unlikely he would have ever met Percival.

Always looking for ways to impress Alvin, Boshell had told him all about the Wickford snooker club, where his girlfriend worked, and suggested that it was a prime target for a robbery. Alvin agreed that the premises were worthy of further investigation and advised Boshell to make mental notes of where the safe was located, where security cameras were positioned and where keys to the gambling machines and doors were kept.

Equally keen to impress the ladies in his life, Boshell was out shopping one day when he noticed that one particular store had no alarm fitted to the front door. He told Alvin about this lapse in security and together they decided to break into the premises. That night Boshell smashed a pane of glass at the front of the shop with a small hammer, put his arm inside and unlocked the door. Laughing at their own ingenuity as they entered, the pair filled two bin liners with garments before returning to Alvin's car, which was parked nearby. Instead of making good their escape, Alvin and Boshell returned to the shop and stole so many clothes that they completely filled the back seat of the vehicle. Only when they were unable to stuff any more into the car did they drive to Boshell's flat to unload their ill-gotten gains.

Not usually the snappiest of dressers, Boshell couldn't wait to show off his finest threads, not only to Carla but also to Emma, who wanted to know how he had managed to afford them. Proud of the ease with which he had broken into the shop, Boshell was only too pleased to inform Emma where, how and with whom he had stolen the clothes. The outrageous flirting that Emma had witnessed between Boshell and Carla and his sudden desire to smarten up his appearance convinced her that his intentions were far from admirable.

A few days after Boshell had committed the burglary, Emma confronted him with her suspicions about Carla and, despite his denials, she left him.

Tensions at work between Emma and Carla soon boiled over and in the ensuing argument Emma was threatened with a snooker cue and warned to stay away from Boshell.

Hell hath no fury like a woman scorned, they say, and in the experience of most men 'they' are more often than not right. Emma, unhappy about the way Boshell had treated her, picked up the telephone, called the police and told them who was responsible for breaking into the clothes shop. The following morning Boshell and Alvin were arrested and the stolen property was recovered. Boshell had little choice other than to plead guilty to handling stolen goods because the clothing was found in his flat, but Alvin denied any involvement and elected to stand trial. Boshell was hoping that the magistrates would sentence him, as they only had the power to impose a maximum six-month term of imprisonment, but to his dismay they declined to do so and referred the matter to the Crown Court.

Instead of rebounding from one lost love into the arms of another, Boshell bounced around the bedrooms of several Essex girls before settling into the arms and lives of two particular females. Neither of these girls was aware of the other until I contacted them recently. Carla was already sharing Boshell's bed before Emma finished their relationship, but the other girl, whom I shall call 'Elizabeth Reece', met him just a short while after he almost became single.

With a prison sentence looming on Boshell's horizon, he decided to secure a job which he could tell the judge about when he appeared in court. He reasoned that it would be unlikely for any young man who had secured gainful employment and was working hard to mend his ways to be imprisoned. Boshell applied for and was given a job as a barman at the Castle public house on Southend seafront. When Boshell was introduced to fellow staff member Elizabeth Reece, the attraction was instant. Elizabeth, a pretty single mum, was bowled over by Boshell's old-fashioned charm and the many compliments that he plied her with. Faithful, sensible and hard-working, Elizabeth represented everything that was lacking in Boshell's chaotic life. Had Boshell chosen a life of normality with Elizabeth over a life of crime with Alvin, he would undoubtedly still be alive today.

After several months of searching, I managed to make contact with Elizabeth by telephone. Initially, Elizabeth refused to discuss her relationship with Boshell because she said she feared reprisals from 'his friends'. After much negotiation, and giving certain assurances to Elizabeth, she finally agreed to tell me her story.

'I was instantly attracted to my friendly and thoughtful new work colleague,' she said. 'We spent our first evening behind the bar together laughing, joking and giving one another those looks you can't explain but both know their meaning. Before heading home that night, Dean and I agreed to meet on the beach opposite the pub the following day. That meeting turned out to be one of the happiest days of my life. Accompanied by my daughter Lauren, I spent an unforgettable day sitting in the sunshine, chatting to Dean and watching the world go by. He was funny, charming and thoughtful, and I just knew he was the man for me.

'Over the next few weeks as I tried to get to know Dean, he refused to say too much about himself other than that he had no contact with his parents but saw a brother named Damon regularly. He introduced me to some of his friends and I met his brother. I could tell that Dean looked up to Damon – he would do anything for him. Unfortunately this included helping him commit what Dean described to me as minor crime. Despite the fact that Dean was committing crime, and I was making my disapproval of this known, we did spend several extremely happy months together.

'I must say that Damon appeared to look after Dean; for instance, he bought him a white Astra to drive. I don't know what, if anything, Dean had to do for Damon in return for this gift.

'In order to provide for my daughter and me, Dean gave in his notice at the pub and got a job with a cleaning company. Like Damon, Dean was extremely generous and became what I would describe as a family man. He would go shopping and buy my daughter treats, walk the dog, do the housework and assist me around the house in any way that he could. His dream, he often told me, was to be part of a proper family. Dean told me once that he had a daughter named Emma. The subject arose because he had the name 'Emma' tattooed on his chest and I asked him who she was. Dean was really upset by my question and began to cry. He said that his daughter's mother wouldn't allow him to see her. Because he had been so distressed by our conversation, I never mentioned his daughter again and neither did he.'

One can almost imagine the sigh of relief that Boshell must have breathed when Elizabeth pledged never to mention his 'daughter' Emma again. Trying to keep his other ongoing relationship with Carla from Elizabeth must have been difficult enough without introducing his ex-girlfriend into the equation.

I genuinely felt for Elizabeth. Apart from Beverley Boshell, she is without doubt the only person that I have spoken to whilst writing this book who truly loved Dean.

In the autumn of 2007, I finally managed to track down Carla Shipton, the other female in the Boshell *ménage à trois*. After going through a now almost routine procedure of reassuring potential witnesses that my intentions were honorable, I arranged to meet Carla at a pub near Basildon to discuss her relationship with Boshell and other related matters. Like most of the women Boshell had romanced in his short life, Carla still held a soft spot in her heart for him and spoke with great affection about their time together.

'One night Dean appeared at the snooker club in Wickford where I was employed as the assistant manager,' Carla told me. 'He said he had just popped in for a drink and we got talking. I liked him instantly; he was really easy to talk to, had plenty to say and was exceptionally sweet. He gave me a lift home in a little blue car when I finished work. He started it with a screwdriver, which didn't fill me with confidence, but he just laughed and said that he had lost the keys. I remember thinking at the time that the rightful owner of the car probably still had them.

'We saw each other regularly after that night and before long we were an item. When I introduced Dean to my parents, they adored him. Mum used to say, "He's lost. He's a sad soul who needs a family around him." She really had a soft spot for Dean. I don't know much about Dean's own family because he rarely talked about them. He did tell me that his mum and dad lived in Basildon, but he said he didn't get on with either of them. He also said that he had a brother and a sister, whom he claimed he adored. To highlight just how much he thought of his sister, Dean told me that he had paid a small fortune to have her hair permed and cut at a top hairdressing salon. I thought that was a really sweet gesture because throughout the time that I knew Dean he never had much money. I have recently learned, however, that he never had a sister. I wasn't surprised that he had lied to me: Dean had a serious problem with the truth. He didn't understand what it was.

'I found out that there was an ongoing dispute between Dean and a former girlfriend of his named Emma, who also happened to work at the snooker club. He said that she had refused to give him his possessions back when they had separated. When I asked Emma about it, she said that he was using it as an excuse to harass her and that she didn't have any of his belongings.

'It was whilst this dispute was ongoing that I met a man called Damon Alvin, whom Dean introduced to me as his best friend. He had been going on and on for ages about this great friend he had whom he always referred to as his brother. I didn't believe Damon was his brother; I just thought it was a phrase Dean used for somebody he thought a lot of. He used to use a lot of phrases like gangster, brethren and homie that he picked up from gangster lyrics by Eminem and other rap artists that he would listen to.

'One Sunday afternoon, Dean announced that he was going to take me to Damon's house to meet him and his wife. The way he was going on about it, I thought we were going to Buckingham Palace to meet the Royal Family. When we arrived at Damon's (not Buckingham Palace), Dean appeared to fall under some sort of spell. If Damon had asked Dean to jump that day, he would genuinely have disappeared through the ceiling. Damon pulled Dean's strings like he was some sort of puppet. I think Dean looked on Damon as a cross between a father figure and a big brother. Damon, on the other hand, looked upon

Dean as a cross between a lapdog and an annoying little brother he didn't have time for.

'After that first meeting, Dean and I would visit Damon's house every Sunday and occasionally during the week. I became very good friends with Damon's wife, Barbara, and in time we began to go out together, mainly to play bingo in Southend.

'When Dean mentioned to me the trouble he said he was having recovering his possessions from Emma, Damon said that he was going to go round to her flat, kick the door in and retrieve them. I have no idea if he ever did that, but he was certainly capable of doing that sort of thing.

'Just two weeks after meeting Dean, I found out that he had been stopped and arrested by the police for drink-driving in his little blue car. I was annoyed with him for being so stupid as to drink and drive but pleased to have it confirmed by the police that he at least owned the vehicle. They didn't inform me as such, I just assumed that he had not stolen it because they didn't take it off him.

'I ended up finding out most things about Dean via the police. He would tell me one story, get himself arrested and only then would I find out what he had really been doing. Knowing what I know now, I am grateful that he habitually lied to me; the truth would have been far too terrifying to contemplate.'

As Mrs Boshell, Carla Shipton, Elizabeth Reece and everybody else I have spoken to who knew Dean Boshell have confirmed, he was totally untrustworthy. He deceived and lied to everybody with whom he came into contact, without exception. Boshell led a double life and constructed well-thought-out lies to fool those he pretended to be loyal to. But Boshell was not the only man guilty of living a double life in Southend at that time. Damon Alvin portrayed himself in public as a family man and a hard-working builder. This facade, however, was no more than a ruse to mask his drug dealing and the cowardly violence he employed to sustain his position in the drug world.

If people have any doubt about the true make-up of Alvin's persona, they only have to ask the elderly man whose ankle he broke, the young man he stabbed in the leg three times, Lee Harris, who was clubbed with a hammer, or an unfortunate man named Malcolm Winters.

Alvin was introduced to Winters through a mutual friend. By his own admission, Winters had a fairly serious drug habit and Alvin had been recommended to him as a supplier of reasonably priced, good-quality cocaine. When Winters first met Alvin, he arrived in a pick-up truck accompanied by another male. Expressionless, Alvin had given Winters a gram of cocaine and demanded £50. Before driving off, Alvin had told him that any time he needed drugs, he should call him. In the months that followed, Winter's cocaine habit had spiralled out of control and he found himself ringing Alvin more often than he could afford. Unable to control or fund his habit, Winters requested and was given cocaine on credit. Within a very short period of time, he owed Alvin approximately £1,000. It might not seem like a lot of money, but it is when you have nothing and you owe it to an extremely violent thug.

One afternoon, Alvin telephoned Winters and said that he needed to see him as a matter of urgency to discuss how the debt was going to be settled. When Alvin swept into the car park where they had agreed to meet, Winters took a deep breath and started to walk towards the vehicle. Forcing a smile, he greeted Alvin, who glared back, said nothing and motioned for him to get into the vehicle alongside him. As he did so, two men, who appeared to be intoxicated, approached the car. Neither Winters nor Alvin had seen the men before. The men asked Winters if he had any spare change, but before he could answer, Alvin 'went ballistic'. He jumped out of the car and head-butted one of the men before punching the other to the ground. Both men were left unconscious.

Winters ran away, whilst Alvin jumped back into his car, slammed it into gear and disappeared out of the car park amidst a cloud of dust and smoke caused by the burning rubber of his tyres. A few weeks after this incident, Alvin contacted Winters again and arranged to meet him outside his workplace. On this occasion, Alvin was sitting in the passenger seat of a BMW and another male was driving. When Winters climbed into the back of the vehicle, he noticed that Alvin was holding a knife, which had a 12-inch-long blade. 'How are we going to sort this out?' Alvin asked, whilst restlessly tossing the knife from hand to hand.

Eyeing the blade nervously, Winters told Alvin exactly what he wanted to hear. He did so because the unprovoked attack on the two drunken beggars several weeks earlier was still fresh in his mind. After accepting an offer to 'pay back some money next week', Alvin told Winters that he was free to go.

The following week, Alvin arrived at Winters' home, accompanied by another male. He took £500 from Winters and gave him a gram of cocaine. Winters was then informed that his debt had started to accumulate interest and if he did not sort it out soon he would be getting another visit and somebody would 'put one in his head'.

THE SOUND OF THE SUBURBS

Nobody knows if Alvin would have carried out his threat and it's fair to say that nobody knows if Lee Harris, beaten senseless for allegedly urinating on Malcolm's grave, was guilty of doing so. Talk is undoubtedly cheap, but as Harris found out and others were to learn, it can be extremely dangerous. Fortunately for Winters, before Alvin could carry out his threat or collect his debt, he had managed to flee from the Southend area and Alvin never did get his money.

Of course, not all threats are veiled or empty; some are followed through with ruthless efficiency. As the first anniversary of Malcolm Walsh's killing drew near, high emotions and the threats against the Tretton brothers and their family intensified.

Emotions were also running high amongst Malcolm Walsh's friends and relatives. There was talk of tossing hand grenades into the Trettons' home, poisoning the milk on their doorstep and shooting them. The majority of this talk was fuelled by alcohol or grief; nobody truly believed that anything would happen. Ricky Percival had added to the personal grief that he felt by doing all that he could to help and comfort Malcolm's brother and three sisters, one of whom, Pamela, had taken his death particularly hard. Her weight plummeted and her general health became a concern for all who knew her. Percival had begun visiting Pamela regularly in the hope that he could help her come to terms with her loss. Two weeks before the anniversary of Malcolm's death, Percival, his brother Danny and their friends were due to go on holiday to Cyprus. This caused Pamela a certain amount of distress because she said she felt alone, but Percival reassured her that she would be OK and made a promise to visit her as soon as he returned.

Whilst Percival was enjoying his holiday, a man whom I shall call 'Gary Baron' arrived at Alvin's home and said that he was looking for Dean Boshell. Describing the incident several years after the event, Alvin said, 'He asked me if he could leave something with me to give to Boshell. I asked him what it was and he answered by opening the boot of his car. I looked in and saw a shotgun wrapped in a jumper. I opened up the boot of my car, and he picked up the shotgun and put it in my vehicle. I said to him that I would give it to Boshell when I saw him.

'Because of all the threats that had been made about attacking the Trettons, I knew what it was going to be used for. Two hours later, Boshell turned up at my house and I told him that Gary Baron had left something in the boot of my car for him. Boshell took my keys, went outside, transferred the shotgun from my car to his and drove home. Five minutes later he re-appeared and gave me back my keys.'

I find it very hard to believe that a villain would deliver a shotgun to a person who was not directly involved in his conspiracy or crime. Firearm offences are very serious matters. Surely Baron would have kept the firearm until he met Boshell in person. Anybody planning to commit such a serious crime would hardly risk involving people who had no reason to know about their intentions.

A more likely scenario is that Alvin had ordered the gun, it had been delivered to his home and he had telephoned for his gofer Boshell to collect it for safe keeping. A few weeks later, on the anniversary of Malcolm's death, Alvin was in the Woodcutters Arms with Boshell and several other men. Ricky Percival was also present, having returned from his holiday in Cyprus. According to Alvin, he didn't recall talking to Percival and even if they did speak, he said, it would have been nothing more than a cursory greeting. When it came to closing time, Alvin claims that he was extremely drunk.

He has since given the police two different versions of what happened when he left the pub. In both, Alvin does his best to distance himself from knowingly being involved in any criminality. Initially, Alvin claimed that he got into a car with Boshell and Percival after asking for a lift home. 'We got into a white Vauxhall Nova. Dean was driving, Percival was sat in the front passenger seat and I noticed that he had a shotgun between his legs,' said Alvin.

If a man cradling a shotgun wasn't enough to alert Alvin that the commission of a crime was in progress, Boshell is said to have informed him that the car they were in was, in fact, stolen. Alvin claimed that if he had known it was a stolen vehicle, he would never have got into it. Considering that the driver didn't have a licence and the passenger was cradling a shotgun, I think that the car being stolen would have been the least of Alvin's worries.

Realising what a totally ridiculous story this was, Alvin changed his mind and said in his second account that after leaving the pub he got into Percival's car and Boshell followed behind in a stolen Vauxhall Belmont. Alvin did not mention seeing a gun at this stage. Knowing that he would have to reintroduce the weapon into his account, he related that Percival had parked his car approximately ten streets away from the Tretton home and then he and Alvin had joined Boshell in the stolen vehicle. They had then driven to a place called Bournemouth Park Road and Percival had got out. Alvin says he heard a car door or car boot slam shut and then Percival returned carrying a shotgun and a rucksack.

When asked how he could have forgotten such important details in his first statement, Alvin replied, 'All I can say is that I got it wrong because of the state I was in that night. I also think it was because it wasn't a job that had been planned with me. I wasn't aware of the routes or what was going on that night; it wasn't my bit of work.'

Regardless of the circumstances, I find it hard to believe that a person wouldn't recall if they had got into a stolen car with a man cradling a shotgun or a car that his friend owned. This 'bit of work' turned out to be, according to Alvin, Percival's plan to take revenge on the Tretton brothers.

After travelling to the vicinity of the Trettons' home in Percival's car and then getting into a stolen car, Alvin claimed that Boshell and Percival were supposed to drop him off at his home.

'I knew they were up to something that night,' Alvin said, doing his best to sound naive. 'I didn't know they were going to actually shoot someone. I knew that Percival was going around to the Trettons' house; I just thought that he would rob them of their drugs and money. Percival and Boshell were just talking amongst themselves on the way; their conversation about the job didn't really involve me. It was common knowledge that Percival was going to knobble Tretton; Boshell had told me that previously.

'On the way to my house, Boshell screeched to a halt at a junction just as a police car was passing. We thought they would turn around, as the front of the car that we were in had entered the junction. Because Percival had the shotgun with him, Boshell sped across the road and we all jumped out of the car and ran in different directions,' Alvin said.

Fifteen minutes after supposedly fleeing from the police, Percival is said to have arrived at Alvin's home. According to Alvin, Percival told him that the police car had turned around and driven past the stolen Vauxhall, but it had not stopped. Percival asked Alvin if Boshell was with him, but Alvin told him that he had not seen him and had no idea where he had gone. Percival is then said to have asked Alvin to show him where Boshell lived, as he had never been to his home.

'We drove to Boshell's flat in the stolen car. When we knocked the door, Boshell didn't answer, but we could see that his television was on upstairs. I climbed into his flat through an open window and found him in the kitchen with his foot immersed in a bucket of cold water.

I asked him what he was doing and he said that he had twisted his ankle as he was running away from the stolen car.

'I went downstairs and let Percival in. He said that he still wanted to do the job, but Boshell refused to assist him, saying that he could barely walk. Percival went on and on about it for 20 or 30 minutes, saying that Boshell was a messer. Eventually Percival asked if I would drive, and I agreed just to shut him up. We left Boshell behind and drove back to the road where we had abandoned the stolen car earlier. Percival got out of the vehicle when we arrived and disappeared into the nearby undergrowth.

'A short while later he re-emerged, clutching a shotgun, then we drove to a park on the opposite side of which was Locksley Close, where the Trettons lived. Percival said that all I had to do was wait and when he had done what he had to do he wanted me to drive him to Pamela Walsh's house in Shoeburyness. I didn't ask him why he wanted to go to Pamela's house. I just assumed that it was an arrangement he had made with her earlier.

'Percival got out of the car and disappeared into the darkness for what seemed like an age; I fell asleep waiting for him. I can remember waking up, getting out of the car and walking into the park to see what, if anything, was happening. I stopped to have a piss and I saw Percival walking across the park towards me. He hadn't done anything; he said that he was concerned about the number of people in the house.

'We hung about for approximately 20 minutes and then we walked towards the Trettons' home. The Tretton brothers were attending a party at a neighbour's house, and so we walked backwards and forwards from the park to their location, waiting for people to leave. Percival kept walking around to the rear of the property to see if he could see who was in the lounge. I knew the owner of the house where the party was being held and I knew that there were children in there. I mentioned this to Percival and he said that it was OK because it was very late at night and they would be in bed.

'I asked him to check, but he said that he was positive there were no children in the lounge. He seemed like he was ready to do whatever he was going to do, so I went back to the car. I can't remember if I drifted off to sleep again, but I was in the vehicle for a while. When I walked back across the park to see what Percival was up to, it was getting light. I think the time was around 4 a.m. Percival was standing motionless outside the premises where the Trettons were and so I asked him what he was doing. He said that he was waiting for the people to leave.

'Getting agitated, he began walking from the front of the house to the back, trying to see through the windows to establish who was where. As he did this, he put the shotgun down by a white picket fence. Somebody must have walked into the kitchen because the light came on. The open kitchen door amplified the sound of music and muffled the voices that were coming from the lounge inside the house. I got the impression that it was pretty lively inside. It was at this point that I told Percival that a woman named Carla Evans lived in the house with her kids. He repeated that it wasn't a problem; the kids wouldn't be in any danger because they would be in bed. I told him that it was late, we had been waiting ages, nothing was happening and so I was going home. Percival replied, "No, just wait. Just wait, I am going to do it, I am going to do it."

'Five minutes later, he had picked up the shotgun, pulled his balaclava down over his face and run up and kicked the front door open.'

6

AIN'T NOTHING BUT A HOUSE PARTY

Raymond Trotton had spent a particularly gruelling day loading and unloading furniture for a household removal company in South Woodham Ferrers, a small new town on the outskirts of Basildon. After finishing work at approximately 6.45 p.m., he visited Jennings, the bookmaker's, in East Street, Southend, where he checked the performance of several racehorses he had backed earlier that day. Finding that he had lost all his wagers, he reasoned it wasn't going to be his lucky day and headed home.

After getting washed and changed, Raymond called on his neighbour Carla Evans. He had no particular reason for going to Carla's – he often visited her home to share a drink and they would talk about their day. At 9.30, Raymond, his sister Christine Trotton, their nephews Stuart and Steven Tretton, a lady named Jenny Dickinson and a friend with the unfortunate nickname 'Vinyl' all went to a local pub called the White Horse. The group spent a quiet but enjoyable evening together before leaving at closing time. As they left the pub, the group were all fairly drunk and acting boisterously. Christine was being particularly loud and this resulted in her having an argument with most, if not all, of the people in her company. Not wishing to get involved in any sort of unpleasantness, Steven and Vinyl bid everyone goodnight and headed home.

The remainder of the group returned to Carla's house. There, they turned on the TV to watch *The Jerry Springer Show* and continued their drinking session with cans of beer. Renowned for his unruly guests, Springer has yet to host anyone as violent as the men who were planning a surprise appearance at Carla's house that night.

While most of the children had retired to bed, there remained a five year old asleep on the sofa and an infant asleep in a baby bouncer. Stuart Tretton was engrossed in a card game that he was playing on a computer and Raymond sat talking to his sister Christine and friend Jenny. After a few hours, Raymond looked out of the window and noticed that it had begun to get light. He could hear birds chirping and whistling in the garden as they prepared to greet the new day.

At approximately 4 a.m., the revellers and the birds' dawn chorus were disrupted by an almighty bang that came from the vicinity of the front door. Raymond jumped to his feet and shouted, 'What the fuck was that?' Before anybody could answer, the lounge door was flung open and two men wearing balaclavas and brandishing shotguns stood before the room full of terrified people. Raymond looked at the gunman nearest to him and, through holes that had been cut in the balaclava, he could see that he was staring straight back at him. The sound of the shotgun's mechanism clicking struck terror in Raymond's heart, but the only words that he could mutter were 'Oh, shit.' The blast that followed threw Raymond across the room and into a wall. His left hand, which he had raised in an attempt to protect his face, was shredded and he suffered wounds to his face, chest and arm.

Between two and five further shots rang out in quick succession, but Raymond had no idea if anybody else had been hit. He was by now in a state of blind panic and was running out of the patio doors into the garden.

Stuart Tretton, who had been sitting in an armchair by the door when the gunmen burst in, had also leapt to his feet. Initially, he thought that the man in the doorway was a friend of his playing some sort of sick joke. When the barrel of the shotgun was aimed at him, Stuart realised that the situation he was facing was very real. As he raised his hands in a vain attempt to shield his face, the gunman opened fire.

Outside in the garden, Raymond attempted to grip the garden fence in order to climb over it and escape, but as he did so he realised that he had lost the ring and middle fingers of his left hand. In extreme pain, bleeding profusely and petrified, he managed to drag himself over the fence and two further fences before coming to rest on the roof of his sister's shed. After catching his breath, he rolled off the roof and lay in his sister's garden, wondering what to do next.

He could hear screams of terror and shouts for help coming from Carla's house, so, rather bravely, Raymond returned to see if he could assist.

Stuart had followed his uncle Raymond out of the patio doors and into the garden, where he climbed over a fence to reach his mother's home. He didn't bother knocking on the door; he kicked it repeatedly in a panic-filled frenzy until it eventually flew open.

Jenny Dickinson had looked at the others in disbelief when she heard the crash that announced the arrival of the gunmen. Witnessing the horror unfold, Jenny had seen Raymond being shot first and then Stuart. Sitting on the settee screaming in sheer terror, she watched in disbelief as one of the balaclava-clad gunmen turned and pointed the gun towards Christine, who was sitting alongside her. In an act of heroism, Jenny grabbed hold of her friend's left shoulder and pulled Christine's head towards her. A split second later came a deafening explosion. Jenny leapt to her feet and fled through the patio doors. As she did so, she felt excruciating pain and realised that the shot aimed at Christine had struck her as she had moved to protect her friend. Instinctively, she ran to her home, where her ex-partner was babysitting their children. When she arrived, she saw that blood was pouring from her left hand and her middle finger was hanging off. Jenny's daughter tried to calm her and administered first aid while they waited for the emergency services to arrive.

Back at Carla's house, Christine had stopped shaking and was sitting up on the settee. She saw that blood was splashed all around the room. A spray of shotgun pellets arched across the lounge wall, and the top of the sofa, where her friends had been sitting, was missing. Getting to her feet, she ran to her sister Lydia's home to raise the alarm.

Christine was unable to recall how she had managed to enter the house, but she next remembers running into her sister's bedroom and shouting, 'We've been shot, we've been shot!' Christine, who had been hit in the shoulder, was totally hysterical and pleaded with Lydia to press the panic button that had been installed at her home by the police following the threats the family had received after Malcolm's death. Lydia could see that her sister's sweatshirt was heavily bloodstained and so she jumped out of bed to assist her.

'Calm down, calm down,' Lydia kept saying, but Christine continued to scream hysterically.

Stuart had entered the bedroom by this time and he began shouting, 'Help me, Mum, help me. I am going to die.' Lydia could see that her son's hand was hanging off and he was losing a lot of blood. He had shotgun wounds to his chest, which she later learned had punctured his lung.

Lydia ran downstairs and dialled 999. Stuart was in extreme shock and throughout the call he was heard shouting for help. When Lydia had finished talking to the police, she went to comfort him but, as she did so, Raymond staggered into the hallway and began calling out, 'Look what they have done to me!' Holding up what remained of his left hand, Raymond kept repeating, 'Look what they have done to me!' Drenched in blood, his face totally expressionless, Raymond suddenly fell silent, turned and walked away.

Wailing sirens and blue flashing lights signalled the arrival of the emergency services. The police cordoned off Locksley Close but exercised caution by not approaching the house where the shootings had taken place. When the ambulances had arrived, they too kept away from the crime scene and so the wounded were forced to walk out of the Close to get assistance.

Realising the nature of the victims' injuries, a police officer asked a friend of the Trettons named Russell Ward if he would return to the house to see if he could find any of the victims' hands or fingers.

Fifteen minutes before Russell Ward had been assigned the grisly task of looking for human body parts, Damon Alvin says that he had watched Percival launch himself at Carla Evans' front door.

'As the door was kicked open, I can remember everything going dead quiet, as though the music had been turned off. Nobody had actually switched the stereo off in the house, it just seemed as though they had. I don't know if it was because my adrenalin was running.

'Seconds later I remember hearing an almighty bang, a fucking loud bang. That was followed by two more loud bangs. It was like bang, bang, bang, and I am on my toes, running towards the car. I was still close enough to hear people shouting really loud and screaming in the house. When I did look back, Percival was running across the park towards me. We got into the car and I drove. Percival had the shotgun with him in the front seat. He was trying to unblock it and said we would need it in case we got pulled. He didn't say that he was going to shoot the police if they pulled us over, but I knew that was what he was implying.

'I told him to put it down because it was clearly visible and I was trying to drive. He told me that he had shot the Tretton brothers. I asked him what had happened and he just said that he had shot everybody. Percival said that he just stood at the lounge door and opened fire; the first person he shot hit the back wall. When he tried to shoot one of them in the chest, they had raised their hand to stop him and he had found this really amusing. One of the people that he had shot on the settee had pulled a girl on top of himself for protection.

'Percival told me that he had shot this particular person in the face. I can remember saying to him, "I thought you were going to do them in the legs?" Percival replied, "Fuck them." He seemed really hyped up, excited almost.

'When we got to Shoeburyness, I parked in a road called Burgess Close near Pamela Walsh's house. As I did so, I said to Percival, "There's a drain there, ditch the gun." Percival got his bag and the gun out of the car, walked to the back of the vehicle and dropped the gun down the drain.

'I know it sounds stupid, but I can't remember if he dropped the gun down the drain or if I did; I know I went too.

'I put the screwdriver in my pocket that had been used to start the stolen car. It was a little dumpy red one, a flat screwdriver. I know I kept it because when I got home I still had it. I had sobered up at this point, but I felt tired and rough.'

Unbeknown to Alvin and his accomplice, a man had been watching them from his bedroom window. Leonard Spencer, a retired gentleman whose home is on the corner of Burgess Close, had been awoken in the early hours of the morning by loud voices and the sound of car doors slamming. Thinking that this disturbance at such an unsociable hour was somewhat suspicious, Leonard had got out of bed and opened his window. Looking to his right, he saw a Vauxhall Belmont and two men who were running from it. After these men had run a short distance, one of them had stopped and returned to the car. Leonard quite rightly assumed that the vehicle was stolen and that the man had returned to it to retrieve something that he had forgotten.

After getting dressed, Leonard made his way downstairs and then out into the street to inspect the vehicle. The doors were not locked and inside he could see that audiotapes and a number of coins had been scattered around the footwell. Returning to his home, Leonard had telephoned the police, who he recalls 'didn't seem interested'. Later that morning, when the police realised the possible significance of the vehicle, they had attended Burgess Close and interviewed Leonard about all that he had seen.

Jogging away from the car without realising the police would soon have their first lead, Alvin claims that he and Percival made their way to Pamela Walsh's house.

'I can't remember if Percival had a key or if Pamela let us in, but we both entered the house,' Alvin said. 'I went to get myself a drink and Percival went upstairs. I could hear him talking to Pamela, but I couldn't hear what was being said.

'When I had finished my drink, I went upstairs and saw Percival standing at the sink in his boxer shorts. He was washing himself with white spirit to remove any traces of gun residue. He splashed the white spirit all over his face, which went really bright red; he kept saying that it was burning his eyes and ears. I found this quite amusing because I had told him before he used it not to do so. I have done a painting and decorating course and I know that you shouldn't splash or soak your face in white spirit.'

Percival wanted to get into the bath, according to Alvin, so he and Pamela went downstairs to give him some privacy. 'Whilst waiting for Percival, I telephoned my brother Darren, who lived in Locksley Close,' Alvin continued. 'There was no answer and so I decided to call a friend of mine who also happened to live there – well, he *was* a friend of mine until he found out that I had slept with his wife! When he answered, I asked him if there was anything going on outside his house. Despite the time, he was already out of bed and well aware that something was going on. He told me that the police were all over the place and had blocked the Close off. He asked me what had happened, but I couldn't tell him, so I said, "Nothing to worry about," and put the phone down. He knew that I was bent as fuck and so wouldn't have pushed the issue any further.

'At that point Percival came into the front room. He had his bag with him and had changed his clothes. He said that he had forgotten to pack a change of footwear and so I said I would get him a pair of shoes from my house. I took Pamela's dog with me, so that I wouldn't look out of place walking along the seafront at that hour of the morning. When I passed the road where we had dumped the stolen car, I saw that a police vehicle was parked next to it. Nobody was in the car; it was just parked there.

'It seemed to be too much of a coincidence and so I made a decision to get rid of the bag of incriminating evidence that I was carrying as soon as possible. I decided to hide the bag under one of the beach huts on Southend seafront. There was a slight gap between the esplanade wall and one of the huts, so I put the bag into it and covered it with shells and sand. After disposing of the bag, I continued to walk the dog.

'When I got home, I sorted out a pair of training shoes for Percival and then drove back to Pamela's, with her dog in my car. When I arrived, Percival was talking to Pamela about being picked up by a guy named Pete Edwards. I think I just left at that point and said I'll see you later.'

At ten past ten that morning, a number of officers from the Essex Police Force Support Unit set up a roadblock in order to seal off the road in which Percival lived. Satisfied that all exits and entrances were secured, PC Noel O'Hara knocked on Percival's front door. When Percival answered it, he was formally arrested on suspicion of attempted murder. A mere six hours had elapsed since the blood-letting orgy in Locksley Close, so one would imagine that Percival and his clothing would have been a forensic scientist's paradise. At that point, his DNA or fibres from the clothing he had worn would be in the getaway car. His fingerprints would be in a number of relevant places, and traces of white spirit would be on every inch of his body.

The shootings were common knowledge by this stage, as BBC Essex Radio had broadcast details of the incident on its ten o'clock news bulletin. Despite the shootings happening only a few hours earlier, the report was extremely accurate and detailed. The newsreader said that a woman and two men had been shot and seriously injured by two masked gunmen in the early hours of the morning at a house in Locksley Close, Southend. An update in the next news bulletin stated that the masked gunmen were, in fact, wearing balaclavas.

After all the talk and all the threats that had been made about avenging Malcolm Walsh's death and the fact that the Trettons lived in Locksley Close, Percival didn't have to be a super sleuth to work out that the shootings being talked about on the radio involved the Tretton family. He had made no reply when arrested by PC O'Hara, but when he was being handed over to other officers for transportation to Southend police station, he had asked, 'Is this about the Trettons?' One of the officers informed Percival that he was unable to discuss the reason for his arrest with him, to which Percival replied, 'Are they dead?' The officer ignored Percival's comments and placed him in a vehicle.

As they made their way to Southend, Sergeant Caldwell, who was sitting alongside Percival, asked, 'Are you all right, are those handcuffs a bit tight?' Percival replied, 'I'm all right, mate, I've got nothing to worry about.'

The sergeant advised Percival to lean forward in his seat so that he would be more comfortable. When Percival had done this, he asked Caldwell, 'What's this all about?'

The officer replied, 'I don't know, we are just the taxi drivers.'

Percival then said, 'I knew this would happen. How are the Trettons? Trouble is, Malcolm knew so many people. One of your officers has already told me that I would be the first one to be nicked if anything like this happened.'

Sergeant Caldwell reminded Percival that he had been cautioned and therefore anything he said could be used in evidence against him, but Percival didn't appear troubled. He asked what the penalty for attempted murder was and when the officer replied that it was life, Percival said, 'I wouldn't want to be the bloke who did it, then. I feel sorry for the bloke who gets caught.'

Whilst Percival was in police custody, officers searching the car that had been dumped outside Leonard Spencer's home in Burgess Close discovered an open bottle of white spirit on the back seat. This information was relayed back to the officers dealing with Percival and they decided that specific forensic tests for traces of white spirit and other materials, such as gun residue, would be carried out on him. Percival's outer clothing and underwear was seized, as were various other items from his home, such as a boilersuit and footwear. These were sent to the Forensic Science Service Laboratory in Chorley for examination.

Despite being arrested less than two hours after Alvin said that he had watched Percival douse himself in white spirit, not a trace of the solvent was found on him or his clothing and not a single shred of forensic evidence linked him to the stolen car, the crime scene or the crime itself.

Percival was not the only suspect police swooped on that day. Malcolm's friend Robert Glover had also been arrested and taken into custody for questioning. He was released after friends and family members said that he had been at home at the time the Trettons had been shot.

Nobody knows what Alvin was doing on the morning Percival was arrested or whom he was with. He claimed that he had gone to work, despite the fact that the Locksley Close shootings had taken place at approximately 4 a.m. He said that he received a telephone call from Danny Percival later that morning, who told him that his brother had been arrested for the shootings. According to Alvin, Danny also asked him if he still had his brother's bag. How Percival managed to tell Danny from within the confines of his police cell that Alvin had a bag of clothing remains a mystery. Percival could not have telephoned anybody and nobody apart from his solicitor visited him at the police station. Make of that what you will.

Alvin says that 'somehow' he ended up meeting Danny later that morning and he took him to where he had supposedly hidden the bag.

At the police station, Percival told the investigating officers that he had spent the night at Pamela Walsh's home. In the morning, his good friend Peter Edwards had given him a lift to his house in Leigh-on-Sea. When officers were dispatched to check out Percival's alibi, both Walsh and Edwards denied seeing him. It looked as if the police had got their man and a very serious crime had been solved in record time. In the interview room, officers confronted Percival with their findings and told him that his friends had deserted him.

'Your alibi has turned out to be false,' they said. 'You might as well tell us it was you who did the shootings in Locksley Close.' Instead of refusing to answer further questions, as one would expect if Percival was guilty, he became frustrated and angry, insisting that he was telling the truth. He guessed that Walsh and Edwards were denying seeing him because they thought they might be protecting him. There was also the possibility that Pamela had denied he had slept at her home because she was in a relationship with a man who might have misinterpreted the situation. Whatever the reason, it is not uncommon for people involved with the criminal fraternity to tell police officers that they haven't seen someone or heard anything. Percival asked the officers to talk to Pamela's children because they would know he had spent the night at their home but, for reasons known only to the police, they refused.

Frustrated, angry and adamant that he was being honest, Percival began to lose patience with the police. Having answered the same questions in two previous interviews, Percival threatened the interviewing officer in his third: 'I'm going to hit you in a minute because you're fucking pissing me off. I'm trying to explain something. Turn this shit tape recorder off before I smash it up.'

After three days of intense questioning and being subjected to numerous forensic tests, the police released Percival on bail pending further inquiries.

Percival had been prosecuted for threatening and abusive behaviour during the altercation with the Trettons' mother at Chelmsford prison.

Percival had been the one who had been warned by a police officer following that prosecution that if there were any further incidents he would be the one that they would arrest. The police therefore, had sufficient grounds to arrest him for the shootings, but the truth is that Percival was at Pamela Walsh's at the time of the incident. Upon his return from Cyprus, Percival had kept his promise and visited Pamela to check on her well-being. The sight he was greeted with was not pretty. It was the anniversary of Malcolm's death that weekend and she had hit rock bottom. Finding Pamela in a terribly emotional state, Percival had agreed to sleep over to help her through what was a very traumatic time. He had spent the evening talking to Pamela and her children and when they retired for the night he had made up a bed on the sofa and went to sleep.

Alvin and others concede that it was fairly common practice for those in their circle to borrow one another's cars. Percival worked as a mechanic for a local company and as a sideline he would buy second-hand cars, carry out any minor repairs that needed doing and sell them on at a profit. This meant that he often had several vehicles at his disposal. Percival says that on the day of the Locksley Close shootings Alvin had asked him to borrow a car to do 'a bit of work'. Percival had told him that he could have the 4x4 Sierra that he had used to drive to Pamela's house. He said he would leave the keys under the foot mat on the driver's side because he had no idea what time Alvin was going to collect the car. If it was going to be late, he didn't want Alvin to disturb Pamela or her children. After talking to Alvin, Percival had telephoned his friend Pete Edwards to ask him if he would give him a lift home the following morning because he knew that he would be going his way.

In the early hours, Percival had been awoken by somebody hammering on Pamela's door. Fearing Pamela and her children would be disturbed, Percival opened the door and saw Alvin standing before him. He realised that he had forgotten to leave the keys to his car under the mat as arranged. Alvin immediately barged his way into Pamela's house and when Percival looked outside to see what, if anything, was causing him to be in such an apparently agitated state he saw two men who appeared to be searching his car. He assumed that they were looking for the keys.

Percival asked Alvin what was going on and he replied, 'If you don't know, you can't be accused of any wrongdoing. Keep your mouth shut and you will be all right.'

AIN'T NOTHING BUT A HOUSE PARTY

Alvin demanded the car keys, which Percival retrieved from inside one of his training shoes, and then left.

That morning, as arranged, Pete Edwards picked up Percival from Pamela's house and dropped him off near his home, where he was arrested shortly afterwards.

Ricky Percival is, by his own admission, two wings and a halo short of being an angel. If he had attempted to murder four people and was then arrested less than six hours later, his best option would have been to remain silent when questioned. Likewise, he wouldn't have asked the police to question Pamela's children about his presence in their home after Pamela had denied that he had been there.

Both Pamela Walsh and Pete Edwards later offered to set the record straight, but they were warned that they could face criminal charges for making false statements and so Percival instructed his solicitor 'not to risk causing them any further grief' and they were not asked to testify at his trial.

The barbaric shootings at Locksley Close had a dramatic effect on Percival and those who knew him. He was catapulted overnight from being an 18-year-old petty criminal in the eyes of a few to being a psychopathic gun-toting madman in the eyes of many. Foolishly – very foolishly – Percival didn't protest his innocence too loudly, if at all, when rumours of his arrest and assumed guilt began to circulate. He chose instead to let the gossip-mongers and the notoriously inaccurate Southend grapevine promote the view that he was guilty so that his reputation as a no-nonsense hard man would be enhanced. Percival ended up with more street credibility than Russian billionaire Roman Abramovich has got cash.

Whilst Percival was bowling around the streets of Southend, enjoying his new-found fame, Alvin was worrying himself sick, thinking the police were going to unearth evidence that would not only implicate him in the Locksley Close shootings but also his sidekick, gofer and occasional best friend, Dean Boshell.

Shortly after Percival was released on bail, Alvin and Boshell returned to Burgess Close to recover the shotgun that had been dropped down the drain. Alvin said that he and Boshell parked some distance from Burgess Close because they feared that the police might have already found the gun and put the area under surveillance. Not wanting to put himself at risk, Alvin indicated to Boshell down which drain the gun had been dropped and sent him to retrieve it. Boshell seemed to be taking his time, so when Alvin was confident police officers were not going to come running from behind the nearby bushes he walked up to join him.

Boshell told Alvin that he had looked in the correct drain, but he had been unable to lift the cover to carry out a thorough search. Together the two men managed to lift the heavy iron cover and then Alvin put his arm in the drain to see if he could feel the gun beneath the water. Still unable to locate the weapon, Alvin told Boshell that the police had probably retrieved it at the same time they had found the stolen vehicle. It's difficult to understand why Alvin and Boshell would risk returning to remove a weapon that had been used in four attempted murders if they had not played any part in the shootings.

In a further twist, Boshell decided that he was going to burn the vehicle that had been stolen for use in the shootings. It had been returned to its rightful owner, but Boshell located it and torched it in the street. Despite Boshell's attempts to destroy evidence that could link him to the shootings, he was arrested a few weeks later for the theft of the vehicle. The police had matched his fingerprints to a partial fingerprint they had lifted from the steering column prior to the car being burned.

Boshell's arrest had caused Alvin to panic, but when Boshell was released supposedly without being questioned about the shootings, he did wonder if Boshell had made the story up.

Thirty days after the shootings, Alvin was left in no doubt that Boshell had been arrested because on this occasion he was handcuffed alongside him. The arrest had nothing to do with the Locksley Close shootings: Boshell and Alvin had been caught breaking into Jewson's, the builders' merchants.

Previously, Boshell would have accepted his fate and served his time, but in the past he had not had a girl who loved him, a daughter he treated as his own or a golden opportunity to fulfil his dream of becoming part of a 'real' family.

Between 1996 and 1998, the courts had rewarded Boshell with discounted sentences for snippets of information that he had given to the police about his criminal associates. Desperate to avoid losing his ready-made family, Boshell asked the officers involved in his case if he could once more trade information for a reduced sentence. No promises were made, but Boshell was told that the judge who was going to sentence him would be made aware of any assistance he offered.

This bargaining process with criminals by police is a fairly common practice, but anybody who agrees to become an informant has to adhere to strict rules which attempt to ensure the information given is genuine and that the informant is not encouraging others to commit crime which he can then tell the police about.

Documentation generated by the police at the time describes Boshell as a 'previously untried source' and suggests that 'the authenticity of any information he may give should be doubted'.

Rules regarding informants had changed since Boshell had first offered evidence to the police in 1996; all informants now had to be registered, which involved their meeting a senior police officer, having the terms and conditions explained to them and then signing the agreement, if deemed suitable. The officer who dealt with Boshell wrote in his notes: 'The source was told in no uncertain terms that he must tell us everything in relation to crime. He was told that if he were arrested, then the fact that he is an informant would not assist him in any way. He was told that there could be, in exceptional circumstances, a situation where he could have minimal involvement in a crime but only after he has been given authorisation by us and not before.'

Rules, regulations and the law had never meant much, if anything, to Boshell. He considered himself to be one of life's players, the type of guy who would agree to go through the motions of any scenario so long as it was ultimately beneficial to himself. Nobody can deny that some of the information that Boshell went on to give to the police proved to be reasonably accurate; likewise, nobody can deny that some of it proved to be entirely false. The problem that exists in the here and-now is that nobody can say with any certainty which evidence falls into which category.

Sadly, Dean Boshell is no more and cannot be questioned about the authenticity of any of the information that he gave. Considering the views of all those who knew him and his inability to tell the truth, everything he told the police should be regarded as unreliable. As his former lover Carla Shipton so eloquently put it, 'Dean had a problem with telling the truth: he didn't know what the truth was.'

7

SNOOKER LOOPY NUTS ARE WE

It became clear from the outset that Boshell was never going to give the police his full cooperation, as he had promised. Instead, he decided to cherry pick crimes with which he could tempt the police. He began to play a bizarre game that he believed would result in the police needing him more than he needed them. Boshell thought that once he had the upper hand, he could then negotiate a better deal when he came to be sentenced for the burglary at Jewson's. The criminal company that Boshell kept meant that he didn't just have a good hand of cards with which to play the police, he had an entire pack.

Testing the water, rather than diving in head first, Boshell initially offered the police details of fairly minor crimes and criminals of which they were already aware. He named one man who was selling stolen tax discs, another counterfeit designer clothing. He also told them the identity and address of the person who stored Alvin's stolen goods for him. Boshell's information was received with thanks but little enthusiasm. The police were told about these sorts of matters more often than time allowed or their limited resources permitted them to prosecute those committing the crimes. Sensing that Boshell was holding back on far more serious criminal activities, his police handler felt the need to remind him – 'in no uncertain terms' – that he had to tell the police everything that he knew in relation to crime if he wished to continue being an informant.

Keen to appear compliant, within a month Boshell had begun telling the police about one of Percival and Alvin's plans to rob a drug dealer from Basildon using guns. He also said that he had information that might be relevant to the Locksley Close shootings. Boshell said that

Alvin had told him that he could lay his hands on cyanide and hand grenades. Asked what Alvin intended doing with such lethal weapons, Boshell said that Alvin had bragged to him, 'The Trettons could end up getting a syringe full of cyanide being injected into a milk bottle on their doorstep, or a hand grenade being thrown through their letterbox.'

Finally, the police appeared to sit up and listen. If Boshell was telling the truth, it would prove that Alvin had a deep-seated hatred for the Tretton family and therefore a clear motive for wanting to shoot them.

Only Boshell knows why he decided to discuss aspects of the Locksley Close shootings with the police. It was a crime that he had been actively involved in. Although he never went so far as to implicate himself in any serious wrongdoing, Boshell must have known that if the police did arrest his accomplices there was a possibility that they would talk about his involvement. Those who knew Boshell have since commented that as the date for him to appear in court approached he became noticeably depressed and increasingly desperate. Boshell was painfully aware that if he was given a lengthy prison sentence he would lose his girlfriend Elizabeth and all that their relationship had promised.

His darkest secrets could, he realised, become his guiding light. If Boshell told the police everything he knew, maybe, just maybe, he could escape a custodial sentence and set up home with the family he longed for. Seven weeks before Boshell was due to appear at Southend Crown Court for sentencing, he concocted a story for the police that was a combination of fact and fiction about the Locksley Close shootings.

He said that he had been the driver of a car on the night of the shootings and his passengers, Alvin and Percival, had been in possession of a double-barrelled shotgun. The inclusion of Percival was an obvious choice for Boshell to make since most people in the area believed that Percival was guilty or at least involved in the shootings because he had already been arrested.

Boshell told the police that the three of them had been 'spooked' by a police car and 'his bottle had gone', so they had abandoned the vehicle. 'Later the same evening,' Boshell continued, 'Alvin had asked me to drive to Locksley Close, but I had refused to do so. Alvin had called me a cunt for not doing as he had asked, but the following day he acted as though nothing had happened.'

The police did their best to convince Boshell to tell them more about the shootings, but every time he agreed to discuss the incident the story seemed to change. In one of his versions of events, Boshell said that Ricky Percival and 'a doorman named Dave' were responsible. Up until this point, none of the officers had heard of 'doorman Dave'.

Beginning to doubt the authenticity of Boshell's information, the police reminded him that he had agreed to be truthful with them at all times. In an effort to prove to them that he was honouring the agreement that he had made, Boshell offered to take the police to the drain in which the shotgun used in the shootings had been dumped. Boshell knew that the gun was not there because he had already searched for it with Alvin. Regardless, Boshell needed to prove that he was a trustworthy informant and so decided to act out his part and feigned surprise that it was no longer there as he stood at the drain accompanied by the police.

In fact, the police also knew that the gun was no longer there because they had recovered it. They just wanted to test Boshell's knowledge of the crime and ensure that he was telling them the truth.

Unwittingly, the police had failed miserably with the second half of their objective: Boshell was now considered to be trustworthy. In reality, he had earned his status by telling the police half-truths and lies.

The general public are in the main of the opinion that if the police know who has committed a crime they should lock them up. Fortunately or otherwise, depending on which side of the fence you live your life, the police are not supposed to be able to do this. *Thinking* that they know who is guilty of a crime is a world away from *proving* that somebody has actually done anything. That is why the police are duty-bound to painstakingly gather all the available evidence before they charge a suspect and present everything to the courts so that the guilt or innocence of the accused can be ascertained by a jury. Because of forensic tests and the time it takes to gather and evaluate evidence, it can be months before any arrests in a major investigation are made. The police had already arrested Percival for the Locksley Close shootings and so arresting him again would have been pointless – Boshell's information was not only contradictory but was also made up of the same gossip that every villain in Essex had been repeating since the incident first happened.

Not wishing to dismiss Boshell's efforts out of hand, the police tasked him to find out all that he could about the incident. Boshell's court date was now only a few weeks away and his chances of securing a reduced sentence were looking increasingly slim. He had taken the information regarding the shootings as far as he dared, so, in a last ditch attempt to win favour, Boshell told his handler that the robbery of a drug dealer, which Alvin had been talking about for some time, was now imminent.

When asked to find out who was going to be robbed, when and where, Boshell said that he had not yet managed to discuss the job in any detail with Alvin because he was away working in Kent. However, he said he would be returning shortly.

Boshell told his handler at their next meeting that he had spoken to Alvin and he had been asked to steal a car. Alvin required a vehicle for use in the robbery and he was prepared to pay Boshell between £150 and £300 for stealing one. Boshell said that Alvin, Percival and a man named Nipper Ellis would be the three men robbing the drug dealer and they would be armed with two handguns. The reason they were going to be armed, according to Boshell, was that their intended target received regular visits from 'trigger happy niggers'. Boshell told the police that Alvin and Percival trusted one another '110 per cent' but neither completely trusted Nipper Ellis. This was because they thought that he was capable of anything after allegedly shooting Essex Boy enforcer Pat Tate the year before he had been murdered in the Range Rover at Rettendon.

Boshell was disqualified from driving, so initially he was told that if Alvin did ask him to drive he was to give an excuse as to why he was not able to do so, like he had to babysit. However, after a risk assessment of the planned crime, those allegedly involved and Boshell's driving ban, the handler was instructed by a senior officer to provide him with a vehicle for use in the robbery. Boshell was offered an estate car, which he refused, but he did accept a Mondeo after explaining that the only cars he ever stole were Fords.

The police plan was that when the would-be robbers had reached the busy arterial road that runs between Southend and Basildon, an armed response unit would stop the car on the pretence of searching for drugs and the occupants would be arrested. Over the next few days, Boshell was constantly on the phone to his handler, giving excuse after excuse about why the robbery hadn't yet taken place. Eventually running out of excuses, Boshell said that he was waiting for a call about the robbery from Alvin but had heard nothing.

For reasons never explained, the robbery, if ever planned, did not take place. When Alvin was asked about this robbery many years later, of course he blamed Percival and Nipper Ellis as the driving force behind the conspiracy. He told police: 'The reason we focused on robbing drug dealers was because they were easy targets. They had what we wanted: money and drugs. We also knew that they wouldn't squeal to the police. Who in their right mind would report the theft of their drugs? I think the first one we planned to do was a mixed-race guy in his 30s. He was quite flash and wore expensive clothes. He mainly dealt in heroin and crack cocaine. He lived in Basildon on one of the council estates. I had met him once in the Woodcutters Arms some time before we ever discussed robbing him. I was aware that Nipper Ellis or Percival knew one of his runners and he had agreed to give us access to the guy's premises so that we could rob him. Various tactics were discussed regarding gaining entry and it was eventually decided that the runner would also have to get a slap so there was no suspicion raised concerning his involvement. One night, myself, Percival and Nipper went round to the man's address to do a reconnaissance of the area.

'Whilst I was in the car, Nipper produced a handgun; it was like an old revolver. I don't know why he was carrying it that night, but it might have been for his own protection, as a price had been put on his head for shooting Pat Tate. We looked around the area where the drug dealer lived. It was near a pub called the Watermill.

'We left shortly after arriving. Nipper still had the gun on him. For some reason, the robbery never did take place, I don't know why. It could have been because we had found another drug dealer who had more money and more drugs than the mixed-race guy. This other dealer also lived in Basildon and we referred to him as JH.

'Again, this robbery was organised by Nipper. I had never heard of JH, but I knew he was an old-time villain in his 50s. There was talk that there would be in the region of £100,000 in his home. We decided that we would watch him and his house for a couple of days so we could get to know his movements. We did this by using different cars and communicating by walkie-talkies. Through our surveillance activities we discovered that he drove a Mercedes and he had another property near Southend. During the planning stage, Nipper said that if we were going to go ahead with the job we would need to arm ourselves, as he believed the guy had firearms in his house. The talk of firearms didn't appeal to me; I thought it was a bit out of my league. I didn't trust Nipper either. I thought he would probably put a bullet in both Percival's and my head if we came out of there with a large amount of cash.

'I decided not to take part in the crime. I can't recall how I got out of it, but there was no further mention of it. It never did take place.'

The reason the robberies never did take place is because they were probably no more than drink- and drug-fuelled fantasies of Alvin's. Boasting to his entourage of impressionable young men like Boshell, Alvin would regularly talk about 'big-time villains' whom he knew or associated with. Unfortunately for Nipper Ellis, he was one man Alvin loved to talk about because he had such a colourful past.

These days Nipper works hard, making an honest living for himself, but more than a decade ago he became embroiled in a dispute that has made him part of Essex gangland folklore. Nipper was initially reluctant to talk to me about his past because he feels the need to move on, but he agreed to do so after reading the 'bloody rubbish', he said, that Alvin had told the police about him.

In 1994, Nipper was friends with Tucker, Tate and Rolfe. I used to see him on a fairly regular basis at the clubs and parties that we all attended and I can only describe him as being a thoroughly decent and polite guy. One day, Nipper made a silly remark in jest about Tucker and one of his numerous mistresses. This got back to Tucker and in a drug-induced rage he decided to teach Nipper a lesson – a lesson from Tucker usually entailed his pupil being beaten senseless or tortured, or both. One particularly troublesome pupil who refused to absorb Tucker's words of wisdom concerning a personal healthcare plan was murdered and his body dumped in a ditch.

What occurred in the weeks that followed Nipper's misdemeanour can only be described as cowardly and disgraceful. Recalling his own particular group session with Tucker and his friends, Nipper explained: 'Tucker stuck a loaded pistol into my temple and threatened to kill me. Tucker, Tate, Rolfe and others then came after me with a machete and threatened to hack off my hand and foot. They looted my home and smeared their shit all over the possessions they left behind.'

Nipper was not the only one these cowards had tried to intimidate: his father and sister were threatened with all sorts of unsavoury punishments and injury.

Nipper Ellis is nobody's fool and, like any man with dignity, he refused to stand by and allow thugs to bully him or his family. He confronted Tucker and Rolfe with a loaded shotgun and they fled to the nearest police station, where they both made statements complaining about Nipper threatening to kill them. Fearing an armed reprisal, Nipper purchased a Smith and Wesson handgun for £600 and a bulletproof vest for £400. Tate, who had been telling anybody who cared to listen that he was going to execute Nipper, was shot soon afterwards. A brick was thrown through his bathroom window and when he went to investigate, he was hit. 'I might be small, but someone had to stand up to those scumbags,' Nipper said.

After the botched attempt on Tate's life, Nipper was invited to meet him in hospital to 'sort out the misunderstanding', but Tate had a gun hidden in his hospital bed and was planning to blow his brains out as soon as he stepped into the room. Nipper found this out and rather wisely didn't bother turning up for the visit. A nurse found the gun when she was making up Tate's bed and called the police, and he was eventually jailed for possessing a firearm.

Nipper was arrested for shooting Tate, but there was insufficient evidence to charge him. He was, however, jailed for seven and a half months for illegally possessing firearms.

'When I was in jail, I received numerous death threats,' Nipper said. 'On one occasion, two men came up to me and told me that a £10,000 contract had been put on my head. As soon as I was released from prison, I was ordered to leave town. I was told that if I ignored the warnings Tucker and his gang would retaliate. A hit man went to my dad's door looking for me. My family were told that Tucker and Tate planned to snatch my little sister and cut off her fingers one by one. She was only 15 at the time and was absolutely terrified. The threats only stopped when Tucker, Tate and Rolfe were murdered at Rettendon in their Range Rover. Those three were nasty, vicious bullies. They are not missed. They were scum and the world today is a better place without them.'

Telling Boshell and others that he was involved with a character like Nipper really boosted Alvin's ego. He felt good thinking that people associated him with some of the country's most infamous gangsters. But the truth was very different.

Nipper said: 'I am not involved in crime any more, but if I was I certainly wouldn't be involved with a loser like Alvin. To suggest that I planned to rob drug dealers with him or anybody else is pure fantasy. What would anybody expect to get off some lowlife drug dealer holed up in a council cave in Basildon – £50? Trust me, if I was going to risk going to prison for ten to fifteen years, it wouldn't be for the worldly possessions of a two-bob drug dealer.

'I did know Alvin, but he was not my mate. I recall being at his ex-partner's house when he turned up clearly out of his head on cocaine. Alvin was ranting about Malcolm Walsh because it was the anniversary of his death. I thought he was trying to look big in front of me by saying, "Tonight's the night those bastards will be meeting Malcolm again." I didn't take much notice of him, but the following day I heard that they had been shot.

'Alvin was like the Pied Piper of Horror around Southend, luring younger, weaker people than himself into drugs so that he could bully, use and discard them. The geezer makes me feel sick. If I had been involved in planning these robberies or possessing firearms, why haven't the police bothered to talk to me? As for Boshell telling his police handler about me, I had never even heard of Boshell at the time. He was obviously just passing on shit he had heard from Alvin.

Alvin knew that burglary had become a crime of the past – safes were just too secure and alarms were becoming too sophisticated. He had noticed that Ricky Percival was making a good living out of selling drugs and so he decided that he would hang up his gloves, put away his crowbar and concentrate all of his efforts in and around the lucrative drug world.

Drug dealing is an extremely risky business: if the police do not bring you down, rival dealers or informants most certainly will. Counter-surveillance techniques have to be employed when combating the police and extreme violence has to be used to deter or destroy rival dealers and informants. Alvin thought he was well equipped on all fronts – what he failed to appreciate was that rival drug dealers will think twice about taking on a powerful man, but drug-dealing informants will have no hesitation whatsoever in passing on information to the police to bring down a man who threatens them.

Somebody else facing up to the problems that a lifestyle change brings was Dean Boshell. Nobody knows for sure if he made the robbery stories up or if he exaggerated beer talk and boasting that he had heard and turned it all into conspiracies that he genuinely believed. What is known is that the police were losing patience with Boshell. The information that he had given had not resulted in a single arrest. Boshell knew he was going to have to come up with something more than idle gossip. He needed to tell the police about a serious crime that he knew was going to be committed or the names of the perpetrators of one that had already taken place. Failure, he realised, would result in him appearing in court with zero bargaining power. A lengthy prison sentence would undoubtedly be imposed and Elizabeth and the family he craved would slip from his grasp.

If affairs of the heart were not enough for Boshell to contend with, his police informant status was about to be exposed.

A man named Mark Bradford was on police bail in connection with the murder of a 24-year-old heroin addict named Danny Davies. A father of one, Davies had died ten hours after being stabbed once in the buttock during a fight over a drug deal in Basildon. Bradford was completely innocent of any involvement in this murder and did not face any charges in connection with it; however, his bail conditions whilst the murder was still being investigated included signing on at a police station every day to ensure that he did not abscond. Waiting to be attended to at the reception desk one day, Bradford saw Boshell walk out of an office accompanied by a man dressed in a suit whom he assumed was a detective.

'Boshell and I acknowledged one another before he walked out of the police station,' Bradford said. 'A few days later, I met Alvin and told him about Boshell being with the police. Initially, Alvin didn't seem too concerned, but one or two days later he rang me up, asking what day and what time had I seen Boshell. He also wanted to know if the man with Boshell had been in uniform or plain clothes. Alvin seemed really concerned about Boshell being in the company of a policeman; he told me that he had found out that he was a grass.'

When Alvin questioned Boshell about what Bradford had seen, Boshell explained that the police had been trying to obtain information from him. Alvin appeared to accept this and told Boshell that he would get in touch with the officer concerned and offer him money to pass on information about police matters that might be of use to him. It is not known if Alvin did actually contact or try to bribe the police officer. Regardless of what Alvin says today, the seeds of doubt concerning Boshell's loyalty to him must have been firmly planted in his mind at the time of this incident.

Seeds grow, so too does animosity, which can fester into feelings of extreme dislike or even blind hatred. Boshell was living dangerously – he knew what the punishment for being an informant was in the Essex underworld – but to save his dream of having a family and escape a lengthy term of imprisonment he was prepared to take his chances.

Boshell would have been acutely aware that the atmosphere between himself and Alvin was changing for the worse. Despite being warned by police that he should not encourage others to commit crime or take part in criminal activities himself, Boshell encouraged Alvin to rob the Wickford snooker club, where Carla Shipton, one of his girlfriends, was working. Whilst conspiring to commit the robbery with Alvin, Boshell also kept his police handler abreast of the plans that he was accusing Alvin of making. The manager was going to be grabbed after he had locked the premises up, his keys taken, the alarm disarmed and the safe emptied. Unfortunately for the police, Boshell claimed that he had no idea when the robbery was going to take place or, apart from Alvin, who was going to be taking part in it, but he admitted that the idea to do the job had been one of his from a year earlier.

After being tasked by his handler to find out more about the robbery, Boshell reported back that firearms would not be used as the manager was an old man, but that they would put him in the boot of a car. In the hope of deflecting his involvement in the planning of the robbery onto Alvin, Boshell didn't mention that his girlfriend was the assistant manager at the snooker club. He did point out, however, that Alvin's wife 'associates with a barmaid from there'.

The information that Boshell was now prepared to give to the police indicated that he was not only trying to secure a reduced prison sentence but was also keen to have his one-time hero, Damon Alvin, removed from the scene. No reason – other than that Alvin had discovered that Boshell was an informant – has ever been given for this.

Unlike the two previous robberies about which Boshell had talked to the police, the robbery at the snooker club did eventually go ahead. Describing the robbery to police several years later, Alvin said: 'Dean Boshell first started talking about robbing the Wickford snooker club about a year before the crime was actually committed. Boshell was dating a couple of girls who worked at the snooker club – one was named Emma, the other Carla Shipton. He went in the club regularly and told me that it was potentially a robbery target. I don't remember meeting Emma at any point, but I do know she shared a bedsit with Boshell in London Road, Leigh-on-Sea. I met Carla – Boshell used to bring her around to my house and we socialised together with my partner. Carla seemed a nice girl, and she and Boshell seemed pretty fine together.

'When Carla used to come to my house, she would always talk about her job at the snooker club. I asked how successful it was, how much money it took, about the alarm system, cameras, panic alarms, and when would be the best time to rob it. Carla answered all of my questions without hesitation and didn't spare any detail. I extracted everything I needed to know from her over a period of time. It must have been obvious to her that I was up to no good and she would have sensed this. As time went on, I then began discussing with Carla how and what I was going to do. I still hadn't involved Ricky Percival at this stage or even checked the premises out.

'The plan discussed with Carla was that she was going to let me in after her shift had ended. I wasn't going to do the job on my own and was planning to get someone in to help me. I think I may have asked Boshell first, as we were good friends, but I can't recall. He may have declined to get involved for one reason or another. At some stage I approached Percival, explained the job to him and what plans were involved. He agreed that he would assist me with the robbery.

'A week or so before the job actually took place, myself and Percival went to the club late at night. I can't remember if we had contacted Carla to let her know that we were coming, but I recall attracting her attention as she left the club. We were sitting in our vehicle in the car park and Carla walked over and got in the back. I don't think Percival or Carla knew each other, but if Carla did know anything about Percival it would have only been things that Boshell would have told her. As she got into the back of the vehicle, she began to tell me about the layout of the building, security issues and any concerns about the manager. I did all of the talking, as Percival did not know her.

'I think we may have met Carla on one more occasion before we carried out the job. It was at the same location, just to go through again what we had originally discussed. Carla agreed with us that when her shift concluded and she was the last remaining staff member on the premises she would leave the front door open for us to gain entry. This would ensure that the manager was alone in the club. I think if there were to be any problems or complications on the night concerning staff and people being left in the club, then I think Carla would have probably rung me.

'I discussed the final details of how we were going to do the job with Percival. We decided that we would take balaclavas and gloves. Percival may have said that he was going to take ammonia. The reason we probably took ammonia was to disable the manager. There are not many people who can fight and still be aware of everything that is going on around them after being squirted with ammonia. I had never carried anything like that before. On the day of the robbery, I picked up Percival from his home address.

'It's possible that when I picked Percival up, I may have seen him with a "squirty" bottle of ammonia. I recall that this was a small, white washing-up bottle. I believe that we may have arrived at the club around midnight, which would have roughly been the time that Carla was due to finish work. Once parked, we got out of the car and walked towards the club. It looked as if it had already closed, as there were no lights on in the entrance area. I can't recall how long we were waiting outside, but it didn't seem long. Carla may have rung me on my mobile to say that she was finishing soon.

'Whilst we were waiting, I didn't see anyone exit or enter the club. I remember approaching Carla from where we were standing and as she held the door open for us I asked her if the manager was alone. She replied, "Yes, he is," and then went on to tell me that he was by the bar drinking. Carla didn't seem at all bothered by what she knew was about to happen. When we had finished talking, Carla walked off, but I don't know if she caught a cab or walked home. Percival and I made our way into the front entrance of the club and hid on the stairs. When we were happy that Carla had left the area, we began to climb the stairs towards the bar.'

The manager of the snooker club had no idea that he was about to be literally dragged into the most terrifying ordeal of his life. Sitting on a stool at the bar with his back to the stairs where Alvin and his accomplice were lying in wait, he sipped his drink as he watched the television.

Alvin continued: 'When we reached the top of the stairs, we waited for about ten or fifteen minutes, but every so often I crept forward to the main entrance to see what was going on. I recall that the manager was sitting with his back to me.

'We still had no plan with regards to what we were going to do, but I remember at some stage telling Percival that I was going to get the manager on the floor. I remember reaching the corner of the lounge bar and then running towards him. As I reached the manager I think I caught him by surprise; I struck him in the face and he fell to the floor. The punch didn't knock him out, so we both grabbed him in an attempt to disable him. Our main aim was to hold him whilst we tied him up. He was swearing, resisting and struggling with us whilst lying face down on the floor. Both Percival and I were trying to get his hands behind his back, but I don't recall this being much of a problem. We were not assaulting him whilst we were trying to do this. However, Percival did squirt him in the head area with a washing-up liquid bottle full of ammonia.

'We managed to get his hands behind his back and Percival produced some cable-zip ties. The manager said we could take whatever we wanted but asked us not to put his hands behind his back, but we still did. Once the ties were on his wrists and secured behind his back, the manager became compliant and I got the impression that he just wanted the whole scenario to be over with. Percival and I got off the manager but ensured he remained face down so he couldn't cause us any trouble. I asked him where the CCTV tapes and the panic buttons were located. He said that there were no cameras and then he went on to tell me that the panic button was behind the bar. I asked him where the safe was and for the keys to open it.

'Once in possession of the keys, I walked into the storeroom where the safe was located. Percival remained in the lounge bar standing over the manager. There wasn't a lot of cash in the safe – I would say that there was only a few hundred pounds – and I was very disappointed about this. I put all of the cash in the safe into a cloth moneybag and went back to join Percival.

'As I approached him, I noticed that he was holding a gun in his right hand loosely by his side. I also noticed that the manager had broken free from the cable ties, which may have been why Percival had got the gun out. I wasn't shocked by seeing Percival with a gun, as I had got to know him a lot more since the Locksley Close shootings and I knew what he was like with guns. I was kind of surprised, though, as he had never discussed bringing anything like that on this job with me.

'I told Percival that there was nothing in the safe and at some point during our conversation we agreed that we would empty the fruit machines. I think the manager must have overheard me telling Percival that there was no money in the safe because he said something about him having already banked it. He must have heard us talking about emptying the fruit machines because he told us which keys were needed to get into them. I had trouble opening the machines and so went behind the bar and picked up a screwdriver. I returned to the fruit machine and began to prise away a corner so I could get my hands in and pull the back off. As I was doing this, the manager began making sarcastic remarks about the damage that I was causing. It's possible that there was more money in the fruit machines than there was in the safe.

'I think in total we only managed to get about £1,000 from the club. When we were finished, I made the decision to put the manager in the storeroom. We got him to his feet and ushered him towards it – I was in front of him and Percival was behind. Once he was inside, I locked the door.

'We then made our escape back out towards the main stairs. We were walking briskly, but I wasn't too concerned, as the manager couldn't get out of the storeroom. During the journey back to Percival's house, I asked him if the gun he had was real or a replica, and he said it was real. We also talked about the amount of money that we had stolen, as we were both disappointed.

'Before we got to Percival's house, he said he wanted to get rid of the gun and the ammonia. He told me to drive to Belfair's woods, which I knew he had been using to hide particular items. When we arrived, Percival hid the gun, the ammonia, gloves and balaclava under some ivy that was growing on the ground. I hid my gloves and balaclava in the same location. After leaving the woods, we went to Percival's house, where we counted the money in his bedroom. We split the money 50–50 and agreed to give Carla Shipton £200 to keep her sweet.'

The day after the robbery Alvin claims that he, Boshell and another man whom I shall call 'Dan Baker' returned to Belfair's woods to retrieve the gun and other items. What Alvin doesn't explain is how Boshell, who had told police that he had no idea when the robbery was going to take place, had become aware that Alvin had carried out the robbery.

It's my belief that it was, in fact, Boshell who accompanied Alvin on the robbery and not Percival. Alvin claims that Boshell and Baker got out of his car to have a cigarette when they arrived at Belfair's woods and he went alone into the undergrowth to retrieve the weapons and tools he had hidden.

'I had trouble locating the items,' Alvin said, 'and whilst I was looking I was joined by the other two, who began searching with me. I don't think I had told them exactly what I was looking for, but they must have guessed, as I believe it was actually one of them who found the items. After leaving the woods, I drove to Percival's house. During the journey I was aware that Boshell was rifling through the bag and handling the gun. He appeared to be playing around with it and examining it up close. He was asking me whose it was, but I can't remember if I told him or not.

'Boshell then passed the gun to Baker, who began to lecture us on his experience with firearms. When we arrived at Percival's, I got out, leaving the other two in the car. I handed the bag containing the items over to Percival and left.

'A day or two later I had a conversation with Carla Shipton on the telephone. She said that the police had interviewed her and she seemed pretty firm in what she had told them, so I didn't think she was going to be a problem to us.'

Carla Shipton had indeed been 'pretty firm' when the police had visited her. She told them that on the night of the robbery she had not been working and had not been expected to do so. The manager had telephoned Carla's home earlier that evening to ask if she was available to work, but she had already gone out with friends. Her brother Clayton, who had answered the phone, offered to work in her place and the manager agreed to this because he had done so on several occasions in the past. At 11 p.m., Carla had driven to the snooker club to give her brother a lift home. When he had finished work, Clayton told Carla that he wanted to buy a kebab and he would meet her outside.

When Clayton was interviewed by police shortly after the robbery, he told them that after he had left the club he had seen 'two males acting strange outside'. He said, 'One of them seemed to stare at me before jumping behind the bin sheds. As I walked past them, one of the men pretended that he was urinating. Crossing the car park, I looked back and saw that one of the men was trying the snooker club door. My sister joined me at the kebab shop shortly afterwards. We spoke about the two men. My sister said that she had only seen one but, from her description, it sounded like one of the same men that I had seen.'

Carla and her brother had discussed calling the police, but as the snooker hall backs onto Wickford High Street, a regular haunt of hoodies and delinquents, they had reasoned that these particular people posed no more of a threat than the usual misfits that plagued the area. They thought no more about it and went home.

Three days after the robbery, Dean Boshell met his police handler and told him that he had been driving Alvin and Baker around when Alvin had asked him to drive to Belfair's woods to pick something up for Ricky Percival. After being directed to an access road on the edge of the woods, Boshell said that Alvin and Baker had got out of the vehicle and returned shortly afterwards with a black handgun, a magazine, fourteen bullets, two scarves, a cosh, two baseball caps and a washing-up bottle containing ammonia. Boshell claimed that Alvin did not tell him what these items had been used for. Everything was put into a plastic bag and, according to Boshell, handed to Percival.

One imagines that after such a serious crime had been committed the police would have descended on Percival's home in the hope of finding the gun and any other incriminating evidence. For reasons known only to the police, neither Percival nor Alvin were ever questioned.

Seven days before Boshell was due to appear in court for sentencing, he contacted the police and told them that he would be willing to become a supergrass and give Queen's evidence against those responsible for the Locksley Close shootings and other matters. In return, he wanted the charges he faced in relation to the burglary at Jewson's to be dropped.

Boshell was advised that the charges would remain in place, but if he was willing to testify against the Locksley Close gunmen and the snooker club robbers 'things could be done for him'.

Undecided which way to fall – because either way fall he must – Boshell went away to consider his options. Before he could reach a decision, fate struck Boshell a cruel blow.

8

A VOICE FROM BEYOND THE GRAVE

Nothing in Dean Boshell's world was straightforward. He deceived everybody that he encountered in life. In the company of his friends he was a criminal, but in their absence he was a police informant. In his relationships, he had pledged his future to Elizabeth Reece and shared his bed with Carla Shipton. He even stole from his own family. Without exception, everybody was a victim of his treachery.

A few days before he was due in court, Boshell, drunk and behaving in a wholly inappropriate manner, got involved in an altercation with a police officer. During the struggle that ensued, Boshell damaged a police car and was arrested. A routine check on the police computer revealed that Boshell had outstanding warrants out against him for a variety of offences and so any chance he might have had of being granted bail was denied. He was taken to court the following morning and remanded in custody to HMP Chelmsford to await sentencing.

When I spoke to Elizabeth about this period in Boshell's life, she felt that his actions that night ruined not only his life but also any future they might have had together. 'Everything was going well between Dean and I until the night he decided to go out with his so-called friends. Dean failed to come home and, as I grew increasingly concerned about him, a police officer knocked on my door. He said that Dean was in his car outside and he needed some clothes. Dean later told me that he had smashed up a police car and he had also been wanted for some time on previous matters. I do not know whether that was true or not. Regardless, Dean was sent to prison.

'We kept in touch by writing every week. In his first letter to me, Dean seemed really sad and down. I have kept all of the letters he sent me and reading them again makes me realise just how depressed and low Dean was at that time.'

In that letter, Dean wrote:

> Thanks for coming down to the police station for me. Now that I am away from you, it's hit me just how much I miss you. Damon is going to go around and see you. I'm not sure if he has been around already. I have got the radio on, just chilling, thinking about all the things I wished I had never done. I can't turn back time – I wish that I could. I keep hearing that R. Kelly song ['If I could turn back the hands of time']. I really wish that I could because I would be at home with you.
>
> Do you still think you might be pregnant? Let me know. I really need to know. It's all I am thinking about. I do want a baby with you. What with my looks and your brain, it will have a head start in life.

'Dean wrote to me regularly and phoned me every day. Apart from me, I don't think he had a lot of contact with people. He used to say that he had written to his mum, but she ignored his letters. His brother Damon had visited him a couple of times, but even he had let him down by not always turning up when he said he would. I did feel sorry for Dean, as nobody really seemed to give a toss about him.

'He did eventually seem to settle down in prison and he began to think about and plan for the future. He told me: "When I get out, all my life is going to revolve around is going to work, being with you and your daughter Lauren and going to the gym. It sounds like a proper family environment, doesn't it?"'

Elizabeth showed me the letter, which continues:

> Damon did not come to see me yesterday, fuck knows why. My fucking mother hasn't written back yet. I don't know what the fuck she is playing at. I can't wait for you to come up and visit me. It seems like ages since I last saw you. I guess that's what love does to you. I don't think I have ever been in love before. Last time I went away I didn't care about my ex, but with you it is totally different because I do nothing but think about you. You're lucky to have me, I know, I know, and I am lucky to have you. I just wish I could be with you now.
>
> My next-door neighbour is really pissing me off. He keeps saying that he can't cope, but what is he telling me for? I am not a Good Samaritan. The worst thing about it is he only has six weeks left to serve. I fucking hate people like that. I might

tell the prison officers that he is bullying me so he has to serve longer – that will shut him up, ha ha ha.

Someone who appeared in court for the same sort of charges as me got two years. I couldn't stand being away from you for that long. I am going to try every scam in the book to get a smaller sentence. I will even give the judge a backhander. I just want to get my judgment day over. I am going to tell the judge that it's not only me that he is sentencing but also my partner and little girl and it's not fair on them. We will just have to wait and see what happens. Just remember, they can't stop time and time is all it will take for me to come home.

You said in your letter that time was dragging, well it is for me too, but we both have to keep our chins up to get through this. I swear to God it will never happen again. If you do fuck me off, I will totally understand, as you deserve better. All I can say is that I love you and your daughter and I hope you do stick by me. I promise I will stick by you for as long as you want me to.

I know I have been in prison a few times, but I never really had anybody to think about before. A few years down the line, I want to give Lauren a little brother or sister. All I want is my own family, someone who is there for me and people I can be there for, too. It will be like a storybook ending, we will all live happily ever after.

Unfortunately for Boshell, Elizabeth did not share his dream. She told me, 'As the date for Dean to be sentenced approached, he grew increasingly fearful of how long he might have to serve. I was becoming more distant with him because it wasn't just my life I had to consider, it was that of my daughter. I didn't want to risk bringing her up in an environment where my partner was in and out of prison like some sort of antisocial yo-yo. I thought the world of Dean, but in my heart of hearts I knew that there would never be any storybook ending because I would have to terminate our relationship. I couldn't tell him whilst he was in prison – it would have destroyed him. I decided to help him through the difficult situation he was in and break the news gently to him when he was released.

'I think Dean knew that I was in turmoil about our future together because he did all he could to convince me that he would not be in prison for long and we could pick up where we'd left off.'

In his next letter to Elizabeth, he wrote:

I saw a probation officer today. I blamed all of this trouble on drugs. I told him about you and Lauren. I said I had just met the right person and then this happens. The probation officer said, 'If there was a magic lamp in front of you and you had one wish, what would you wish for?' I said that it would be to be at home with you and Lauren. I put on the old tears; I think that worked, ha ha ha. I think he will give me a cracking report. Let's hope so. My solicitor said that I could get anything up to four years. I said you must be joking, but she said I have to always expect the worst.

She said I probably won't get that much as I have got an excellent probation report, plus she's going to ask for rehabilitation because I have said I have a drug habit. Depending on the judge, I could be given probation and a drug course, which means if I stay clean for a year I stay out of prison. That won't be hard because I never touch drugs. I am knocking drinking on the head when I get out because I always end up in prison as a result of it.

Damon never came up today; he is coming next week instead hopefully. I have had only one visit since I have been in so, like I said, when I get out everyone can kiss my arse because none of them are my friends. They are just wankers and when I get out if I see any of them the motherfuckers can go to hell. When I get out it's going to be about me, you and Lauren and one in the oven. Not straight away, though, but I hope you do want another kid because I would like you to have one.

When the day Boshell had been dreading arrived, he delivered his mitigation speech to the court whilst stuttering and showering those within striking distance with flecks of phlegm. His anxiety accentuated his stammer, making it impossible to understand what he was trying to say. The judge thanked Boshell 'for that' before sending him to prison for two years. The moment Elizabeth heard, she knew that Boshell's life would spiral from being dangerously erratic into some sort of suicidal free fall. All his hopes, plans and dreams would have been trashed.

'I'm not for one moment saying that he didn't deserve to be sent to prison,' Elizabeth said to me. 'Those that commit crime should face the consequences of their actions. I am just saying that maybe, just maybe, Dean's cries for help should have been given a little more attention when he was younger.

'Once sentenced, Dean's mask slipped; he no longer talked about mending his ways. He went back to talking about all of the things I do not like, such as violence and revenge.'

In a letter bristling with anger, Dean had written:

> I swear to God that if any man comes near you, I would go off my fucking head because you are all I have got and you are all I want. If anybody tries anything, God help them.
>
> I am sorry I am talking like this, but I have got a lot of things on my mind at the moment. There is you, Lauren and my mum has not wrote back to me yet. I have got all of these things building up and I am sure I am going to explode soon. I am reading a book at the moment about the IRA, it's called *Killing Rage* and it is really good. I might join the IRA, ha ha ha. You know, I smashed up that police car? Well, we have got the address of the person who grassed me up. He lives in Victoria Road, but the top end, fucking wanker.

Elizabeth said that when Boshell was released from prison he went to her home. 'We were polite and pleasant enough to one another,' she said, 'but he sensed that something was troubling me. When I said it was over between us, Dean became very defensive and said that he'd had enough of Southend and was going to disappear back up to Leeds, where he said his friends and some of his family were. I felt he was showing a bit of bravado, seeing if I would ask him not to go. I didn't, and shortly after gathering up his meagre possessions Dean left.

'He did come to see me a couple of times after that, just to see how I was and to say hello. He told me that he was very happy and doing well and I was genuinely pleased for him. Dean was a kind and caring person who loved my daughter and me. There isn't anything that he wouldn't have done for either of us. Dean only ever wanted a future with my daughter and me; he craved for a normal, everyday family life. Unfortunately, he looked up to his brother Damon as some sort of hero. I just wish I knew what sort of business or mess Dean ended up becoming involved in. Whatever it was, it would have been something that he was dragged into by Damon.

'On the anniversary of his death each year, I go to the spot on the beach where we spent our first day together to reminisce about him and the good times that we shared. News of his murder really shocked me. I cannot imagine why anybody in this world would have wanted to hurt him. The Dean I knew was so kind and gentle.

'In a way, I blame myself for his death. If I had found the strength to stand by him, Dean might have kept out of trouble and, more importantly, kept away from Damon. Had that happened, I have no doubt whatsoever that Dean would still be alive today. I have learned that it's not what you have in life, it's who you have that counts.'

Carla Shipton, the other woman in Boshell's complicated love life, had also stood by him whilst he was in prison. Rather than go out alone and risk being accused of having affairs, Carla had socialised with Alvin's partner Barbara. Occasionally, Alvin would go out with Barbara and Carla, or give Carla a lift to the prison to visit Boshell. For all his apparent faults, Damon appeared to Dean to be the perfect friend. If he wasn't supplying his daily newspapers, giving him money, electronic games or giving Elizabeth and her daughter gifts, he was looking after Carla.

Alvin had even approached Ricky Percival to ask him to supply Boshell with a course of protein supplements, as he had taken up bodybuilding whilst in prison. Percival had given Alvin the products free of charge on the basis that he was helping the friend of a friend. He later learned that Boshell had given them to Essex Boy Chris Wheatley. Boshell should have been eternally grateful for the apparent favours that his friend Alvin bestowed upon him, but Boshell only cared about one person and that was none other than Dean Boshell.

Not long after Boshell had been sentenced he was visited in prison by the police, who were hoping that he would continue to provide them with information about his criminal associates. Boshell told them that his 'best friend' Alvin was importing large amounts of cannabis from Amsterdam and another guy named 'Spanish Frank' was smuggling an ounce of heroin into the prison every week.

No one knows what prompted Boshell to do what he did next. Some say it was guilt, others believe that it was fear, but, as soon as the police officers had left the visiting room, Boshell rang Alvin and told him that he ought to be extra vigilant because the police had been to the prison and wanted to know all about his business. What Boshell failed to mention was the fact that he had supplied the officers with the information that they had requested.

Alvin's initial thoughts on Boshell warning him about the police interest in him was that it was an act of loyalty. This reinforced his trust in Boshell rather than making him wary of his sincerity. After asking Boshell the names of the officers who had been to the prison, Alvin immediately phoned them to ask what it was they wanted to know about him. He advised the officers that if they wanted questions answered about his business in the future, they should contact him and not Boshell.

Alvin did not get any sort of satisfactory response from the police and he heard no more about it. Perhaps it was drug-induced paranoia or simply intuition, but however hard Alvin tried to put the incident to the back of his mind he kept wondering, toying with the idea that maybe, just maybe, his friend Boshell was informing on him to the police. Alvin wondered if Boshell might have only told him about the visit because he could have been frightened that a fellow inmate might have seen the officers talking to him. Whatever conclusion Alvin reached, his relationship with Boshell was never the same again. Trust was replaced with open hostility. Fearing that he had been found out, Boshell refused to talk to the police ever again and concentrated on rebuilding Alvin's trust in him.

Boshell's Judas-like behaviour towards his friend was without question despicable, but Alvin's was not much better. His outward display of affection for Boshell masked a sinister and deceitful pattern of behaviour that can only be described as abhorrent. When Carla Shipton was alone with Alvin, on more than one occasion he tried to lure her into his bed and he regularly ridiculed his so-called friend Boshell in her company.

Carla told me that when it was coming up to her birthday Boshell had asked Alvin if he would buy her a card on his behalf, sign it and hand it to her. His prison income didn't stretch to a card and a gift, but he didn't want to ignore her special day.

'Damon agreed to do this for Dean and, as an additional favour, he said that he would enclose some money, say it was from Dean and tell me to get myself a present,' Carla said. 'I, of course, did not know anything about this at the time. When Damon gave me the card and I opened it, there was a two-pence piece inside. "What's this for?" I asked. He started laughing and said, "That's all your boyfriend could afford to give you." I didn't know what to say or do; Damon was still laughing and so I pretended to see the funny side of it, but inside I felt sick.

'Occasionally, Damon would give me a lift to the prison to visit Dean. One time, the prison drug-detection dog, which is led past all visitors, barked when it reached Damon. He was taken out of the queue by an officer and I was also asked to step aside, simply because I happened to be with him. We were told that the dog had indicated that one or both of us was carrying or had been in contact with controlled substances and we would either have to leave the premises or have a closed visit. Ordinarily visits take place at a table in a large hall, which permits private conversations and physical contact between prisoners and their visitors. Closed visits are conducted within the confines of a small room. Prisoners and their visitors are separated by a glass partition, which prevents any physical contact, and conversations are monitored.

'Damon and I, not wishing to disappoint Dean by not seeing him, opted for the closed visit. When we sat down to talk to Dean, Damon began laughing and joking with him about drugs. They began talking about smoking huge spliffs and snorting really long lines of cocaine off the visiting-room table. At the time, we did not know that our conversations were being monitored, but we found out as soon as the visit was over. Two detectives greeted us as we opened the door to leave. "Would you mind accompanying us?" they said to Damon and me. "We think you might know what this is about." One officer led Damon away and the other escorted me through the prison. I was taken from one office to another because they were trying to locate two female prison officers so that I could be searched.

'Images of big, butch lesbians with gnarled spade-like hands flashed through my mind, striking terror in my heart. Fortunately before my worst nightmare could become reality, the officer with me was informed that drugs had been found on Damon and he had confirmed that I had no knowledge of them. I'm wrong when I say drugs had been found *on* Damon – they were actually found in him. Damon had secreted cannabis that he had intended to give to Dean in his anus.

'Disappointment at not being able to kiss my boyfriend that day quickly turned to relief, and thoughts of mouthwash, toothpaste and violent scrubbing with a hard toothbrush.

'Having extracted the incriminating evidence from Damon, we and "it" were taken to a local police station "to be processed". After what seemed like an age, Damon and I were eventually released. Damon was in a foul mood. He said he'd been charged with possession of cannabis with intent to supply and the likelihood was that he'd be sent to prison. I wasn't particularly pleased myself. Despite doing no wrong, I was informed that I was now banned from visiting anybody in that particular prison. Dean would not be happy with this news but, because his hero Damon was involved, I knew that he wouldn't say much, if anything.

'When Damon appeared before magistrates in Norwich some time later for this incident, he was sentenced to three months' imprisonment.

'On the way home from our disastrous visit with Dean, Damon said that he had to stop off at Woolworths to spend some gift vouchers he had. It was near Christmas time and so I assumed that he was going to buy some presents. When he came back to the car, he seemed to have cheered up. He started asking me about my relationship with Dean, then started groping my leg. I was really shocked and demanded that he stop at once, but he ignored me.

'I got quite scared and kept saying that I was going to be late for work. I was really upset because I was his wife's best friend and he was supposed to be Dean's. I didn't dare tell Dean or Barbara what Damon had tried to do because they both would have been devastated. I put it down to Damon having a little too much Christmas spirit and decided to try and forget about it.

'When Barbara's birthday came around, we celebrated it by going out clubbing in Southend. I was getting ready at Damon and Barbara's house when the phone rang. It was Damon. He told Barbara that he was sending a man to the house for a change of clothing. He wanted Barbara to have a set ready and told her not to ask any questions when the man arrived to collect them. Not long afterwards a man did come to the house, Barbara gave him the clothes and he left without saying a word. When Damon eventually arrived home, he was wearing the clean set of clothing.

'Barbara told him, "I've made you chilli con carne for your dinner. It's in the saucepan," but when Damon lifted off the lid and looked at the food, he said, "I can't fucking eat that, it looks like the geezer's head I've just done." Nobody dared to pass comment.

'We went out shortly afterwards and ended up at a nightclub called Tots, in Southend. Barbara appeared to be upset by whatever Damon had done to the person earlier; she certainly wasn't herself. We went back to their house when the club closed and Barbara went upstairs for some reason. I went into the kitchen to put the kettle on. Damon came in behind me, put his arms around my waist and tried to shove his hand down the front of my trousers. There was a large mirror in the lounge and as I turned to face Damon I could see Barbara in it coming down the stairs. I pushed him away and said, "Get your hands off me. Have you no respect for Barbara?" At that moment, she walked into the kitchen, totally oblivious to what had been going on.

Damon looked at me with a sneer and walked off into the lounge.

'I thought Damon was sick for behaving the way he did, especially as it was Barbara's birthday and it was her best friend that he was trying to seduce. The fact I was Dean's girlfriend and he worshipped Damon made it even more disgusting. I really wanted to tell Barbara, but Damon would have sweet-talked his way out of it and probably blamed me. I decided once more, for everybody's sake, to keep quiet about it. I continued to socialise with Barbara after that night, but I always ensured that I was never left alone with Damon.

'When Dean was eventually released from prison, he rang me up and we arranged to meet at Damon's later that night. Barbara and I assumed Dean would be going out to celebrate his release with Damon and they wouldn't be home until late and so we went to play bingo. When we returned, Damon was home and he said that he hadn't seen Dean. I rang Dean's mobile, but he never answered, so I waited up all night for him. He didn't arrive. The following morning I was in a foul mood. I rang his mobile again, but there was still no answer. I got so annoyed I stormed round to his old flat and hammered on the door, but there was no response.

'Disheartened, I turned to walk away, but as I did so I caught a fleeting glimpse of a figure behind the net curtain of an upstairs window. I began pounding on the front door with the flat of my hand and continued until I saw somebody approaching through the frosted glass. When the door opened, a large black male said, "I am Lester, who are you and what do you want?" I didn't answer; I pushed past him and hurried upstairs. Dean's bedroom door offered no resistance, as I barged it open. Two young girls lying naked on the bed stared up at me in total shock. They were too afraid to speak. "Where is he?" I demanded. "Where is Dean?" The girls averted their eyes from me and glanced at an old wardrobe in the corner of the room.

'As I approached it, the doors opened and Dean stepped out, dressed in just his boxer shorts. "You bastard," I shouted. "How could you do this? These girls are only about fourteen!"

'Dean didn't answer. He just shrugged his shoulders and put his hands out as if to say it's a fair cop. I glared at him in total disgust and walked out of the flat. I decided there and then that I wanted nothing further to do with him. He would ring me occasionally to apologise when he was pissed, but I was determined not to renew our relationship. I continued to socialise with Barbara, but even our friendship dwindled and died before too long.

A VOICE FROM BEYOND THE GRAVE

'I was sad about all that had happened, but none of us can change the past. Dean chose others over me and I couldn't accept that.'

Carla Shipton is, of course, right: we cannot change the past. Today's decisions mould our future and so we should always think hard before we embark upon any particular path. A life littered with lies, deceit and deception had left Boshell's dreams for the future in tatters. What he couldn't have known was that his chosen path was about to end his short life.

9

INTO THE ABYSS

Pretty 19-year-old Kate Griffiths was the former girlfriend of Daniel Langley, one of Damon Alvin's closest friends. During their relationship, the couple used to go to the Woodcutters Arms to socialise and it was there that Griffiths was introduced to Malcolm Walsh's younger brother Kevin. Following the break-up of her relationship with Langley, Griffiths began dating Kevin. Romance blossomed between the two and before long Griffiths was living between her mum's house and Walsh's flat in Shannon Close, Leigh-on-Sea. Life for the couple revolved around regular, mundane visits to the Woodcutters and work. Griffiths managed a launderette that she and her father owned, and Walsh was employed on a casual basis in the construction industry. That was until Dean Boshell washed up at the pub one night after being dumped by not one but two girlfriends.

Boshell was in the company of his friend Damon Alvin and his partner Clair Sanders. Alvin had somehow convinced Sanders to allow Boshell to live in their home until he was able to secure an address of his own. On his release from prison Boshell had hoped that he could take up residence with either Carla or Elizabeth, but he had soon learned that his shoddy behaviour had resulted in both of those bridges being burned. Homeless and unemployed, he had turned to Alvin in desperation.

Thinking that Alvin had resolved his accommodation problem, Boshell began to celebrate and it wasn't long before he was staggering around the pub drunk out of his mind. Sanders was outraged when she saw the state Boshell had got himself into. Pulling Alvin to one side, she told him that under no circumstances was Boshell to go near their home.

Embarrassed but too weak to oppose Clair's will, Alvin told Boshell in front of everybody that his invitation to stay had been withdrawn. Despite Griffiths and Walsh having only been introduced to Boshell earlier that evening, they felt deeply sorry for him. 'Don't be like that,' Walsh said to Alvin. 'He's just got out of jail and has nowhere to go.'

'Fuck the cunt,' Alvin replied. 'If you're so fucking worried about him, you take him home.'

Rather than leave Boshell roaming the streets, Walsh invited him to stay at his flat until he found a place of his own. Once installed in Walsh's home, Boshell appeared to be in no hurry to resolve his housing problem – he would hang around the flat all day and ask Walsh's friends to buy him drinks in the Woodcutters Arms at night. Because he suffered from a stutter, Boshell was subjected to a degree of light-hearted banter from the locals, but he gave back as good as he got.

His choice of female company was also the butt of many jokes because he appeared to care little about size, species or their origins. One of his many lovers was described as 'five-foot-three tall, three-foot-five wide, woolly-haired and possibly human'.

Regardless of all the mickey-taking Boshell endured in the Woodcutters Arms, those who knew him say he was genuinely well-liked and he never once complained about the treatment he received.

It took a month for Boshell to secure his own accommodation and he only achieved this with the assistance of Alvin. Ever prudent, Alvin had employed jobless Boshell initially as a labourer; however, once Boshell had become financially dependent upon Alvin, he was easily coaxed into selling cocaine, ecstasy and cannabis for him.

To avoid any large quantities of these drugs being found at Alvin's home, he had decided it would be a good idea to provide Boshell with his own flat where the drugs could be stored and distributed from. Alvin paid the £350 deposit on the flat on Elmsleigh Drive in Leigh-on-Sea and Boshell moved in later the same day. To thank Walsh and Griffiths for accommodating him, Boshell invited the couple round to his flat and made them dinner. Neither Walsh nor his partner showed any sort of animosity towards Boshell during his rent-free residency at their home; in fact, Griffiths has very fond memories of him.

'I thought Dean was really sweet. He spoke to me a lot more than he spoke to Kevin. He was really easy to talk to. He was definitely better at talking to girls than men.

'He never talked much about his past, but he did tell me that he was from Beverley in Humberside and that he didn't get on with his family. He said he had two sisters, but I can't ever remember him going to visit them.

'All in all, Dean was a really nice bloke, but he could sometimes be a bit unreliable. The one thing I didn't like was that I knew he was seeing other girls as well as my friend Natalie. He had loads of girls' numbers stored on his phone and kept asking me not to tell Natalie if he went clubbing in Southend. After he moved to his new flat I seemed to see less and less of him.'

The reason Griffiths was seeing less and less of Boshell was because he was getting more and more involved with Alvin and the murky drug world that he was striving to control. Every weekend Boshell would visit the pubs and clubs that litter Southend seafront, plying Alvin's illicit substances. On Friday and Saturday nights, the town is awash with revellers and so Boshell had no shortage of customers, drinking partners or pretty girls to choose from. He would flit from bar to club to bar feeling something that he had never felt before: important. Everybody, it seemed, wanted to be his friend, not because they liked him but because the drugs he was selling were of good quality and reasonably priced. Having experienced hard times himself, Boshell was not unknown to give drugs to people on credit, so long as they promised to pay him the next time they met. Unfortunately for Boshell, the chance of a drug debt being honoured that was agreed in a nightclub when both parties were pissed is about as likely as world peace.

Boshell didn't help himself by acting out his fantasy of being a gangster to impress the steady stream of females he was constantly trying to seduce. He would supply them with free pills or free lines of cocaine, or peel off notes from a wad of Alvin's drug money to buy them drinks. Before Boshell knew it, he was accumulating numerous small debts that amounted to him owing Alvin one large one. Tensions between the two men were becoming more intense, not only because of Boshell's playboy lifestyle but also because of Alvin's own excessive use of cocaine. He started to believe that he was somehow invincible and treated everybody he met with contempt.

One night, two girls, Lisa and Donna, were making their way home after an enjoyable evening out in Southend when, as they passed Tots nightclub, Lisa was grabbed around the waist by a man. Laughing, he said, 'Hello, Nicole.' It wasn't a case of mistaken identity; people often remarked how much she resembled the Hollywood actress Nicole Kidman.

The person who had accosted Lisa was in the company of another man named Sean Buckley and a female, who walked off as soon as she saw what had happened. 'My name's Dean Boshell,' the man said as he released Lisa's waist and held out his hand. After talking for half an hour in the bitter cold, Boshell invited the girls to join him and Sean for a drink at his home. When they arrived at Elmsleigh Drive, they went up to Sean's flat, which was above Boshell's in a converted house. Boshell began to play Eminem on the stereo and told the girls it was his favourite music because he loved gangster lyrics.

In a statement made later to the police, Lisa said, 'After a while, Dean said to me, "Do you want some charlie?" I didn't really know what he meant by this. He then got up and disappeared down the stairs to his flat. When Dean came back up, he was holding a clear plastic bag that was about the size of a 2 lb bag of sugar. He held it up and said, "That's charlie, you know, coke?" It was then that I realised he was holding a bag of cocaine. I wasn't at all comfortable with this. He then put a line of powder on the table, rolled up a £10 note and snorted it up his nose. Sean did the same, but Donna and I refused to have any of it. I also noticed that Dean had a big roll of cash, about £600. I don't know why, but he did tell me that this was not his money. Dean asked me if I wanted to go down to his flat; I agreed, and left Donna with Sean. There wasn't a lot in the flat. He had a mattress for a bed, a three-piece suite, a TV and a video. Dean did wear nice clothes, though. They were all designer labels. And he also wore a thick gold chain and a Krugerrand sovereign ring.

'Dean went to have a shower and I went into the kitchen to make a coffee. As I looked around, I saw a further three bags full of white powder on top of the freezer. These were the same size as the bag Dean had brought up to Sean's flat earlier. I don't know a lot about drugs, but I do know that the amount of cocaine Dean had must have been worth a lot of money.

'When Dean came out of the shower, we both sat on the settee and had a cuddle. Dean was initially stuttering, but very soon relaxed and started to talk normally. I asked Dean about the cocaine and he said that whilst serving a prison sentence for burglary he had been bullied by two men who had forced him to deal drugs for them. He told me that one of these men was called Chris. Dean explained that these people used to smuggle pills into the prison for him hidden in the butts of cigarettes and he would then have to sell them to other inmates.

'Dean said he wasn't happy with the situation, but he didn't have much choice other than to go along with their demands. When he was released from prison, Dean said the people he'd been forced to work for had tracked him down and made him continue to sell their drugs. That's how he came to be in possession of so much cocaine – it belonged to these people.

'Dean seemed to be under extreme pressure. He said they were blackmailing him and had threatened to harm his brother. He clammed up when I asked about his family – he said that he never talked about his mum or dad. He told me he had a daughter.

'I sensed that Dean had many regrets about his family, particularly regrets concerning his dad.

'I remained with Dean until Sunday morning and then went home. Dean and I spoke to one another on the phone every night thereafter. The following weekend Dean picked me up from my home in a cab and we went to Clouseau's pub, had a few drinks and then went back to Dean's flat. When we sat down, Dean really opened up to me. I was quite shocked by how emotional he was. He said he was stuck in a situation that there was no way out of. He started crying, saying he was suicidal and wanted to get a gun. He kept saying he had a problem that he desperately needed to sort out and that he was really frightened. "I need to face up to this and get it sorted," he said.

'It really upset me to see how distressed Dean was. Unfortunately, he refused to go into detail about just what his problem was. The following morning I went home. During the next couple of weeks, Dean would text or telephone me at all sorts of silly hours. He would either be stoned, drunk or both. Sometimes he would be fine with me, but other times he would say that he needed help or that he missed me a lot. He would say things like, "I'm stuck in a situation that I want to get out of" or "I'm going to have to deal with this problem, so that I can settle down with you."

'The next time I saw Dean was in the Chameleon nightclub. He was really off with me and moody; I wasn't happy with his attitude at all, so I left the club and went home. At about 3 a.m., he phoned me. I told him I was unhappy about the way he had behaved and he apologised. I never saw him again; however, he continued to text and telephone me. One message I received said: "Miss you. I am not a liar. You are special. I need to sort business out once and for all. Be in touch." I tried to phone him back, but he didn't answer.'

The story that Boshell told Lisa about being forced to sell drugs for a man he had met in prison named Chris was in part true. He was selling drugs for a man he had met in prison – but his name was Alvin, not

Chris. The only Chris that Boshell had encountered whilst in prison was ex-Essex Boy member Chris Wheatley.

He had been released from his seven-year sentence for drug dealing around the same time as Boshell. On 14 November 2000, two weeks before Boshell had met Lisa, Chris had collapsed with heart failure after a particularly strenuous workout at a Southend gym. He was rushed to Basildon hospital but pronounced dead on arrival. The cause of his death was determined as bronchial asthma.

Boshell had been lying when he told Lisa that he was working for and being threatened by Chris, but he certainly feared somebody. Shortly after meeting Lisa, somebody kicked in his front door and he disappeared from his flat. His landlady made enquiries about his whereabouts amongst his associates and in the local pubs, but nobody seemed to know where Boshell had gone or why he had left so suddenly. When the landlady had exhausted all avenues of enquiry, she arranged for the broken door to be repaired, packed Boshell's belongings and handed them in at the local police station before re-letting the flat.

It is still a mystery why Boshell left or why his flat had been broken into. What is known is that Boshell was admitted to Southend hospital around this time suffering from a severely swollen testicle.

Alvin claimed that he inflicted the injury during a bit of horseplay whilst Boshell was working for him as a labourer. 'It was lunchtime and my wife had dropped off some sandwiches for me,' Alvin said. 'Dean grabbed a sandwich without asking and so I grabbed him by the bollocks. I took it off him and he ended up in hospital. I was only fucking about. He rang me the next day and said that his bollocks were hurting. He had a couple of days off work and then he admitted himself to Southend hospital. I remember going up to see him. I took him in a phone and a McDonald's meal. He stayed in there for a few days and then he rang me and said that he was staying with some girl.'

Alvin's explanation of Boshell's hospitalisation did not ring true to me and so with the kind permission of his mum I obtained her son's medical records from the hospital. They make very interesting reading.

Boshell declined to give a reason why his testicle was so grossly enlarged 'that he had trouble walking'. His pain factor recorded by hospital staff on a rising scale from one for minimum pain to ten for extreme pain was ten. Testicular injuries of this magnitude are, I am informed, divided into three broad categories based on the mechanism of injury. These categories include 1) blunt trauma, 2) penetrating trauma, and 3) de-gloving trauma. Blunt trauma refers to injuries sustained from objects applied with any significant force to the testicles. This can occur with various types of activity, such as a kick to the groin or an injury sustained in a motor accident. Penetrating trauma refers to injuries sustained from sharp objects, such as gunshot and stab wounds. De-gloving (or avulsion) injuries are less common. One might occur if scrotal skin is sheared off, for example, when a testicle becomes trapped in heavy machinery.

Boshell was clearly not shot on this occasion nor had he been trapped in heavy machinery, so one must assume that Alvin's playful tweak had the force of a hard kick. If Alvin's explanation is to be believed, then Boshell's behaviour when he was eventually released from hospital several days later can only be described as puzzling.

Instead of returning to his old haunts and continuing to work alongside Alvin, Boshell left Leigh-on-Sea and moved to Southend. He walked into a café on the seafront and asked the man behind the counter if he could offer him any work. The thousands of pounds worth of cocaine and the wad of money he had shown Lisa just weeks earlier were suspiciously absent.

'I'll do anything,' Boshell pleaded. 'I will wash up, clean the tables or cook the food.'

Halil Osman, the man Boshell had spoken to, knew that the café proprietor was short of staff. He was hired and given the menial task of washing up. While he worked his probationary period, he was paid cash in hand. The hours were long and extremely tedious. He would start his shift at 1 p.m. and wash dishes and cutlery until the café closed at 3 a.m. or 4 a.m. For working five nightshifts, Boshell was paid the princely sum of £70 – hardly the sort of money a one-time well-to-do drug dealer would toil all night, five times a week to earn. It cannot be denied that Dean Boshell was trying to make a completely new life for himself, free of drug dealing and the influence of Damon Alvin.

Halil Osman worked alongside Boshell for just six or seven days, but during this time Boshell confided in this relative stranger that he was interested in guns. When Halil asked him what he meant, Boshell claimed that he had recently acquired a gun.

'Dean told me that he and his brother had gone to London to buy the gun,' Halil said. 'He had purchased two guns because it was cheaper to buy a pair. He'd paid £500 for them. He said, "Normally, a clean gun would cost £300 or £400 each." Because he'd been kept waiting a long time, they had got them cheap. I asked him if he kept them at his home address and he said, "No, I'm not that stupid!" He said he'd bury it or keep it round someone else's. I couldn't make up my mind if Dean was actually telling the truth.'

There is no way of knowing if Boshell did buy a gun in London with 'his brother', but Halil is not the only person who claimed to have had a conversation with Boshell about guns.

After he had left the Leigh-on-Sea area, via Southend hospital, Boshell had moved into a flat at the rear of the café where he worked. Not really knowing anybody in the area, he would occasionally visit his old haunts along Southend seafront seeking out company. One day he bumped into a man I'll call 'Paul' whom he had met whilst serving one of his many prison sentences. Through Paul, Boshell was introduced to a group of people that included Stacie Harris, her brother CJ McLaughlin and a man named Jason Spendiff-Smith. Boshell and Spendiff-Smith got on well and they began to go out drinking together.

Spendiff-Smith was experiencing a fairly low period in his life when he first encountered Boshell. After being asked to leave his family's home because of irresolvable differences with his parents, Spendiff-Smith had drifted around Southend's bedsit land and jumped from one disastrous relationship to the next. At the time he met Boshell, he was with Stacie Harris, but she had just announced that her ex-partner was due to be released from prison and that they were going to get back together.

Boshell confided in Spendiff-Smith that he was in need of money to honour a debt and invited him to go on a job that would have earned him about £1,000. 'I cannot remember exactly what his words were,' Spendiff-Smith said when trying to recall the conversation, 'but he said that he and his brother were going to break into a house in Westcliffe and steal a load of drug plants. He said that the house was surrounded by fields and it would have to be done in the dark. He mentioned that the owners of the house were not very nice and not from around here. I assumed from that description that they were foreigners. Dean said he knew that the people were going to be away or out of the house at the time.

'He told me that the job was planned to take place the following Thursday and that he would be getting paid at least £2,500 for doing it. I didn't have any money or anything to do, so I said I'd think about it.

'The following day Dean asked me if I'd go with his brother and him to drive past the house where they were going to do the job. I agreed because I was bored at home, but his brother never turned up. For some reason, the job didn't take place the following Thursday, but on the Friday Dean told me that he was going to meet up with one of his mates to pick up a gun. I didn't really think much of it; I just thought it was Dean being all mouth.

'On Sunday, Dean and I went out to the White Horse pub for a drink. On the way, we called in at Dean's flat because he said he wanted to show me something. Dean asked me to close the door and he lifted up his mattress. I could see that he had a gun and three bullets hidden underneath it. I was surprised to see a gun, as I thought it had just been talk from Dean. He said, "Go on, make a man of yourself and hold it. It's not loaded." I didn't want to touch it and felt a bit uneasy seeing it.

'After that we walked to the pub to have a drink. It's quite a long walk from his flat and on the way I told Dean that I didn't want to get involved in the job he had planned. "You're such a pussy," he said. I replied, "I don't care, I don't want to do it. I don't care if it's a thousand pounds or a million pounds, I'm still not going to get caught for that or go around killing people."

'I automatically thought Dean was going to use the gun on this job – for all I knew, he could have gone out and killed himself, or maybe killed me.

'At some point during the evening he received a call from his brother, the one he always spoke to. He said he was going outside to meet him to get some money and make sure the job was still on. I assumed Dean was talking about the break-in.

'When he came back in five or ten minutes later, he said something like, "I love my brother," and took some money out of his pocket which I assumed he'd been given. He said the job was still on and told me to look out of the window at his brother's car, a red Audi convertible. I couldn't see the driver, but there was a blonde female in the passenger seat and I think a little girl in the rear. Dean then told me the job was going to be done on Tuesday, which was only two days away.'

The following day Boshell didn't see Spendiff-Smith because he was working at the café. During his shift, Dean was working with Ishmael Mehmet, who was also employed to wash up in the kitchen. Ishmael recalled that during the evening Dean received a number of calls on his mobile phone. At eight o'clock, when Dean's phone rang again, he appeared to recognise the caller and walked out of the café to continue his conversation. This was the only call that Boshell felt he needed to take out of earshot of Ishmael and the others. Analysis of phone records by the police later proved that this call was made from Alvin's girlfriend's phone.

Following this call, Boshell asked Ishmael if it would be OK to have a couple of hours off the following night. It wasn't up to Ishmael but he told Boshell that he didn't think their employer would mind if he asked.

Out of curiosity Ishmael asked Boshell why he needed the time off.

'I need to do a job,' Boshell replied. 'I'm going to rob some drugs in Chelmsford that are worth around £100,000.'

Without any prompting, Boshell went on to elaborate. 'Me and my brother are going to rob a house in Chelmsford. It's in a little village. There's a barn at the back. It's full of skunk, and me and my brother are going to take the plants.'

Ishmael says, not wishing to become in any way involved in criminal activity, he didn't press Boshell for any further information and quickly changed the subject.

At 4 a.m., Dean's employer closed up the café and said goodbye to Boshell as he left. Turning, Boshell raised his hand and shouted out, 'I'll see you tomorrow, mate.'

Spendiff-Smith later told police that at about nine-thirty that same morning, he and Boshell visited the social security offices. 'We had no money and so we were going to try and get what they call a "crisis loan". Dean was refused the loan and so we went back to the flat. I asked Stacie to borrow me some money and although she had none herself she said she'd get some off her boyfriend to lend me. Stacie left the flat to find him and about ten minutes later Dean and I went to meet her in town.

'Stacie never did arrive at the place we had agreed to meet and so we didn't get any money. As we were walking around town, Dean said, "I've not been to see my probation officer for ages." I didn't think much of this at first and so said nothing as we walked down towards the Probation Service offices.

'Standing outside, Dean announced that he had a warrant out for his arrest. He hadn't kept the terms and conditions of his probation, so he could have and should have been arrested as soon as he set foot in there. He obviously knew this, but he didn't seem bothered. I haven't got a clue if he was trying to get himself arrested on purpose or not. He said, "I want to make sure that I'm wanted by the police." I think he was trying to look big in front of me.

'I would say Dean was in the probation office for only a few minutes before coming out. He said his probation officer had been surprised to see him because he'd missed a number of previous appointments. A warrant had been issued recalling him back to prison, but other than that, he said no more about it. We then returned home.

'Dean needed to borrow some dark clothing for doing the break-in, so I sorted him out with Adidas trainers, a dark-blue puffa jacket and a pair of blue jogging bottoms. He then left the flat, saying he was going home to get changed and get something to eat. About 15 minutes later, he came back and told me he was expecting his brother to phone and said if he dozed off not to answer the call but to wake him. We began to watch the Brit Awards on TV, but Dean soon fell asleep.

'At about 8.45 Dean's mobile rang and I nudged him awake. I could hear him talking – he was asking the caller what time he was going to meet him. Nine o'clock was mentioned. As soon as the conversation ended, Dean got up, saying he had to go and meet his brother, who was picking him up at Lidl's supermarket.

'Just before he left, I was having a laugh with him, saying, make sure you bring back loads of fags, loads of food and things, and he replied that he would. He then left with his phone and I never saw him again.'

Nobody can say what was going through the mind of Dean Boshell that day. What is known is that he appeared to be extremely concerned about something.

If Boshell was planning to commit a crime that night for which he was to be paid £2,500, why would he apply for a £70 crisis loan at 9.40 a.m., and why would he hand himself in to his probation officer at 3.39 p.m. knowing that there was an outstanding warrant for his arrest?

Boshell's behaviour had changed dramatically after he was admitted to hospital suffering from injuries to his testicle caused by Alvin's alleged 'playful prank'. He had abandoned his flat in haste shortly after being discharged and left Leigh-on-Sea, severing all contact with his friends there. He had given up selling drugs and labouring for Alvin and to substitute that income he had taken a menial job washing up at night in a café. On the 8th, 14th and 27th of February, he had pleaded with the social security department to grant him crisis loans, as he was desperate for cash. Nobody can say what he was going to do with this money, but he had talked about returning to Leeds.

Alvin had been in contact with Boshell by phone on a sporadic basis and Boshell had talked about doing a job with him. However, Boshell had wept whilst explaining a situation that he was in to Nicole Kidman lookalike Lisa. He had told her that there was no way out of it and that he wanted to get a gun because he was really frightened.

I would suggest that Boshell had been dealing drugs, and the large amounts of cocaine seen by Lisa would support this theory. The fact that his flat was ransacked and he ended up in hospital would suggest that Boshell had upset somebody. Fleeing Leigh-on-Sea and associating with an entirely new circle of friends adds weight to this possible version of events. Boshell gave no explanation as to why the theft of the drugs from the barn had been cancelled – perhaps he had agreed to do it to work off a debt and then changed his mind at the last moment?

What is interesting is that Alvin phoned him using his girlfriend's mobile. Boshell took the call out of earshot of his colleagues when he realised whom he was speaking to. A friend of Boshell's who was interviewed during the police investigation said that Dean rarely got calls but a week or two before his death he was receiving several each day. This, to me, indicates that Boshell had been trying to avoid Alvin, who then used his partner's phone to call him. Dean would have recognised Clair's number and, having no reason to fear talking to her, answered it. Realising it was Alvin and not Clair on the phone, Boshell had then taken the call outside the café to prevent anybody overhearing what was being said. Once he had spoken to Alvin, Boshell immediately asked his employer for time off to do 'the job'.

During my days with the Essex Boys firm, there were many occasions when we were trying to contact people about debts or grievances and out of fear they had acted in exactly the same way as Boshell. They duck, dive and avoid your calls, but when you lure them into talking to you, they become very compliant. Boshell's nervousness and reckless visit to the probation office, knowing that he could be arrested and returned to prison, suggests to me that the last thing he wanted to do was meet Alvin that night. Why? We shall never know for sure, because Boshell did meet the man he had referred to as his brother that night, but he was found dead several hours later.

10

GANGSTER'S PARADISE

Colin Todd was employed at the Manchester Drive allotments in Leigh-on-Sea as a general maintenance man. Apart from young people fornicating in the bushes or breaking into the numerous garden sheds that cover the ten-acre site and crops being stolen or damaged, very little of interest ever happened.

There had been one unusual problem during the spring of 2001 – a keen plot-holder had taken to racing along the tracks that divide the allotments on his tractor. This had caused his fellow gardeners to become so concerned that they had strategically placed metal spikes in an upright position along the track to prevent him from driving at speed. In a rage, the man had attempted to manoeuvre his machine through the slalom of spikes, but had failed miserably. The plot-holders had found the punctured tyres on the disabled tractor extremely amusing. Its owner, however, failed to see the funny side of the trap and had abandoned his plot in protest shortly afterwards.

On the morning of Wednesday, 28 February 2001 at approximately 9.20 Colin Todd and a colleague were walking along one of the spike-laden tracks when they came across the lifeless body of 24-year-old Dean Fergus Boshell. The blood-soaked corpse was lying with the right side of the face on the ground and the knees slightly drawn up. Todd could clearly see that the person on the ground was dead. He called the police and the paramedics, who arrived amidst a deafening chorus of wailing sirens and blue flashing lights. They too recognised that the body was lifeless and so summoned Dr Goodchild to the scene, who certified Boshell as being dead at 11.28 p.m.

It was clear from the amount of blood that had poured from the victim's head that this death was, at the very least, suspicious and so the police erected an air tent around the body to contain and preserve any evidence that might have been present.

For reasons known only by the police, one of the metal spikes that had been used to slow the tractor driver down on the allotments was never forensically tested as a possible weapon. In the crime scene photos, it can be clearly seen lying close to Boshell's head. A long, thin wound across the back of his head looks as if it could well have been made with this bar.

Boshell had been squirted in the face with a substance and shot. If he had also been beaten with a bar, it would suggest that two or more people had murdered him.

The body was examined by a coroner's officer, who described the clothing worn as Adidas trainers, black trousers, a black anorak and a grey jumper. After the scene had been photographed, the body was placed onto a large plastic sheet, which was then sealed. When they raised the body to put it onto the sheet, an officer noticed a hole in the ground below the right side of the victim's face. This hole was 'probed' by one of the men present, who eventually recovered from it a fired .38 calibre lead bullet.

At 5.05 p.m., the sealed sheet containing Boshell's remains was put inside an undertaker's body bag and taken to the mortuary at Southend hospital. That evening, between 7.55 p.m. and 9.56 p.m., Dr Rouse, a forensic pathologist, performed a post-mortem on Boshell's body to determine the cause of death. Ten detectives, two coroner's officers and a ballistic forensic specialist were also present to witness any findings. The doctor's examination revealed that Boshell had been shot three times in the head. Two of the bullets were still in his head – one was lodged in the soft tissue of his right temple, the other had come to rest in his upper left nostril.

It was also noted that the entry wounds to the head were blackened, two wounds to the left of the skull more so than the one to the rear. This was consistent with the gun being in contact with Boshell's head when the shots to its side were fired and at close range when the shot from the rear was fired. Dr Rouse could not be certain, but he said that the likely scenario had been that Boshell was shot in the back of the head and then shot twice in the side of the head 'to make sure'. The victim would have been on the ground when the second and third shots were fired.

Dr Rouse concluded his examination by stating, 'What can be said with certainty is that this was not an accidental killing in the course of a struggle. This was an execution.'

The doctor's examination also revealed that Boshell had suffered lacerations behind his left ear and on his forearm and wrist. There was also an area of skin rash with some skin loss around the left side of the face and neck.

A forensic toxicologist took various blood, urine and tissue samples from the body to determine whether or not Boshell had been intoxicated or under the influence of drugs at the time of his death. These all proved to be negative. Ballistic tests carried out by the firearms' expert found that the weapon used to fire all three bullets was most probably a Colt revolver. At the conclusion of the post-mortem, the body was reconstructed, cleaned and placed in the mortuary storage facility.

The allotments where Boshell's body was discovered are surrounded by houses, and so the police decided to conduct door-to-door inquiries to find out if any of the residents had seen or heard anything of significance the night before.

Number 94 Randolph Close, approximately 300 metres from where Boshell's body had been discovered, was the home of Gordon Osborne. When the police called at his home, Osborne told them, 'Half of me thinks that I might have heard a bang, but I couldn't be sure.' He added that he didn't know what time he might have heard this noise, but it was 'possibly between 11 p.m. and 11.30 p.m.'

The only other person in the neighbourhood who recalled hearing anything of note was a lady named Hansel Andrayas. Her home backed onto the crime scene and was less than 100 metres from the spot where Boshell's body had been found. If anybody had heard anything significant, the likelihood was that it would have been Andrayas or one of her neighbours.

Andrayas told the police that around 2 a.m. she recalled hearing 'a loud bang and echo, then further noises, like a fence being climbed or broken', which she said woke her youngest daughter. Andrayas then described hearing a van driving at speed. She said that it had made skidding noises a few minutes later, as it disappeared down the road.

With so little evidence to work on, detectives turned their attention towards locating and interviewing Boshell's family, friends and associates.

At 6.30 the morning after Boshell's body had been found, Damon

Alvin says that he was awoken by his phone ringing. The caller, Boshell's friend Sean Buckley, said that he had arrived home earlier that morning and found the police standing outside his flat and his front door kicked off its hinges. After asking the police what they were up to, Buckley was told that instead of forcing an entry into Boshell's old flat, in error they had kicked in Buckley's door. Even if the police had raided the correct flat, they would have found that Boshell had vacated the premises three or four weeks earlier. When the police did eventually find and search Boshell's flat in Southend, they didn't find much of significance other than his address book, which contained four different telephone numbers for Alvin and one for his girlfriend, Clair. There was none for Percival. The police hadn't had the greatest start to the investigation and their luck appeared to deteriorate the longer it went on.

Officers had advised Buckley to go to the police station and register the mistake and damage to his front door. However, Alvin claimed that Buckley had phoned him en route to the police station and asked him to repair the door instead. Another pressing problem Buckley had faced that morning was that Alvin had left several thousand pounds at his flat in a carrier bag and he wanted to know what to say if the police discovered it. Buckley was told by Alvin to say that the money was his.

At approximately 10.30 a.m., Alvin arrived at Buckley's flat. As he climbed the stairs, he was confronted by several police officers whom he claims recognised him immediately. The officers said that they were investigating the murder of Dean Boshell and asked Alvin for a contact number because he was a known associate of the deceased and they wanted him to make a witness statement. Alvin explained that he had a new mobile number, which he couldn't recall or retrieve from his handset, and so he gave them his wife's number.

The officers asked Alvin where he had been on the night Boshell had died and he told them that he had been in the company of Kevin Walsh, Kate Griffiths and Ricky Percival. A brief note was made of this information and an officer advised Alvin that there was no need for him to repair the door as they were going to contact a contractor themselves.

Because Alvin said that he had been in Percival's company on the night Boshell died, the police asked Percival to make a formal statement. He felt he had nothing to hide and so he agreed. Percival told the police that in 1999 Alvin had introduced Boshell to him as a friend, but their acquaintance had been short-lived because Boshell had been sent to prison.

Percival said: 'Damon told me that he was keeping in touch with Dean in the jail. Boshell had asked him if he could get any weight-training supplements. I didn't mind getting them for Alvin to give to him because he was the friend of a friend. I was aware that Boshell was released from prison around the end of 2000. He turned up at a couple of places where I was socialising, such as the Woodcutters Arms. We didn't say a great deal to one another as we had little or nothing in common. He thanked me for getting the protein supplements for him. I would describe Boshell as a bit of a ponce: he was always borrowing, not from me but from others. He would always drink but never buy his round. I referred to him as "Dopey Dean".

'There was nothing nasty about Boshell; he was never offensive or rude. On the night Boshell died, I went to visit my friend Kevin Walsh at his flat. It was around seven or eight o'clock when I arrived. Alvin and a man named Sean Buckley were already there. We all left the flat shortly afterwards and went to the Woodcutters Arms. I went there in my car and the others travelled to the pub in Alvin's red Audi convertible. After an hour or two, Alvin and I left the pub. I went home, had something to eat and then drove to Alvin's house in Rochford to give him a lift to Kevin's flat. He had gone home to drop his car off because his partner doesn't like him to drink and drive. I left Kevin's flat alone around 11.30 p.m. because Alvin said his girlfriend was going to pick him up later.'

The police thanked Percival for his assistance and told him that they would be in touch if they had any further questions.

The following day the police asked Alvin to make his witness statement concerning his knowledge and relationship with Boshell. He told them that he had first heard that a body had been found on the allotments after it had been reported in the local newspaper and on the radio and that it wasn't until Kate Griffiths had telephoned him that he learned the body was Boshell's.

'I was quite upset when I heard this,' Alvin said. 'I know of no reason why someone would want to kill him. I would describe Dean as a friend – he was friendlier towards me than I was to him. He would confide in me if he was in trouble. The last time I spoke to him he was quite happy; he didn't appear to be worried about anything. Dean would contact me on my mobile. I can't remember the number, as I've misplaced it since the weekend and bought a new phone, but I can't remember that number either.

'I've let it be known in the area that I will pay £500, as will Ricky Percival and Dean's friend Lester, to any person who can help catch the person responsible.'

After completing his statement, Alvin offered the police a possible 'off-the-record' motive for the murder. Doing his best to sound concerned and looking to appear helpful he informed them, 'There's a possibility that Dean was having an affair with a married woman or sleeping with someone's underage daughter, he was like that.'

Percival's and Alvin's statements led officers to the door of Kate Griffiths, who was also asked to detail her knowledge of Boshell and her movements on the night that he died. Without realising the severity of the situation she was walking into, Griffiths agreed to make a statement.

She told the officers that she had spent the day of the murder working at the launderette that she and her father owned. At around 7 p.m., she said she had locked the premises up and caught a taxi to her mother's house.

'I sat down with my dad and sorted out the paperwork for the takings for that day,' she said. 'After having my dinner, I went to the Woodcutters pub, where I met Damon Alvin, Ricky Percival, Sean Buckley and my boyfriend Kevin Walsh. It was really quiet in the pub that night. I can't recall what time it was, perhaps quarter past, half past nine, but Damon and Ricky left the pub before Kevin and me.

'About ten o'clock, we decided to buy a few takeaway beers and go home to watch the television because the pub was really quiet. Half an hour after we arrived at the flat, Damon and Ricky turned up in Ricky's car. They came in and we all just sat watching the television and chatting. Everything was really normal, as far as I was concerned. Around midnight Ricky went home. Roughly half an hour later Damon's girlfriend Clair beeped the car horn outside the flat. Kevin went to the kitchen window and told Damon that Clair was outside. Clair was driving Damon's red Audi. He got into it and they disappeared.

'It wasn't unusual for Clair to pick Damon up from our flat. Clair would do it when she had finished work because she didn't like him drinking and driving.

'At approximately 1 a.m., Kevin and I went to bed.'

Griffiths, an honest girl of impeccable character, was very fond of Boshell and had absolutely no reason whatsoever to lie to the police. Little did she know that her willingness to assist would later result in her facing ruin.

Gangster's Paradise: the original Essex Boys murder scene

Your name's not down, you're not coming in:
O'Mahoney at HMP Chelmsford, Essex

Bernard O'Mahoney and Beverley Boshell reading Damon Alvin's letter

The Woodcutters Arms in Leigh-on-Sea, where Percival, Alvin, Walsh and Boshell socialised

Dean Boshell, taken at the Woodcutters two weeks before his death (courtesy of Beverley Boshell)

Darren Kerr following
the acid attack

The Wickford snooker club:
the scene of the robbery

Kevin Walsh on home leave from prison, October 2007

Boxers: (back, left to right) Danny Percival, John McDermott, Mark Potterand; (front, left to right) Danny Williams and Julius Francis at The Big 5 press conference at the TKO Gym in London (© Empics)

Danny Percival (standing) and brother Ricky at their home (courtesy of Sandy Percival)

O'Mahoney with Martin Hall, friends and former doormen
at Raquels nightclub in Basildon

Former Detective Sergeant
John Moran

Carlton Leach (left) and Ricci Harnett (right), who played Leach, on the set of *Rise of the Footsoldier* (© Carnaby Films International)

John Marshall's estranged daughter, Stacie Harris

Ricky Percival at home shortly
before his arrest
(courtesy of Sandy Percival)

O'Mahoney outside
HMP Gartree after visiting
Steve Penfold

Dean Boshell's body:
Note the iron bar lying near
the long, thin wound at the
back of his head
(courtesy of Beverley Boshell)

Sean Buckley, whom the other witnesses had also mentioned, made his statement after the police had raided his flat in error. He said he had left the group early in the evening and had no contact with Boshell and so proved to be of little use in the investigation.

Walsh had spent the evening in Griffiths's company and so when he made his statement it unsurprisingly turned out to be almost identical in content to hers.

When officers visited Clair Sanders and asked her to give an account of her movements on the relevant night, her statement agreed with everything in Alvin's. However, for reasons known only to Sanders, she refused to sign the declaration that her testimony was true to the best of her knowledge.

Within weeks of the murder, Boshell's funeral had taken place at Pitsea Crematorium, near Basildon. The hearse carrying Boshell's coffin passed the last resting places of Patrick Tate and Craig Rolfe, two victims of the infamous Essex Boys murders, who were buried as they lived, side by side. It would also have passed the grave of Kevin Whitaker, an innocent young man murdered on a whim by Rolfe and Tony Tucker. Dean Boshell's dream of being just like one of the 'big boys' had finally come true. He was young, dead and being buried full of bullet holes, just like his heroes.

The unwarranted reputation Ricky Percival had revelled in since his arrest for the Locksley Close shootings was to come back to haunt him with a vengeance as soon as Boshell was dead. Twenty-year-old Jason Spendiff-Smith, who had never met Percival but had heard all the rumours about him, was about to drag him onto centre stage of the murder investigation.

Shortly after Boshell's murder, Spendiff-Smith telephoned his uncle, who happened to be a serving police officer. In a complete panic, he had explained that he might be in trouble because he knew that Boshell had been planning 'a job' and he had provided dark clothing for him so that he could carry it out. Spendiff-Smith's uncle advised him to calm down and contact the police immediately. After doing so, Spendiff-Smith was asked to make a witness statement, the contents of which resulted in his being asked to make several more. The numerous statements that followed never did quite make sense to detectives. Every time he talked about events surrounding Boshell's death his story changed dramatically. Thinking he was involved in the killing or shielding the killer, the police decided to arrest Spendiff-Smith on suspicion of murder.

During interviews made under caution, Spendiff-Smith gave a fairly detailed account of his movements during the day of Boshell's death. He told the police how he had given dark clothing to Boshell for use in a crime which, he understood, involved the theft of drugs from a farm building. This evidence was important when linked to statements made by Boshell's work colleagues at the café. They said Boshell had told them that he had purchased guns and planned the theft of the drugs from a farm building with 'his brother'. Detectives had, by this stage, established that more often than not Boshell referred to Damon Alvin as his brother.

Unfortunately for the police, just as they thought Spendiff-Smith was making himself useful he would tell them something that they knew was blatantly untrue and, in doing so, he would totally discredit himself. Spendiff-Smith had only been required to give a straightforward account of his knowledge of Boshell and matters that might have had some bearing on his murder, but he soon proved to be totally incapable of telling the truth.

He told officers, 'When Dean said, "My mate has organised the job," I believed that he was referring to Ricky Percival. I thought this because, apart from me, Percival was the only other person that he referred to as his mate.'

When detectives pressed him for more details about Percival, he said, 'I got that wrong. At no time did Dean mention Ricky Percival – that was only an assumption. Sorry about that.'

The police effectively had to tear up Spendiff-Smith's statement and ask him to make another. In the account that followed, the police were told about a gun that Boshell had supposedly shown him, which had been hidden under the mattress of his bed. Remarkably, he had failed to mention this in his earlier statement and, when asked to explain how he could forget such an important detail, he replied, 'I was worried because I didn't want to get Boshell into any more trouble.'

When the interviewing officer pointed out that getting Boshell into any further trouble was most unlikely because he happened to be dead, Spendiff-Smith meekly replied, 'Oh, yeah.'

Despite the officers repeatedly explaining the need for total honesty, each of Spendiff-Smith's statements continued to be riddled with inaccuracies or lies. One moment the detectives were elated by the prospect of a major breakthrough in the case, the next they were deflated, realising they had just been told yet another barefaced lie.

Spendiff-Smith told the by now weary detectives that on the night

Boshell left his flat he had received a very strange call on his mobile phone. He was asked to describe this call. 'At about 9.20 p.m., my phone rang and I saw that the caller had withheld their number,' he said. 'When I answered it, a bloke said, "This is Rick, Dean's mate Rick. Is Dean there?" I replied, "No, he has gone out." Rick had then said that if Dean came back, I was to tell him to meet him at 9.30 p.m. at the same place. Rick then started to talk to me about football; I told him that I supported Manchester United, which he said he didn't like. He asked if I had found a job yet and asked me how my friends were. The call lasted about five minutes. The voice was that of a male and was deep and husky.'

The officers asked Spendiff-Smith if he thought this caller was Percival and he replied, without hesitation, 'Yes, because he said he was Dean's mate, Rick.'

In order to give the story a little flavour, Spendiff-Smith added, 'It sounded as if the caller had been on something, you know, all hyper.'

Spendiff-Smith claimed that the day after Boshell's body had been found, he had received a second call from a withheld number and that this caller had also said that his name was Rick. They had exchanged greetings and then Spendiff-Smith alleged that Rick had told him to 'keep his big mouth shut'. After asking what he was supposed to keep his mouth shut about, Spendiff-Smith says that he was subjected to a torrent of abuse and threats.

'He was saying, "I know where your parents live, I am going to fuck your mother then cut her up. Keep your big mouth shut or you're going to get your throat cut. I will do it or get somebody else to do it." Only then did it hit me what these calls were all about,' he said. 'When I saw it in the paper about Dean's death, I started getting worried. I formed the opinion that Ricky Percival had either killed Dean, had something to do with Dean's death or perhaps was present when he died. I was very frightened and still am. These calls went on for days; he was wasting his phone credit really, because I had heard him the first time. He started saying that he was keeping an eye on me and I had better not go to the police. "I will find out where you live," and stuff like that. That's why I didn't go to the police at first because if he found out that I had I was in trouble.

'Dean regularly spoke about Percival and mentioned that he had a nasty streak. He told me he wasn't a nice person and would kick you in if you did anything against him. He said he'd been with him once and he'd fired a sling shot at one of the doormen at Tots nightclub because they hadn't let him in. If it was Ricky that had killed Dean, then maybe he was going to get me as well. I took these threats so seriously that I sold my phone, and I loved my phone.'

The sound of Percival's name being linked to such damning evidence must have been like music to the ears of many in the police service, but, sadly for them, Spendiff-Smith had already proved himself to be a complete fantasist. To the credit of the interviewing officers, they questioned Spendiff-Smith meticulously until he was forced to concede that he had not received any threatening calls whatsoever. He also admitted that he had lied about the reason he had disposed of his phone. 'I sold it for eight or nine pounds,' he said, 'because I needed the money.'

The reason for this catalogue of lies, according to Spendiff-Smith, was that a senior police officer had mentioned during one interview that if he knew anything about Boshell's murder that he was scared to talk about he could possibly get supergrass status on the witness-protection programme.

Spendiff-Smith told the interviewing officer, 'I decided to lie so that I would get that protection and be able to start my life off anew, as mine at the moment is awful; in fact, it's horrible, absolutely horrible. That's what I have wanted to do for ages, start a new life, but I have never had the money to do it. If I told you I had only got one call, it wouldn't have sounded as though I was in any danger and you might not have helped me.'

Like most revellers who frequented the pubs and clubs around Southend, Spendiff-Smith's knowledge of Percival would have been gleaned from alcohol-fuelled gossip and rumours about the Locksley Close shootings. This isn't speculation on my part: during his marathon of interviews, Spendiff-Smith had told the police: 'I sold my phone because I had people coming up to me in nightclubs, saying, "Sorry about your mate dying, but the bloke who did it should not be fucked about because he's not a nice person." When I asked whom they were talking about, they said, "We all know who did it – Ricky Percival. You don't want to be on the wrong side of him. If he can make contact with you in any way, make sure you're not there." I automatically sold my phone. I'm still scared of the bloke now and I don't even know who he is.'

Clearly, Percival had been tried and convicted by the good people of Southend long before the police had even considered him as a suspect.

Little wonder that as time went by everybody 'knew' who had killed Boshell.

After weeding out what police believed to be the lies, hearsay and innuendos that had formed the basis of Spendiff-Smith's statements, the officers finalised an account from him that a jury was asked to believe. Spendiff-Smith claimed that Boshell had talked about the proposed theft of cannabis from a farm with his brother, he had been shown a gun by Boshell and he had given him dark clothing to wear the night of his death, but, other than that, everything else he had told the police had been discarded.

Three and a half months after he was first interviewed during the door-to-door inquiries, Gordon Osborne was asked to make a further witness statement. Unlike his first rather vague recollection of the night of the murder, Osborne was this time able to recall events with extreme clarity.

'I went to bed about 9 p.m.,' he said. 'My bedroom is at the rear of my house and overlooks the allotments. At about 11 p.m., I was awoken by the sound of two or three shots coming from the direction of the allotments. My bedroom window is always open and I got up to look out of the window towards the allotments, but could not see anything, as it was pitch black. I can say from my experience in the armed forces that the shots I heard were from a handgun and not a shotgun. I did not see anything at all that night. The following day I learned that a person had been found dead on the allotments.'

Osborne claimed that he had heard two or three shots, which was consistent with the number of gunshot wounds Boshell had suffered. Detectives, therefore, assumed that the shots Osborne had heard were the shots being fired into Boshell. They thought it would be unlikely that he would be mistaken; he had boasted that because of his military training he could distinguish the sound of one particular firearm from another. It followed, therefore, that Boshell must have met his death at around 11 p.m. With an approximate time of death established, the police were able to begin constructing their case. They knew that Boshell had left Spendiff-Smith at approximately 9.30 p.m. and so anybody who had been in his company up until the time of his death, a mere two hours later, would be considered a suspect.

Officers had always harboured a niggling doubt about Alvin's story regarding the loss of his mobile phone. It seemed to be too much of a coincidence that he just happened to lose it on the very day Boshell had died. The fact that Alvin had replaced it so early the following morning was equally suspicious. Most people would search high and low before accepting their handset was truly lost.

Curious to know why Alvin might not have wanted detectives to examine his phone, they investigated further and learnt of his number by simply asking his friends.

Boshell's mobile phone was also missing, but 'CJ' McLaughlin, who had been in Spendiff-Smith's flat on the evening of the murder, had told police that Boshell had used his phone at 8.32 p.m. to call a friend that he was going to meet. Detectives retrieved the number Boshell had called from McLaughlin's mobile and soon established that it belonged to Alvin's missing phone. This was the first concrete evidence to link Alvin to Boshell on the night he died.

Officers were extremely encouraged by the breakthrough because Alvin had claimed that he had not seen or spoken to Boshell that day. The icing on the detectives' cake was CCTV footage seized from within the Woodcutters Arms, which showed Alvin answering his mobile phone at the precise moment that Boshell made his call.

The decision by police to gather all the CCTV footage they thought might be relevant proved to be an extremely significant and constructive one. At 9 p.m. on the night of the murder cameras had recorded Boshell and McLaughlin walking to Woodgrange Drive in Southend and waiting outside Lidl's for Boshell's friend to arrive. At 9.15 p.m., CCTV at the Woodcutters had recorded Alvin leaving the premises.

McLaughlin told police that at 9.26 p.m. Boshell had telephoned his friend's mobile from a public telephone situated on Woodgrange Drive. Telephone records revealed that this call had also been made to Alvin's phone. McLaughlin said that Boshell's friend had turned up not long afterwards in a red car. Detectives knew that Alvin drove a red Audi convertible.

There was genuine excitement amongst officers involved in the inquiry. It appeared that Alvin was lying about his whereabouts after leaving the Woodcutters Arms. He had said that he had gone straight home to drop off his car, but the police now had evidence that he had driven to Southend to pick up Boshell to commit a crime that involved the use of guns.

Osborne's evidence – that he had heard three gunshots approximately two hours after Boshell had been seen leaving Southend alive – could have sealed Alvin's fate had it not been for evidence given by Griffiths, Percival and Walsh. They had all given him an alibi from approximately 10.30 p.m. to midnight. Detectives believed that Alvin and those who had given him an alibi had to be lying, but despite their best efforts they could not disprove the witness statements. For a while, the investigation ground to a shuddering halt.

Six months after Boshell's murder Alvin married his first love, Clair Sanders. It was a rather lavish affair, funded in part by sections of the local community. That is, Alvin's drug clientele. Amongst the guests were the Percival family, Kevin Walsh and Alvin's good friend Tony Staunton. When Staunton first heard about Alvin's wedding plans, he asked Alvin to remember his invitation. Alvin laughed and replied, 'You can have Boshell's. He won't be needing it!'

Guests at the event have all said they had never seen Alvin looking so happy. Having outfoxed the police, established his drug-dealing empire and married the girl of his dreams, Alvin probably never had been. After settling into married life, Alvin settled back into supplying his friends and associates with drugs. Darren Wall, a long-standing friend and customer of Alvin, asked him if he could supply large quantities of cannabis. Alvin had consulted Percival and he had said that he would be able to get as much cannabis as Wall required. Deliveries ranging from twenty to thirty kilos of the drug were later made to Wall by Alvin, via Percival, on at least four occasions. As is the norm in the world of business, Wall realised that by cutting Alvin out of the supply chain he would be able to purchase the cannabis at a far more attractive price and so he started dealing with Percival direct.

Having removed Alvin from the equation, Wall ordered 60 kilos of cannabis from Percival. After agreeing on a price, the handover was arranged to take place near Southend. According to Alvin, Percival had sourced the drugs from a notorious crime family in the North London area, whom he had not yet paid.

Wall and his partner in crime, a man named John Ling, met Percival as arranged and approximately 240 bars of cannabis were loaded into the boot of their car. Wall and Ling had not been required to pay for the drugs at this meeting, as payment was expected to be made within the following two days. Once the cannabis had been safely stored in their car, Wall and Ling drove to a safehouse in Leigh-on-Sea. Whilst they were checking the quantity and quality of the drugs in the kitchen, the police stormed the house. Wall and Ling were arrested and charged with possession of cannabis with intent to supply. Wall was sentenced to 18 months' imprisonment and Ling received a non-custodial sentence.

When Wall was released from prison, Percival demanded approximately £30,000 from him, which he said was owed for the cannabis. Wall had other ideas: he felt his imprisonment and the loss of the cannabis were Percival's fault. The police had placed Percival under surveillance following Boshell's murder – it was no secret that they were monitoring his every move – so Wall reasoned that he was responsible for the police becoming aware of their deal.

Fair play and understanding are not attributes embraced by those involved in the world of drugs; the rules the players live and often die by are hard and fast. 'I give, you pay' are all they appear to amount to.

Percival, unsurprisingly, didn't see things in the same way as Wall. He argued that if he had been under surveillance that day surely the police, who appeared to be more than keen to see him behind bars, would have swooped on him whilst he was still in possession of the cannabis.

Out of prison, out of pocket and out of luck, Wall's last attempt to negotiate a settlement involved him approaching his friend Alvin. After they had discussed the situation, Alvin asked Percival on Wall's behalf if Wall could be given a discount in light of the circumstances. Wall was quite a passive person and certainly not the kind of man to stand up to Percival or give him grief and so it was agreed that because he had suffered, through no fault of his own, he could pay for the cannabis at cost price.

Despite this being an extremely reasonable offer, Alvin advised Wall not to pay Percival. He said that the drugs had only been in Wall's possession for five minutes and if it had been him in that situation he would have refused to pay. Wall thought for a moment, looked Alvin up and down, and reminded himself that this was the man who used to bully Percival for fun. But all hope of salvation drained from Wall when he remembered that the North London crime family who had supplied Percival with the cannabis would probably be chasing him for their money also. Did Wall really want to fall out with them and Percival over cannabis that he was never realistically going to get out of paying for?

Wall bit his trembling lip and scraped together £10,000. His partner, Ling, also managed to come up with the same amount of cash. This £20,000 was then handed over to Alvin and he gave it to Percival, who in turn passed it on to his supplier. As far as everybody involved in the rather disastrous deal was concerned that was the end of the matter. To many people reading this, Percival may appear to have been a hard and difficult man to deal with. He doesn't deny that he was – in the drug world he inhabited, one had to be to survive.

GANGSTER'S PARADISE

Being a bully, as Alvin undoubtedly was, is a world apart from being a hard man. A bully would have squeezed every possible penny out of Wall and Ling. A bully certainly wouldn't have accepted a settlement that left him breaking even on a deal that had caused him untold grief. Percival was acutely aware that bullies do not survive in the Essex underworld. Tucker, Tate and Rolfe were testament to that.

Following the furore caused by the arrest and convictions of Wall and Ling, Percival decided to take a much-needed vacation. The pressure created by the Boshell murder inquiry had become more intense since suspicions of Alvin's guilt had begun to circulate. Percival was a known associate of Alvin and was thought to be a purveyor of drugs and the madman who had blasted a house full of revellers with a shotgun. Common sense told him that the police were bound to focus their attention on him at some stage.

He had made a reasonable amount of money over the previous year but the activities going on around him would ensure that he would make very little more. The thought of lying on a beach in sunny Spain for a month or two suddenly sounded very appealing.

A few days before he departed, Percival bumped into an old friend of his named Kim Webber. He was in the company of a mature, grey-haired man whom Percival had not seen before. As soon as Percival made eye contact with Webber, he knew something was wrong.

'Hello, Ricky,' Webber said, almost shouting out, 'this is an associate of mine, he is a copper and his name is John Moran.'

Percival was stunned at first – Moran was one of the detectives working on the Boshell murder inquiry. Fortunately for Percival, Webber had been prudent enough to blurt out the fact that Moran was a policeman before Percival had started talking about the mess his friend Alvin appeared to be in.

Sensing Percival wasn't happy about conversing with a policeman, and perhaps less than happy that a friend was out strolling with one, Webber explained that he and Moran worked together on the board of a local football team. Relieved that his friend hadn't crossed over to the other side, Percival excused himself, bidding both men goodbye, and continued on his way.

When he arrived in Spain, Percival met up with several nightclub doormen and faces from Essex who were out on the Costas soaking up the sun. One of these men was the legendary Frankie Wright, who is respected throughout Essex and the East End of London.

One evening, Percival and Frankie were enjoying a drink at a bar when a group of Liverpudlians entered. Cheap, vulgar and abrasive, the Scousers began glaring at Percival and making derogatory comments about cockneys and southerners. Choosing to ignore their juvenile behaviour, Percival continued his conversation with Frankie.

The waitress had been enjoying a bit of harmless flirting with Percival and Frankie up until this point, but as the Scousers got louder her mood changed. Percival and Frankie tried to reassure the terrified girl that there wouldn't be any trouble, but she insisted that she was going to remain behind the bar until the men had gone.

Noticing this, one of the Scousers shouted across to Percival and Frankie that the waitress was with him and so they had better stop talking to her. Frankie Wright was no fool and he quite rightly took exception to the attitude of these people. He wanted to teach them a lesson in respect, but Percival, who had gone to Spain to avoid confrontation and stress, had sensed the situation was deteriorating rapidly and suggested to Frankie that they should leave.

As they walked out of the bar, one of the Scousers started walking behind Frankie, so Percival shoved him in the back and asked him what the fuck he thought he was doing. 'He is an old man,' Percival shouted. 'Grow up, you fucking Scouse mug.'

As he was remonstrating with this individual, Percival felt a blow, as if he had been kicked in the backside. Turning quickly to face his attacker, Percival tried to grab the man but he was already fleeing in the opposite direction.

As he stepped towards the vehicle, Percival heard something fall to the floor. Looking down, he saw a blood-stained knife. He instinctively placed his hand where he thought that he had been kicked. It was at that moment that he realised he had, in fact, been stabbed. The knife had been plunged between his legs and had cut a gaping hole in his scrotum.

Sitting in the passenger seat of the car, Frankie was totally oblivious to what had just happened to Percival. That was until Percival, who was bleeding profusely, lowered himself into the driver's seat and told Frankie that he had to get to the nearest hospital. Driving at speed away from the scene, Percival soon became weak because of the amount of blood he was losing. He thought he would be OK to make it to the hospital, but lost consciousness and collided head-on with an oncoming vehicle en route. Two Spanish locals and Percival were seriously injured in the accident, but, sadly, Frankie Wright lost his life.

As soon as Danny Percival heard the news, he flew out to Spain to be at his brother's side and there he remained for several weeks. Throughout this period there was talk that the Spanish authorities were considering charging Percival with manslaughter, so, as soon as he was fit enough, Danny escorted his brother back to Essex.

Percival had endured several difficult years since the death of his friend Malcolm Walsh. His arrest for the Locksley Close shootings, the suspicion surrounding him regarding the murder of Dean Boshell, the botched cannabis deal with Ling and Wall, then being stabbed in Spain and the death of Frankie Wright had all been extremely stressful events. But compared to what the future held for Percival, I imagine he will look back on those traumatic times and think of them as the good old days.

11

THE FOOL ON THE PILL(S)

On April Fool's Day 2003, Damon Alvin was arrested at gunpoint in possession of a kilo of cocaine. And who said that the police don't have a sense of humour? The arresting officers were members of the murder inquiry team rather than regular drug-squad officers. After informing Alvin of his rights, he was transported to Basildon police station, where he immediately contacted his solicitor. Several hours later, Alvin was interviewed, but he refused to answer any questions. Instead, he read out the following prepared statement:

'I would like to confirm that I was in possession of a quantity of cocaine when I was arrested. I had fallen into debt with loan sharks from whom I had borrowed £15,000 to finish refurbishments at my house. I fell behind with the payments and pressure was put on me to pay the money back. Eventually, the loan sharks threatened that they would cause physical harm to both myself and Clair. My wife is pregnant and has a seven-month old baby; she knows nothing about my business activities.

'Eventually, and in fear of our safety, I agreed to collect and deliver what I believed to be a quantity of cocaine on behalf of these loan sharks. I collected the drugs from a contact yesterday morning with directions to deliver it to Canvey Island. I was arrested with the drugs in my possession en route. The scales were with me to check the weight before delivery and were provided for me, with the money, which I received the night before. I have a cocaine habit, which I have suffered from for the past two years. Any drug paraphernalia found at my home address relates to my habit. My wife has no knowledge of my habit or of any drugs that may have been found at my home address.

'The £31,420 found in my washing machine by police officers was cash given to me to pay for the cocaine once I had completed my delivery to Canvey Island. Other amounts of money found at my address relate to my wife's savings, recent employment and monies I kept at home to pay for refurbishment material deliveries. I accept that the Taser gun found at my home is mine. I found it in a car I bought a few months ago. I realised it was a prohibited weapon and so I put it on top of my fridge freezer. I have since forgotten about it.'

Alvin would have known that the penalty for possessing and conspiring to supply such a large amount of cocaine was likely to attract a sentence of approximately six years' imprisonment. The very thought of losing his liberty after getting married and having a child, and while his wife was expecting another, must have been too much to bear. Whatever it was going to take to get Alvin out of the predicament he faced, he knew that he was going to have to do it.

The problem for Alvin was that the police were aware of his state of mind and his dilemma. The evidence they had so far gathered had left them in no doubt whatsoever that Alvin was at least present at Boshell's death. They had heard rumours that Percival might have pulled the trigger, but they needed leverage or some sort of trigger mechanism to get Alvin to start talking. When they had received intelligence that Alvin was going to be involved in the supply of a kilo of cocaine that morning, they knew that if they caught him with it, the threat of a lengthy prison sentence would provide the bargaining tool they needed. It was suggested to Alvin that if he was prepared to assist the police with their inquiries, they might be able to assist him with the jail term he now faced.

At 8.32 p.m. on 2 April 2003, having already been charged with the possession of a kilo of cocaine with intent to supply, Alvin agreed to give an intelligence interview to DS Carter and DC Staff on the condition that the judge sentencing him for the drugs would credit him for his cooperation.

There is absolutely nothing wrong in law or police procedure with these types of agreements; however, the credibility of anybody giving evidence or intelligence in return for any type of reward has to be, I would suggest, at best questionable. It was explained to Alvin that he was not under caution or arrest and he was not under any obligation to say anything at all. He was then reminded that the charge he faced in relation to the cocaine was a serious one and that it was likely to be dealt with by means of a lengthy prison sentence when he finally appeared in court. In plain English, Alvin had been told: 'Help us, or face six years inside.'

DS Carter told Alvin, 'There are a number of things that we can do to assist you in relation to that prison sentence that are governed by the judiciary. Basically, the judiciary agrees that if anybody turns to assist the police and we go along to court and behind closed doors say to the judge, "This person has assisted us," the judge is then duty-bound to reduce the sentence. That is written in the judiciary. Whatever help you give us, a decision will be made on what help we can give you and there are a number of options open. But again, it's down to you to decide whether you want to speak to us or not.'

I cannot imagine Alvin agonising over the decision he was going to make for too long. Shall I serve six years in prison and risk losing everything, or shall I give these people a load of bullshit information and secure a reduced sentence? He did refuse to talk initially, but only because he didn't want what he had to say being recorded. After being reassured by the officers that the tapes would never be used, Alvin agreed to tell his story.

Having read the transcripts of the interview tapes, it is apparent to me that Alvin was not concerned about the finer details of his story, his safety or the pursuit of justice. His main concern appears to have been that the authorities were going to try to seize his home under the Proceeds of Crime Act. This legislation was introduced to show criminals that crime really does not pay, even if they are not caught initially; any money or assets that a criminal cannot prove he has earned or funded legitimately can be seized by the courts at any time.

It would have been fairly clear to the officers who had arrested Alvin and found £31,420 in his washing machine that the vast majority of his sizeable income was anything but legitimate.

'What guarantees can be made that my wife will be able to keep the house?' Alvin had asked.

'No guarantees at the moment,' DS Carter replied, 'because I don't know what you are going to tell us. The bottom line is you will go to court tomorrow and you will be remanded in custody. We can then get you out of prison on a production order so that we can sit down and talk in more depth. I can't give you any promises whatsoever; we can only help you if you help us.'

Alvin paused. Images of his home, his car and his pretty wife must have been flashing through his mind.

'OK,' he eventually said. 'There is an officer at Rayleigh police station giving out information to people close to me about certain crimes that have been committed. I'm not sure of his whole name – I think it is Strongholm. He is about to retire and is on the board of governors at Brentwood Football Club. I've never actually seen him and I can't describe him, but he shouldn't be hard to find. All I know is that he works on the murder squad. He is known to me through a person called Kim Webber, who also sits on the board of governors at the football club.

'Strongholm received a payment for information from one of my friends, who I cannot name, for an offence that occurred a few weeks back. Someone was charged with possession of 60 kilos of cannabis and my friend was advised to leave the country because he was going to be arrested on the 29th of this month. Darren Wall and John Ling are the guys who were arrested with the 60 kilos of cannabis and my friend was supposed to have been videoed by the police delivering it from the boot of his car to Darren Wall's.'

The detectives pressed Alvin for his friend's name because they wanted to identify the officer he was alleging was corrupt, but Alvin repeatedly refused to do so. Alvin told them, 'I can't name him because he is in with the people that I owe money to.'

The officers reminded Alvin that unless he was prepared to assist them, they would not be able to help him when he appeared in court for sentencing.

'It all relates back to Kim Webber,' Alvin said. 'He's the supplier of the stuff. And the people that I owe the money to – I don't know their names, I only know where they work. There's a car showroom up in Hadleigh. It's run by Carlton Leach and some pikeys. They were meant to go to Spain to meet some Liverpool people out there. An incident occurred between the Liverpool drug dealers and them. Somebody got stabbed up; I think one may have died. That was two weeks ago, I believe. A shipment of about a ton of cocaine was meant to come into the country within the next three weeks. I don't know everybody involved; I just know Leach and Webber were. They are the ones who are making me pick up the drugs and drop them off.'

Alvin's dramatic story regarding the importation of a ton of cocaine, an alleged corrupt detective selling information to villains, and Kim Webber and Carlton Leach forcing him to work as a drug courier was not initially received with the enthusiastic response Alvin had hoped for. DS Carter remained silent for quite some time; it was as if he was gathering his thoughts.

'What we are going to be looking at is this,' he said finally. 'If we go down the road of you helping us, you're going to have to be 100 per cent honest. We cannot work on half-truths.'

Unfortunately for DC Carter and his colleague, who were undoubtedly doing their utmost to spell out the need for Alvin to be truthful, he was already trying to weave together half-truths and lies. He was thinking up a story that would not only reduce his prison sentence but also save him from losing his home.

'I don't hear names. It's hard to,' Alvin lied. 'You can't blatantly ask these sort of people who they are and where they are from. If you do, it looks suspicious. It's all on a need-to-know basis. They're not idiots, they're all serious people. There's nothing that I can tell you that I know is 100 per cent true, apart from the information about the corrupt police officer. That is 100 per cent.'

Alvin repeated that he had never actually met the officer, but his friend had told him that he had been 'open to losing evidence' in relation to the 60 kilos of cannabis that Darren Wall had been arrested with. The evidence Alvin's friend was allegedly hoping to have lost was a police video of a bag containing cannabis being transferred from his car boot to Darren Wall's. Just what use such evidence, if indeed it ever did exist, would be to the police is highly debatable. A man putting a sports bag into somebody else's car would hardly be sufficient evidence to prosecute. One might ask why the police didn't stop and search the man and his bag at the time, instead of just videoing the event, if they thought it was important.

Alvin's credibility as an informant was fading fast. Not one of his remarkable stories had a shred of concrete evidence to support it. The mystery detective, who he said was bent but whom he had never actually met, might have been called Strongholm, 'or something like that'. He owed money to people, yet he didn't know their names. And he had mentioned a friend, whose name he couldn't give, who was hoping the insignificant camcorder evidence would be lost. This was all Alvin had so far divulged.

Losing patience with Alvin, DS Carter pressed him for information that he and his colleagues could act on or at least investigate. 'I am going to ask you who your friend is, not because I am looking to go and nick him, but it could help to identify the police officer. If I know who your friend is, I can work out who his associates are. If there is a corrupt officer, then we want to get him off the force because he is no good for us and no good for you. If we have people playing both sides of the fence, it becomes very difficult.'

Alvin still refused to name his friend. It was as if he was stalling the detectives, trying hard to rack his brains for a name, a face, anybody who would fit the tales he had invented and was preparing to tell. No credible story and no information would mean no deal and that would result in a long prison sentence for Alvin and the possibility of losing his home. Whatever else happened, that disastrous scenario could not possibly be allowed to happen.

'You're talking about something we know nothing about. If your friend is on video, he will get nicked anyway,' said DS Carter. 'We would never use what you are saying here in evidence because this is an intelligence interview. If we know who your friend is, we can then work out who the detective is because there will have been contact between the two.'

'So this won't be used?' Alvin asked.

'No, you will never give evidence against anybody. The only people who are going to know are us three in here and a couple of our bosses.'

'Straight?'

'Yeah.'

Alvin began to talk without giving the consequences of doing so much thought. The next two words out of Alvin's mouth were to set in motion a chain of events that would result in his saving his own skin but losing everything and having to flee to a place of refuge never to return again.

Alvin named his friend Ricky Percival.

Alvin said that Percival was the man who had been videoed handing over the 60 kilos of cannabis to Darren Wall and it was Percival who was involved with the alleged corrupt detective apparently named Strongholm.

Alvin was confident that he was entering into a deal that he could not lose. He had been given complete assurances that he would never have to give evidence against anybody and whichever friend he named would never be prosecuted.

Percival was on holiday in Spain at the time and therefore out of harm's reach in any event. Alvin was fulfilling his part of the deal, which would reward him with a reduced prison sentence and prevent his house from being seized.

THE FOOL ON THE PILL(S)

Despite naming Percival, Alvin still hadn't actually revealed anything of evidential value to the interviewing officers and so they pressed him further. DS Carter asked Alvin what, if any, incriminating evidence existed regarding Percival and the 60 kilos of cannabis. He also wanted to know how he knew for sure that Percival was involved with Strongholm. Alvin was unable to provide any link between Percival and the cannabis, but he claimed that Percival had discussed paying the corrupt detective with him.

'I went to see Percival; he was doing community work at the time. He told me that he was going to leave the country. For some reason, he wanted to finish his community work off first. Percival said that he was going to put it to the corrupt officer that he would pay him substantial amounts of money if he lost the evidence. This offer was going to be made through Kim Webber, who was friends with the officer. As I was leaving, Webber was pulling in down the road to meet Percival. Webber said that the officer had advised him that the police had been checking where Percival had got his cars from, whether he had paid cash for them and stuff like that.

'The police report detailing the results of these inquiries had ended up on the corrupt officer's desk and when he read that Webber had been seen in Percival's company, he had warned him to stay away from him.'

Alvin was asked if he was involved in any way with Percival. 'He's a friend,' he replied. 'I grew up down the same street as him.'

When asked if he was involved in any criminal activity with Percival, Alvin replied, 'No, he is in a different league. He's in with Kim Webber, Carlton Leach and the pikeys. He gets off on the fact that he thinks he's for real.'

Asked if the 60 kilos of cannabis had anything to do with him, Alvin's answer set the tone for many of the interviews that he was going to have with the police in the future: 'No, nothing, 100 per cent. I wouldn't have mentioned it if it was.'

This makes it crystal clear that there was no way he was going to give incriminating evidence relating to crimes he had been involved in personally.

Before ending the interview, the detectives reminded Alvin once more that the degree of assistance they could offer him depended entirely upon the quality of information he could give them. They told him to think about it and they would chat again at a later date. Alvin said that he would try to remember things, but he was having difficulty because 'that shit [cocaine] has fucked my head up half the time'.

DS Carter concluded the intelligence interview by telling Alvin, 'What might seem trivial to you might mean something important to us. It might be that we have a lot of intelligence about somebody, and something you say might make it all fall into place.

'Whilst we wouldn't use you in evidence – unless you actually come fully on board and say, "Right, I'm going to clear everything up that I have ever been involved in and I am going to name these people," and then obviously you would go down the path of being what is commonly termed a supergrass – you would have to make statements and you would have to be prepared to stand up in court. Obviously, there are advantages to you that can be put in place. It's been done many times.

'I was involved with Darren Nicholls, who was the supergrass on the Rettendon murder job. He still went to prison for his involvement, but he became a protected witness. I'm not going to press you today because we now have something to work on and we need to check you are not spinning us a line to try to get something. There has to be a trust thing between us.'

Damon Alvin has never understood the word 'trust'. His mind was already focused on how he was going to overcome the next hurdle between himself and the freedom he was prepared to do anything to secure. He knew he would have to start fabricating evidence to make the story he had given in mitigation plausible.

On Thursday, 3 April 2003, Alvin was remanded in custody to HMP Belmarsh in south-east London to await a hearing at Basildon Crown Court for sentencing. A few weeks later, he was taken from the prison to Gravesend police station in Kent, where he was formally arrested for the murder of Dean Boshell.

Alvin underwent two interviews, during which he refused to answer any questions other than his name, address and date of birth. In the break between the two 'no comment' interviews, the officers said to him, in the presence of his solicitor (who made notes on the subject), that they believed Ricky Percival was responsible for the murder of Dean Boshell. In a statement made later about this incident, Alvin recalled, 'They called Percival the "shooter" as opposed to the murderer. They went on to say that if I was prepared to tell them what had happened the night Boshell died, protection would be offered to my family and me. My wife came to the police station and it was explained to her what assistance could be given if I was in a position to confirm what they suspected. I was then allowed time alone with my wife in a room divided by a screen.

'My wife and I discussed our options. I told her I knew what had happened that night and that I was involved. She made it plain she did not want to be away from her family – she was pregnant at the time and was scared. She left it up to me, however, to make the final decision. I was allowed the night to think about it.

'By the following morning I had decided to remain silent because I was concerned for my safety, the safety of my wife, her family and mine.'

I do not believe that people facing an allegation of murder should be assisted or offered deals by the police. If that person is later convicted of murder, a judge can only pass one sentence and that is life imprisonment. It is non-negotiable under any circumstances and so I fail to see just how the police intended to assist Alvin if he agreed to assist them. This offer by the police suggests to me that, despite the evidence pointing towards Alvin being guilty of involvement in Boshell's murder, officers were doing their utmost to encourage Alvin to implicate Percival. It was wholly inappropriate for the police to even suggest that they 'knew' Percival was the shooter. How could they possibly know such a thing unless they had been present during the murder? No gun had been found, no witness had made a statement saying that Percival was present at the scene and no telephone records or forensic evidence had linked him to Boshell. This assumption by the police and their offer to help Alvin has led to what I believe is the most blatant miscarriage of justice of recent times.

Just before Alvin was returned to HMP Belmarsh, he was asked 'off the record' why Boshell had been murdered. Without any hesitation, Alvin had replied, 'Because he was a liability.'

Alvin says that whilst at Gravesend he was desperate to tell the police the full story regarding Boshell's murder, but he was too scared. Of whom he does not say – Percival was in Spain and so one can only assume that Alvin feared the drug-dealing loan sharks whom he says he owed £15,000.

All decent police officers dislike nothing more than the suggestion that one of their colleagues is corrupt. Such allegations impact not only on each and every officer who has dealings with the individual concerned but also upon the police service as a whole. The detectives who interviewed Alvin were extremely keen, therefore, to research and discover the facts behind the alleged antics of Detective Strongholm, but all their inquiries had been fruitless. The reason they had been unable to find Strongholm was simple: he did not exist.

Alvin was aware that Kim Webber dealt in drugs and he had heard that one of Webber's colleagues at a football club he helped to run was a detective. Creating a story involving both men was quite easy for a man as devious as Alvin. However, in the heat of the moment, he had made three major errors. The intelligence that Alvin had given the police regarding the officer's name being Strongholm and the name of the football club that he ran being Brentwood both proved to be false. The video evidence that Percival had allegedly been trying to purchase from Strongholm was proven to have never existed.

In an effort to get his story back on track, Alvin claims that he employed the services of a friend, Tony Staunton. According to Alvin, Staunton was a major player in the Essex underworld who also had connections with the Provisional IRA (PIRA). Alvin received regular prison visits from Staunton, who happened to be in regular contact with Kim Webber. There was nothing sinister in this: Webber and Staunton simply shared the same circle of friends. Alvin claims that it was during a prison visit that he had asked Staunton to help him. He said he wanted Staunton to find out who the policeman was that Percival had been talking to so that he could give the name to the intelligence officers.

Acting upon Alvin's instructions, Staunton apparently found out that Webber was the vice-chairman of Basildon United Football Club and the chairman was Detective Sergeant John Moran. Staunton then visited DS Moran's home, which happened to be just a few hundred yards from Alvin's, and wrote down the make, model and registration number of his car, along with distinguishing features, such as the car's headlight being cracked. Staunton passed this on to Alvin on his next prison visit and it was eventually presented to the police as information that Alvin knew personally.

I say 'eventually' because Alvin's first attempt to divulge DS Moran's name was a total debacle. During intelligence interviews at HMP Belmarsh, Alvin told the police that the corrupt officer was a man named John Weaver. When asked if he was sure, Alvin had replied, 'No, no, it's John Moran. I knew a guy called John Weaver and so I made a mistake; it just threw me. I was trying to remember what name Staunton had told me.'

THE FOOL ON THE PILL(S)

Having polished his story, to a certain extent, Alvin told the police that it had been towards the end of 2002 or the beginning of 2003 that Percival had begun to associate with DS Moran. He said Percival hadn't told him DS Moran's name at first; he just claimed that he had 'a tame old bill' who was a high-ranking officer on the murder investigation team. Alvin said that Percival had been warned by Webber that he was being investigated for very serious matters. DS Moran had initially tipped Webber off because Webber had been seen in Percival's company, and so he had subsequently also been flagged by the police as a man worth watching. DS Moran's advice had been that Webber should distance himself from Percival or risk being arrested with him. According to Alvin, Percival had asked Webber if he could set up a meeting with DS Moran to discuss this and Webber had said that he would see what he could do to arrange it.

'Initially,' Alvin said, 'DS Moran refused to meet Percival, but eventually a meeting did take place in a café.'

Alvin said that as soon as the meeting with DS Moran was over, Percival had arrived at his house. He had boasted that if Alvin was unsure about anybody he sold drugs to Percival now had a policeman in his pocket who would be willing to find out if they were registered informants. All Alvin had to provide was the person's date of birth and name.

Despite stating that he had never seen DS Moran or known his name in his initial intelligence interviews, Alvin told detectives, 'One afternoon Percival was around my house and asked me to give him a lift home. On the way, he said he needed to stop off at a place called Hadleigh. I pulled into a car park at the back of the Iceland store and he got out of the car. He walked up to a blue Carlton Omega and got in. I could see that a broad male was sitting in the driver's seat.

'I remember looking over, and I could just see his head and shoulders. He had grey hair. When Percival came back to my car, he told me that he had just met with DS Moran and paid him £4,000. He said he had been advised to leave the country. He also told me that surveillance was being moved from him to me, as I had become the prime suspect for Boshell's murder. Apparently Percival was difficult to monitor because he was a single man who had no routine, and his friends and associates lived a similar lifestyle. Because I was married with a settled home life surveillance on me would be easier.

'Percival was particularly good to me after that. He would sell me large quantities of cocaine at a very cheap rate. He also sold me designer clothing and a pair of Rockport boots very cheaply and gave me a £300 speed-trap detector as a present. I believe he only did all of this to retain my friendship. In January 2003, I gave up dealing in drugs because of all the attention on me.'

Alvin's explanation as to why he says Essex police switched surveillance from Percival to himself is laughable. If the police are watching two suspects and one goes home to his wife and kids every evening after work and the other is dashing about meeting people and committing crime, why on earth would they put any resources into sitting outside the family man's house? It might be easier to watch the family man, but the police wouldn't solve many crimes. Regardless of the criticisms from some sections of the public, I believe the police are a little wiser than that.

Alvin was correct in describing DS Moran as having grey hair, but, as he lived just a few hundred yards from the detective's home, he may have known this for some time. It's more than probable that Alvin had been advised at some stage by one of his countless criminal associates that he had 'old bill' living on his doorstep. He might not have been told the officer's name, but he would have been told roughly where he lived and what he looked like.

I have spoken to Tony Staunton, who Alvin claims assisted him, and he has asked me to remind Alvin that the year these fictitious events allegedly occurred was 2003 – the PIRA called a ceasefire in 1997 that has remained intact ever since, so how Staunton could have possibly been involved with them six years later remains a mystery to him. He assured me that he has had no involvement whatsoever with the PIRA 'before, since or ever'.

'As far as I am aware,' Staunton continued, 'the PIRA were never active around Southend. Maybe Alvin drinks in different bars to me, or maybe he's simply full of shit. I did visit him in prison because he wanted me to give his pregnant wife a lift to ensure that she was safe travelling into London. That is gentlemanly conduct or kindness, not proof of a conspiracy. There's no way I went snooping around on his behalf. I had never heard of DS Moran before this. Alvin was in a corner; he couldn't face what was coming like a man, so I suppose he concocted this ridiculous story to get out of it.'

If Alvin was being entirely honest with the interviewing officers and everybody else was lying, it raises the question: if he gave up dealing in drugs in January 2003, as he claimed, how did the police manage to arrest him with a kilo of cocaine in April of that year?

THE FOOL ON THE PILL(S)

As for Leach being involved with Percival, he had been involved in drug dealing in the past but turned his back on crime in 1995 after the murder of his closest friend, Tony Tucker. Percival was an associate of Leach, but their mutual interest was bodybuilding and fitness at a gym they both used rather than any sort of criminality. At the time Alvin was describing Leach, he was involved in a successful and legitimate car sales business in Essex. He has never been questioned about the allegations made by Alvin, I assume, because the police know they have no substance.

In 2002, Leach published his autobiography entitled *Muscle*. In 2007, a film covering aspects of Leach's life and the Rettendon murders was released, called *Rise of the Footsoldier*. It's fair to say that as a result of the book and the film Leach is a very well-known character in Essex and Alvin would have heard of him.

In Leach's book, which was published the year before Alvin's arrest, he details his escapades as a football hooligan, nightclub bouncer and drug dealer. In one incident, Leach and others fly out to Tenerife to resolve a dispute between a bar owner and a friend. The affections of a female were at the heart of the matter, but Leach was able to sort the problem out without too much fuss. Whilst in Tenerife, Leach says that he met fellow Essex Boys Jason Draper, Big Joe Wright and his father Frankie Wright. Because Leach had written about drug importation and meeting Frankie in Spain, this may have given Alvin the means to spice up the story he told about Percival's holiday in Spain and him being forced to courier drugs for Leach when he was caught with the kilo of cocaine. Instead of a sadly all-too-common drink-fuelled stabbing incident, Alvin was able to portray Percival as being stabbed and the terrible accident that followed as a Mafia-type drug deal gone wrong that had resulted in the death of Wright. Knowing Alvin and his desire to emulate the gangster lifestyle, it is more than likely that Leach's name was added to Alvin's story after he had read his book or he had discussed it with one of his fellow wannabes. His story about Leach and Webber forcing him to sell drugs was later proved to be an absolute lie.

Before someone is sentenced in these days of equality and justice he or she is interviewed by the Probation Service so that a report detailing personal circumstances can be presented to the judge. The homeless or unemployed, or those otherwise in genuine need, are generally sent to prison and those with a wife, children, a job and a home are often spared the indignity of incarceration. The thinking is that jailing a family man will cause his innocent wife and children to suffer. Society as a whole is apparently punished if a taxpayer is jailed because the public purse has to fund his upkeep whilst he is inside. Those with nothing are decreed to be an existing strain on the limited resources of the welfare state and so sending them to jail seemingly affects nobody. The fact that a person with a stable background should have thought long and hard about the consequences of his actions before risking losing it is generally ignored.

When Alvin met the probation officer appointed to write his report, he knew exactly what he was required to say in order to attract maximum credit. He was going to have to claim that he had acted under duress and that any punishment he received would punish his innocent wife and child more than it would punish him.

Alvin told the probation officer that following the death of his good friend Dean Boshell he had become very low and depressed. He claimed that he was diagnosed as suffering from depression and his condition had become so dire he began to 'self medicate' with cocaine. Initially, he only used the drug socially but after moving to the Benfleet area of Basildon he had become increasingly involved with heavy cocaine users. As a result Alvin's habit had spiralled out of control to the point where he was using up to £250 worth of the drug per week, though he said he had managed to conceal his drug dependency from his wife. When refurbishments were required at his home, he had secured a £10,000 loan from drug dealers with whom he associated and a further £5,000 from them at a later date.

At first there were no problems with the arrangement, but Alvin said as his drug habit escalated he fell behind with the repayments and relations between him and his creditors began to sour. In December 2002, matters came to a head when Alvin was confronted by a number of men from this gang who demanded their money back. Alvin had asked them for more time to pay, but the men refused to listen.

Alvin said that he was stabbed in the leg and then beaten with a hammer. As he lay on the floor bleeding, he was told that if he did not pay or somehow work the debt off, future attacks would involve not only him being hurt but also members of his family.

As he told the shocked probation officer his story, Alvin had struggled to keep his composure. He said he had initially refused to comply with the gang's requests, but when they threatened him and demanded the full amount he reluctantly agreed to work off some of the debt by making a delivery of cocaine. It was whilst transporting a kilo of the drug from Leigh-on-Sea to Canvey Island on behalf of the gang that he had been arrested.

Alvin said that while he was in prison his wife had been accosted by gang members and forced to withdraw £20,000 from their savings in order to repay the debt. Despite handing over this money, his wife continued to receive threatening phone calls and death threats, one of which was a funeral wreath delivered to her address with a card which read, 'With deepest sympathy for you. Tell him to keep his trap shut or these will be yours. May it help you to remember that friends are always there.'

In a note posted through her letterbox, which had been made using letters cut from a newspaper, the gang had warned, 'We want our fucking money. Sort it, or we will sort you.'

Alvin claimed that these threats against his family were intended to dissuade him from giving information to the police about the gang and that was why he had refused to answer police questions when he had been arrested.

After hearing Alvin's tale of woe, the well-meaning probation officer wrote in his pre-sentence report: 'Given the circumstances surrounding this offence and further information provided within this report, if the court feels that only a custodial sentence can be justified I would ask that any term of imprisonment imposed be as short as possible in order to limit further pressure upon Mr Alvin's family, who have already suffered significantly as a result of this offence.'

Knowing the importance of shoring up a fictitious story with factual evidence, Alvin produced a medical certificate to 'prove' that he had been stabbed and beaten by the loan sharks to whom he owed money. This certificate stated that he had attended a doctor's surgery around Christmas 2002, suffering from cuts to his hands and leg. These were, the document said, 'allegedly caused by a knife'. Alvin's wife had already reported the death threats, letters and funeral wreath she had received to the police, so it's unlikely that any judge would have doubted the authenticity of Alvin's dreadful plight at the hands of such an evil drug gang.

On 10 July 2003, Alvin appeared at Basildon Crown Court for sentencing. When asked by the judge if he had anything to say in mitigation, Alvin acknowledged that he was aware that the only sentencing option available to the judge for such a serious offence was a custodial sentence; however, he begged the judge to consider how much he had changed in the past few years of his life.

'My past offending is shameful,' he said, 'and I'm far from proud of my previous convictions, but I have changed in the past few years. I have got married to a wonderful, caring woman and together we have bought a house. We have a baby and have another on the way. I started my own business three years ago, which has been steadily growing, and I normally employ up to six people. I know the offence I committed was both stupid and irresponsible, and I have no one else to blame but myself. I know this is no excuse, but I got myself into a position I didn't know how to get out of. I now realise I could have, and should have, done things differently.

'I am now clean from drugs and am receiving help with the depression caused by the murder of my friend [Boshell], which led to my habit. I have helped the police to the best of my ability with everything I know. I ask you for one last chance and for you to consider giving me a shorter term of imprisonment. When I'm released, I want to show that I can live a normal law-abiding life and continue with my business.'

There wasn't a dry eye in the courtroom by the time Alvin had finished delivering his emotionally charged speech.

But the Damon Alvin sympathy show was not over just yet. Pregnant and dabbing at her eyes with a tissue, his wife Clair listened intently as a letter she had written as an encore to her husband's performance was read out on his behalf:

> I am living between my own home and my parents' house because I am scared to be at home alone with my son due to the threats that I have been receiving. I have had an alarm and panic button installed, but I still feel unsafe. I have lost my husband, who I love and miss very dearly. We have never been apart before and I'm finding it hard to cope. We are a very close couple and, although I don't condone what Damon has done, I do feel that I now understand the reasons why he did it. Both myself and my young son are still suffering, as Damon is away from us, and we are still living with the threat that he tried to resolve.

Taking into account the information that Alvin had given to the police, the circumstances that supposedly led to Alvin being forced to courier drugs and the fact that he had been 'beaten, stabbed and his family left traumatised', the judge sentenced Alvin to thirty months' imprisonment instead of the expected six years.

THE FOOL ON THE PILL(S)

A confiscation order was also made against him for the £31,420 that was found in his washing machine and a further £18,000 from his savings was seized. Justice, on the surface, appeared to have prevailed. Damon Alvin had broken the law and Damon Alvin had seemingly been made to pay. The truth was that Damon Alvin had mocked justice and deceived everybody. He had learned a valuable lesson about doing deals with the police in order to save himself. It was a lesson he was never going to forget.

12

THE SMELL OF CONSPIRACY

Detective Sergeant John Moran and Kim Webber came under intense police
scrutiny as a result of Alvin's intelligence interviews. Their cars had
covert listening devices installed and their phone calls were monitored.
The few calls that were intercepted between the two men turned out
to be totally innocent: they discussed the business of Basildon United
Football Club and little else.

DS Moran was the Basildon United chairman, with Webber the
vice-chairman. There was nothing sinister in the fact that they
happened to know one another; the pair shared a professional working
relationship rather than any sort of unethically cosy bond. Both had
been democratically elected by the club's members and so one assumes
that everybody at the club, who happened to have known them for
years, had no doubts about the integrity of either man.

Being wrong is not yet a crime in this country, though I am sure
there is a government minister somewhere looking into this problem.
Fixed-penalty fines for errors of judgement will no doubt become a
feature of our lives one day.

Webber had been a very close friend of Pat Tate and Tony Tucker.
He wasn't involved in any of their illegal activities, but he witnessed
many of the unsavoury incidents that brought about their notoriety. In
the mid-1990s, Webber had got involved in an altercation with a man
at the Southend Flying Club. Both parties traded punches, but Webber
had ended the fight by plunging a beer glass into his opponent's face.
As a result of this incident, Webber had found himself serving a prison
sentence when Tucker and Tate had met their deaths. When Webber was
eventually released, he learned that the drug empire his fallen friends

had once controlled with an iron fist was now a relatively free market. Anybody and everybody was getting involved in what appeared to be a fairly easy route to getting rich quick. Rather foolishly Webber decided that he too would join the herbal gold rush. Previously anti-drugs, Webber reasoned that if the police were not too bothered about people smoking the stuff, he should not worry himself too much about selling it.

Unfortunately for DS Moran, who was totally oblivious to Webber's personal business, a police surveillance team had watched a man named David Ferguson loading packages into the boot of Webber's Mercedes in a hotel car park. The police had followed Webber, who later met a man named Raymond Marten. Officers observed as the men unloaded the packages from Webber's car into Marten's van. This van was later stopped and searched in the village of Aylesford, Kent. Inside, police found three parcels containing nearly 50 kilos of cannabis. I say this was unfortunate for DS Moran because the find proved that Alvin had been telling the truth about Webber, and so it was logical to assume that he was probably telling the truth about DS Moran also.

At 5 a.m. on Tuesday, 14 October 2003, more than a hundred police officers swooped on just six people in dawn raids across south Essex. Three vanloads of officers dressed in operational overalls stormed the clubhouse of Basildon United Football Club with sniffer dogs. In simultaneous raids, other officers, some armed, burst into a flat, a car dealership and a farmhouse. DS Moran, one of those arrested, was subjected to almost forensic scrutiny. His bank accounts were examined, his home was searched and he was interviewed under caution on ten separate occasions, but not a hint of wrongdoing or inappropriate behaviour was found. It wasn't for the want of trying by some of DS Moran's overzealous colleagues.

They had covertly watched and listened one evening as DS Moran had given a friend of his a lift home. This man, David Cusack, had been a professional footballer throughout the 1980s. It was through his love of football that Cusack met DS Moran, who had spent years trying to improve the facilities and fortunes of Basildon United.

Aged 16, DS Moran had joined the club as a striker and was named as their Sportsman of the Year just 12 months later. When Moran had turned 18, he had joined the Police Force. As well as his policing duties, he played for the Basildon Police football team and won six league titles, four Challenge Cups and eight inter-police titles. Whilst still serving with Essex police as part of their major investigations team, DS Moran was elected Basildon United's chairman. Some time later Dave Cusack was elected club secretary and, inevitably, their friendship was reinforced.

DS Moran had been working at Rayleigh police station one day when Cusack had been brought in for an allegation of drink-driving. Once Cusack had been charged and processed, DS Moran had met him by chance in the reception and offered him a lift home.

When DS Moran was arrested months later following Alvin's allegations, the police accused him of tampering with the evidence against Cusack and suggested that this had 'led to his acquittal'. DS Moran strenuously denied doing any such thing. Because DS Moran was refusing to 'come clean', Dave Cusack was interviewed by police. In answer to questions about how he had managed to evade justice, the ex-footballer replied: 'The answer is quite simple. I didn't evade justice, I pleaded guilty at the earliest opportunity and was banned from driving.' Embarrassed but not deterred, the officers began to seek out other evidence to support Alvin's claims.

He had told them that DS Moran had sold Percival information about the identity of police informants and they obviously knew that Boshell was a registered informant. This led some officers to believe that Percival might have learned of Boshell's status from DS Moran and decided to kill him. This motive for Boshell's murder was certainly presented to the jury during Percival's trial. Unfortunately for Percival, what his defence team did not know and therefore the jury did not hear, was that DS Moran was no friend of Percival; in fact, the detective was actively working towards having him prosecuted.

I have learned from an official and extremely reliable source that DS Moran acted professionally and with integrity in all matters relating to Percival, Webber and the Boshell murder inquiry. When Percival visited Spain, DS Moran also happened to be visiting the country with his brother and a friend. DS Moran's brother has a holiday apartment near a golfing complex and they had gone to decorate it. When they had finished their task, the trio had spent two or three days playing golf and enjoying a few beers in the sunshine.

Webber knew that his friend Percival was in Spain and had heard through his colleagues at Basildon United that DS Moran had also recently flown there. Adding two and two together and coming up with six, Webber believed that DS Moran had gone to Spain to carry out surveillance on his friend. When Moran returned to England, Webber phoned him, in what has been described as a 'fishing expedition'.

Webber wanted to know where DS Moran had been in Spain, with whom he had travelled there, whom had he seen out there and, more importantly, the purpose of his visit. DS Moran thought that Webber's questions were extremely suspicious – so much so that he filed an intelligence report detailing the call.

When DS Moran heard about Percival's involvement in the death of Frankie Wright in Spain, he thought it would be an ideal opportunity to prosecute him. It was certainly no secret that Percival was high on the priority list of persons Essex police were keen to see behind bars. DS Moran had therefore submitted a report to his superiors suggesting that Percival should be extradited from Spain for the manslaughter of a British subject and put on trial in this country.

For reasons known only to Essex police, DS Moran's proposal was ignored. A few weeks later, DS Moran was walking around a parade of shops near his home when he met Big Joe Wright. DS Moran offered Big Joe his condolences and mentioned that there was a possibility that the man driving the vehicle when his father died might face manslaughter charges in England or Spain.

'He won't face any charges in Spain,' Big Joe replied. 'We have just helped to bring Percival home.'

As soon as DS Moran returned to the police station, he filed a report about the conversation he'd had with Big Joe and the fact that Percival had returned to the UK. DS Moran's actions were those of a policeman dedicated to doing his duty. His only failing appears to be that he was courteous and polite to everybody he met regardless of his or her background or history. It's a pity not all police officers have the same 'flaw' in their personality; if they did, people might start respecting them. It's ridiculous to suggest that DS Moran was protecting or was somehow in league with Percival.

If the jury at Percival's trial could have heard the truth about DS Moran's professional conduct, it's unlikely that Percival would ever have been convicted. Despite Alvin's allegations and the way in which they were investigated, DS Moran's unblemished and distinguished career with Essex police remains intact and untarnished.

After being cleared of any wrongdoing, DS Moran told his local newspaper, the *Evening Echo*, 'I had worked for the police for 30 years. It was my whole way of life; it was destroyed and turned upside down. The allegations that I had sold information about the Boshell murder investigation to Percival for thousands of pounds were found to be baseless. There was a thorough investigation by the anti-corruption squad. They took away the computers in my house and all of my documents concerning bank accounts. Every penny that I had – and that wasn't a great deal – was accounted for. I must admit I was very disappointed by the way the matter was handled. An allegation was made and I fully understand and accept that it had to be investigated. It was the way it was investigated that troubled me. I have always been professional in my approach to cases and I therefore know that the way this particular allegation was handled was anything but professional. As far as I'm aware, I've never met Damon Alvin. I know the name because it was me who put his name forward as one of the two people responsible for the murder of Dean Boshell. When you do that in a job where you are dealing with gangland people and killings, sometimes the people who put names forward are going to have their own names dirtied.'

Webber was sentenced to serve fourteen years' imprisonment, but this was later reduced on appeal to ten years. Ferguson and Marten were both sentenced to four and a half years for their part in the plot. A fourth man named Francis Sims was sentenced to ten years' imprisonment for his role in the conspiracy.

Commenting after Webber had been sentenced, DS Moran said, 'I guess that will teach him. It's what you should get for dealing in drugs. He was a member of the football club and managed to get himself elected on to one of the committees. I would never have guessed that he would have been involved in such a drugs conspiracy. In fact, at the football club he was always verbally against drugs and drug-taking.'

Eight brief months after being sentenced to serve two and a half years' imprisonment, Damon Alvin was released from prison on the condition that he agreed to wear an electronic tag for a period of four months. These tags are tuned into an electronic box in the offender's home, which sends a warning signal to the police if the person is not within a certain distance of it at designated times. Rather than having low-risk inmates inhabiting prison cells that could be being used for housing more dangerous criminals, the idea is that they are tagged and effectively put under house arrest. This allows them to work during the day but prevents them from roaming the streets at night.

After three long, seemingly inactive years, the Boshell murder investigation appeared to be going nowhere. That was until 2004, when the Labour Government announced the introduction of new legislation. The then Home Secretary, David Blunkett, said that a new strategy to tackle organised crime was needed and this would include a revamp of the supergrass system. The proposals were aimed at 'getting a grip on gangs who control drug-running, people-smuggling, prostitution and financial rackets'. Criminals who 'turn Queen's evidence could win immunity from prosecution or have their sentence cut by more than two-thirds if they shop their gang bosses,' Blunkett said. 'Existing criminals who turn Queen's evidence already have their sentences reduced and are often given new identities, but this will be the first time that this approach has been formalised in an Act of Parliament.'

Nobody knows if Essex police already had a strategy for the Boshell case simmering on some back burner or if news of this new legislation prompted officers to think again. Coincidentally, or otherwise, the police decided to re-arrest Damon Alvin.

At 4 a.m. on the very morning that Alvin was due to have his electronic tag removed, the police stormed his house and took him into custody for the murder of Dean Boshell. At the same time, Kevin Walsh and Kate Griffiths were arrested for allegedly conspiring to pervert the course of justice.

Ricky Percival's address was also raided, but he was not home at the time. His brother Danny had just got back from a night out when armed officers who mistakenly believed that he was Ricky dragged him naked from his bed. Bleary eyed and confused, Danny, who had retired to bed just half an hour earlier, tried to explain to the police who he was, but it took him 30 minutes to convince them.

Alvin was taken to Harlow police station for questioning, but on the advice of his legal representative he made no comment when interviewed. He did, however, produce a written statement. In this he explained that he liked Boshell and had no reason to fall out with him, and certainly had no reason to want to kill him. Vehemently denying that he had planned to commit a burglary with Boshell on the night of the murder, Alvin added, 'If I was doing something really serious like that, I would not have relied on Dean.

'I simply do not know who killed Dean,' he continued. 'When I was taken out of prison to Gravesend police station, the officers told me that they knew I had nothing to do with the murder. They said they believed it was Ricky Percival who was responsible for the killing. They offered me all sorts of deals, which I refused. I said I didn't know anything about Dean's death and so was unable to do a deal and implicate Ricky, even if I had wanted to.

'I have heard various rumours about Percival's involvement in criminal matters. I know nothing of these matters and believe that many of these rumours have been put about by the police. Further, I believe that I have only been charged to put pressure on me to give the police information about Percival's possible involvement in Boshell's murder. Unfortunately, I do not know anything.'

In an effort to appear helpful, Alvin offered the interviewing officers his second 'off the record' motive for the murder – that Boshell might have been involved in gun-running and drug dealing with immigrants in the Southend area.

When the police had finished questioning Alvin, he was bailed to reappear at Harlow police station two months later, pending further inquiries. Walsh and Griffiths were interviewed at separate police stations and both reiterated the accounts that they had given previously concerning the night Boshell died.

The police had formed the opinion that the couple had either been coerced or threatened by Percival or Alvin, or both men, to give them an alibi at the time Boshell was shot. The unofficial time of death had been calculated by the police by considering the time Boshell was seen leaving Southend and the second statement of Gordon Osborne, who claimed that he had heard two or three shots being fired between 11 p.m. and 11.30 p.m. Boshell had not been seen alive again after leaving Southend. He had suffered three gunshot wounds and, according to the police, nobody other than the gunman would have known this. Osborne's evidence, therefore, must have been accurate. Convinced that either Alvin or Percival, or both, was responsible for Boshell's murder, the police were left in no doubt that Griffiths and Walsh were therefore lying. In their view, they had to be because they had both said that Alvin and Percival were in their flat at the time Boshell was believed to have been murdered.

Kate Griffiths, a hard-working young woman of good character, was seen by the police as the weakest link in the alleged plot to provide Boshell's killers with an alibi and so she was subjected to intense questioning over two days. Laughing nervously when they accused her of lying throughout her numerous interviews, Griffiths insisted that she was telling the truth.

In an effort to break her resolve, one of the officers said that he wished to outline all the evidence they had unearthed, which proved Alvin, at least, was involved in Boshell's murder. 'If Alvin is lying,' the officer said, 'you must be lying, and so, after considering this evidence I am now going to read, you might wish to reconsider your statement.

'Our understanding is that when Malcolm Walsh was stabbed to death by Terry Watkins, it caused a great deal of friction. A year after Malcolm's death, two males in balaclavas burst into a house, which was full of women, children and men. They were armed with shotguns and started blasting away, seriously injuring a number of people. It is believed that this was done as a favour to the Walsh family to avenge the murder of Malcolm. That crime was committed by Ricky Percival and another man, possibly Damon Alvin. What I am trying to emphasise here, Miss Griffiths, is the cruelty that these people are capable of. We have spoken to a number of Dean Boshell's friends in the Southend area and they say he might have been a drug user and a drug dealer. A witness has seen him with cocaine. They have also explained that he had very few friends.

'The only people that he talked about were his girlfriend, Damon Alvin, or his brother, as he referred to him, and Ricky Percival. They are the only three people who would phone him or have anything to do with him.

'Early in February 2001, Boshell asked a friend to go on a job with him. Boshell said that he and his brother were going to break into a house in Westcliffe and steal a load of skunk plants. He said that he would pay this friend £1,000 out of the £2,500 that he was expecting to be paid. Two days before Boshell died, he showed this friend a revolver and three rounds of ammunition that he had under his mattress in his flat. Boshell also told the person who employed him at a café that he and his brother had purchased two guns. Apparently, it was cheaper to buy a pair and so they had paid just £500. Boshell was at work the night before he died and he told his employer that he was planning this robbery. He added that he was intending to do it with his brother on the 3rd or 4th of March. Later that evening, he received a telephone call from Clair Sanders' phone. We know that Alvin did not have any credit on his phone and we know Sanders had no reason to call Boshell, and so the likelihood is Alvin was using Sanders' phone to call him. Immediately after that call, Boshell asked his employer if he could have Tuesday night off work, as he had a job to do.

'When Boshell left work, he confirmed to a friend that he had a job to do and asked if he could borrow some dark clothing. At 8.31 p.m., phone records show that Boshell called Alvin from his friend's mobile phone. Alvin is seen answering this call on CCTV footage recorded in the Woodcutters Arms. Later that night, Boshell is recorded on CCTV wearing the dark clothing his friend had given him. At 9 p.m., the footage shows Boshell and another friend walking towards the Lidl general store on Woodgrange Drive.

'At 9.26, a telephone call is made from a public kiosk at Lidl's to Damon Alvin's mobile phone. We have CCTV footage of Alvin leaving the Woodcutters pub at 9.15. Shortly after the call to Alvin's mobile phone, a red car pulled up outside Lidl's and Boshell said to his friend, "See you tomorrow." The friend watched as Boshell got into the vehicle and then he walked away. Dean Boshell was never seen alive again.'

The policeman interviewing Griffiths said that phone records showed that at 11.17 p.m. and 11.47 p.m. Kevin Walsh had been trying to call Damon Alvin's mobile phone. The calls had only lasted a second or two and had not been answered. However, these calls were made at a time when all concerned, including Griffiths, had said that Alvin was with Walsh at his flat.

'Why would Walsh telephone Alvin twice on his mobile phone, if they were in the same room?' the officer had asked. Barely pausing for breath, the policeman continued to read out the evidence to Griffiths who, despite her solicitor's advice to remain silent, commented on points throughout his recital.

'Between 9.44 p.m., which is the approximate time that Alvin was seen picking Boshell up, and 11.29 p.m., which is around the time the murder had allegedly taken place, Alvin's mobile phone was switched off. At 11.48 p.m., Clair Sanders had received a call on her mobile phone from the phone kiosk located directly outside Boshell's old flat. This kiosk also happens to be adjacent to the allotments where he was murdered. Sanders said in a statement that she refused to sign that this call was from Alvin and he was asking her to pick him up from Kevin Walsh's flat. How could Alvin be at the allotments and in the flat with you at the same time?' the detective asked.

There was a brief silence in the interview room before Griffiths replied, 'I know what you want me to say, but I cannot say it. Every time that I have spoken to the police, I have told them the truth, 100 per cent.' Griffiths' words fell on deaf ears.

'Alvin had claimed that he and Percival had arrived at the flat around 10.45 p.m. and Walsh has said their arrival time was 11 p.m.,' the officer continued. 'When Percival was asked what time he had arrived, he said that he didn't recall. That smells, to me. That stinks of somebody making things up. Sorry, it just doesn't work. There has been some collusion; you've had a chat. I don't know if you've been told what to say, someone's had a go at you, you thought you were doing somebody a favour or you were put under pressure. I don't know, but people don't take a guess at a time and get the same time. They are all wrong because we can prove they're wrong, and yet they all say the same.'

With the benefit of hindsight, the officer may no longer believe that he could prove that all four people were lying. It may have since occurred to him that four people who give the same account of an event are actually being honest.

Kevin Walsh was undergoing a similar interrogation to Griffiths. He, too, was insisting that he was innocent, but the police officers interviewing him were far from convinced.

When the police had completed their questioning, Griffiths and Walsh were bailed to reappear at Harlow police station, pending further inquiries.

Shortly after the arrests of his three friends, Percival had handed himself in at a police station and was arrested for the murder of Dean Boshell. Later that same day, after giving a no-comment interview on the advice of his solicitor, he too was bailed to return to Harlow at a later date.

On 21 October 2004, all four suspects attended Harlow police station, where Alvin was formally charged with the murder of Dean Boshell; Percival, Griffiths and Walsh were charged with conspiracy to pervert the course of justice. Later that afternoon they appeared in court. Griffiths and Walsh were released on bail to await trial, but Percival and Alvin were remanded in custody to HMP Chelmsford, where they were placed in the same cell.

Recalling those early days in custody, Alvin said, 'At that stage, we felt that there was little or no evidence against us. A month after being remanded in custody, the case papers were given to us and we began to consider our defence. After reading all of the evidence, we realised that the case against us was not as weak as we had originally thought.'

The most alarming evidence for Alvin had been given by the very man he had been accused of murdering. This evidence, which caused Alvin many sleepless nights, was a bundle of contact sheets that a police officer had compiled after Boshell had given information about his criminal associates. These detailed the alleged involvement of Alvin, Percival and others in a range of both serious and rather trivial offences.

'I had absolutely no knowledge that Boshell was informing on me before I read those notes,' Alvin said. 'Nothing about Boshell being an informant had ever been mentioned to me in any of the police interviews. I was flabbergasted. It didn't seem like the sort of thing that Dean would do because he always seemed so fond of me and loyal. I cannot think why Dean would inform on me. We were friends. I was never arrested on any of the so-called information that Dean gave to the police. I don't know what he got out of doing it. Perhaps he made it up to sound more important than he was, or he wanted to be known to hang about with "big criminals". I think Dean was a Walter Mitty character who liked to pretend he moved in gangster circles. I don't think he had even met Percival at the time he gave some of the information about him.' The case papers contained lots of damning evidence concerning Alvin, much of which he was unable to dispute.

Mobile telephones are made up of small radio transmitters and receivers. They operate by sending and receiving signals to and from the masts that we see dotted all around the country. The phones are designed to automatically make contact with the mast that has the strongest signal. This is invariably the mast that is closest to the mobile phone. Some of these masts contain antennae that are positioned to face in different directions. The mobile phone companies are able to identify the antenna to which a phone has connected and therefore provide a rough location for that phone when it has made or received calls. Using this method to track Alvin's movements, the police were able to show that after leaving the Woodcutters Arms he had travelled towards the centre of Southend. In Alvin's own words, the telephone evidence, which proved that he had visited Southend at the time Boshell was picked up, was 'of major concern to us'.

'I had told the police that I had driven straight home to Rochford,' Alvin said. 'We had to come up with a story to explain why, after leaving the public house, I had gone in that direction. It was agreed that I would give one of the following reasons: either I was dropping cocaine off, collecting money due for drug deals, going to a pub or going to see my brother. There was a variety of excuses I could have used, but they all would have contradicted my original witness statement.'

Desperate to avoid being convicted of Boshell's murder and spending his life in prison, Alvin said, 'We agreed that we would use the available evidence to try and construct a case against others that we could blame for the murder. There was a witness called Lisa who had stated that Boshell had told her that when he was in prison two men had bullied him into selling drugs. When he was released, these two men were supposed to have tracked him down and forced him to continue selling their drugs. We decided to say that one of these men was Chris Wheatley because Lisa had said that one of the men who had bullied Boshell was called Chris. The benefit of having Wheatley as a suspect was that he was dead and he couldn't defend himself.'

Alvin's constant use of the word 'we' implies that Percival was a co-conspirator in his plot to evade justice; at no time has Percival hinted or admitted that he was party to any such conspiracy. He has asked me to point out that none of the evidence highlighted by Alvin as damaging has any bearing whatsoever on his own personal innocence or guilt because at that time it was Alvin facing the charge of murder.

Constantly trying to come up with a scenario that would clear his name, Alvin was seen by fellow inmates and prison staff scribbling down ideas and then scrapping them with the stroke of a pen before starting anew. In these notes, Alvin had written:

> Ask legal team to make more of the allegation that Boshell had been bullied into selling drugs by Chris Wheatley. See statement by Lisa that said the same people tracked him down when he was released from prison and he had to store and supply drugs for them and that they were blackmailing him, saying that they would harm his brother if he did not comply. Wheatley died very shortly before Boshell, so it's likely that Boshell kept the cocaine that Lisa had seen. Boshell possibly hid the drugs in the allotments and moved to Southend because Wheatley's associates would want the cocaine back and were after Dean. Thus leading to the murder?

Other ideas dreamt up by Alvin to deflect blame from himself included portraying Boshell as a paedophile who had been murdered by one of his victims' families, or as a drug dealer murdered by a rival gang.

Alvin wrote:

> Dean had a picture of a young girl in his cell when I was locked up with him. He also told lies to people about him having a daughter. Dean seems to latch on to or date girls with young daughters. Is this evidence of grooming?
>
> It's my belief from the statements gathered by the police and rumours going around that Boshell had for a few months prior to his death been robbing drug dealers. Dean would camouflage these robberies by telling friends when they saw him with drugs that he was looking after or selling drugs for other people. This way if any dealers came to find out about Dean having drugs, he would just repeat the story they were not his and he would be left alone. I believe this was the motive for Dean's death. This motive may not be known to the police because

no dealer is going to report their losses to the authorities. This would explain the anger used in Dean's murder as beating and shooting someone of this magnitude is personal.

Dean's robberies obviously caught up with him and he was executed by the persons he had robbed. Dean always spoke like a big player and bigged himself up into something he wasn't. A couple of months prior to his death, he became more distant and we saw less of each other. This was more Dean's choice. He seemed to be moving on and into different circles.

The more Alvin read, the more he realised that the police evidence indicated his guilt. Alvin became increasingly desperate to find the scenario, the motive; the ill-fitting pieces of the jigsaw that he needed to portray himself as innocent. Pondering endless conspiracies in his prison cell that he hoped might help set him free, Alvin wrote that in order to explain the phone evidence, which contradicted his police statement, he would tell the police that he had lost his phone during the weekend of the murder.

'I was most likely chatting to a friend and left my phone in their car,' Alvin said. 'That person then probably drove to Southend with my phone.'

But realising this excuse would prompt the police to ask for the names of any friends whose cars Alvin had sat in that particular week, Alvin decided to tweak his story. 'It is clear my phone was lost on the night of Dean's death, because no more calls were received or made by me after that. It's my belief that I left my phone on the roof of my car whilst unlocking it. Then, on exiting the Woodcutters pub, it fell off and would have been in full view of a number of people who were using the shops in the parade adjacent to the pub. Anybody could have found it.

'Whilst in Walsh's flat, I realised that I never had my phone with me. I couldn't recall what I had done with it, so I borrowed Walsh's phone to call mine. The call was unanswered and I was told to try again by the pre-recorded message, which I did and again there was no answer.'

Unfortunately for Alvin, the police had established that despite 'losing' his phone on the day of the murder, he certainly had it in his possession a few days later.

The temptation for Alvin to introduce yet another miraculous happening must have been great, but instead he revisited his notes and all the witness statements to ensure the continuity of his lies before coming up with a synopsis for his defence, which he hoped would clear him of the murder charge.

'I received and made a number of calls whilst in the pub the night Dean died. I received a call from my girlfriend, Clair, who asked what I would like for dinner. Before she hung up Clair reminded me that I had to switch the tortoise lights on as I had forgotten to do it before leaving home. I breed tortoises and the lamps used to keep the eggs warm need to be turned on each night, but even more so when the weather is cold, which it was that night. The tortoise eggs are quite valuable; I was expecting to sell each egg that hatched for £350. I told Clair that I would do it and asked her to pick me up from Walsh's flat when she had finished work. Clair agreed that she would.

'Shortly after this call I told Walsh that I had to return home quickly, but I would be back. Walsh said that because the pub was quiet he was going to take a few beers back to his flat and I was welcome to join him. I said that I would.

'Whilst I was in the car park, Percival came out of the pub and I mentioned that I was going home. I asked if he was going around to Walsh's flat later and he said he was. We spoke about getting hold of cocaine for the evening and I said that I could get some. We agreed on getting a gram each. Before parting company Percival asked if I wanted picking up from my house. I said I did because I could then leave my car at home as Clair was picking me up from Walsh's flat later.

'I drove to a friend's flat in Leigh-on-Sea to buy the cocaine, but when I arrived there was no answer, so I drove to a pub in Southend where he usually hangs out. He wasn't there either. I thought about trying to get it off somebody else but decided to get myself home instead to sort out the tortoises.

'I arrived home about ten o'clock, did what I had to do and was cleaning up in the kitchen when Percival arrived. I let him in, gave him a dozen or so bottles of beer out of the fridge and he put them in his car. We then drove to Walsh's flat together. We arrived at about 10.45 p.m. I recall Katie Griffiths came down the stairs to let us in.

'We sat around drinking for a while, just killing time until Clair had finished work. Percival left around 11.30 p.m. I left about half past midnight, when Clair picked me up.'

When cornered, Alvin has proved himself to be an extremely intelligent and cunning individual. Rather than raise his hands and accept his fate, he requested over one thousand statements and documents from his solicitors whilst in custody. He rehearsed what he was going to say at his trial by cutting out flash cards for himself containing questions and answers about the case. His cell has been described by prison officers as resembling a CID investigation room, with telephone billing, photographs and charts taped to the walls. Nobody can argue that Alvin did not know inside out every shred of available evidence about the case. If anyone wished to fabricate a convincing story about the murder of Dean Boshell, Damon Alvin was undoubtedly the man to do it.

As his confidence grew, Alvin's belief that he was going to escape justice became evident. Not only did Alvin laugh and tell jokes about Boshell's demise to inmates and prison officers, but he also boasted about terminating Boshell's life.

A man named Michael Brown was first introduced to Alvin in 2002 after a friend had recommended him as a reliable cocaine dealer. During one of his regular residences in Her Majesty's prisons Brown had found himself housed in the same part of the prison as Alvin. As they had known one another prior to their incarceration and had been brought up in the same area, the pair rekindled their friendship. It was while discussing their recent fortunes and mishaps that Brown claims Alvin told him that he had stabbed himself in the leg with a Stanley knife to prove to the Probation Service and the courts that he had been attacked by loan sharks.

'He said he stabbed his upper thigh,' Brown said. 'He didn't tell me if he had gone to hospital. Damon was making out that he received this injury from a member of the Adams family. The Adams family is a very violent family from North London. Because of him dropping their name, I found the story unbelievable. I could see on his left hand that he had a number of scars on his knuckles and fingers. Damon told me that the Adams gang had bashed him over the hands with something.

'I have since learned that these scars were the result of a domestic dispute during which Damon punched the glass out of his windows. He also told me that his wife was cutting letters from newspapers and sending threatening letters to herself, saying things would happen to her if Damon did not pay what was owed and if he didn't keep his mouth shut. He said he and his wife couldn't stop laughing whilst they were doing all of this.

'Damon had asked his wife to take these letters to the police station, which she did. Following his instructions, she went to a cashpoint and withdrew a large amount of money. She then told police that the people he owed money to had forced her to withdraw it. I pointed out to

Damon that there were flaws in his story because you can't withdraw that sort of money from a cash machine in one go.

'I think he told me these stories because a lot of the inmates thought it was suspicious that he had only received a two-and-a-half-year sentence after being caught with a kilo of cocaine. Many of these people thought he was a grass and wanted to sort him out. I thought Damon was telling me all this to reassure me and them that he was a Jack the Lad and had not given information.

'One day Damon and I were walking around the exercise yard. There were three other people present – one was an Australian we called Ozzie, and I can't recall the names of the other inmates. I said to Damon, "Have you got any other worries, anything outstanding that could possibly bite you in the arse?" to which he replied, "Only the shooting at the allotment in Southend."

'I believe that Damon was referring to the murder of Dean Boshell, which I had read about in the newspapers. I automatically told Damon to shut his mouth. Damon was talking loudly in front of the other inmates. He didn't mention it again during the exercise period. We discussed Boshell's murder on a number of occasions after that in our cells. Damon told me that he had actually done it, but I didn't believe him. I honestly didn't think that he was capable of murder. I thought he must have just been saying it to boost his reputation.

'Damon told me that he'd picked Dean up that night. As far as Dean was concerned they were going to pick up some drugs, and so he walked of his own free will into the allotments. Damon was boasting and said he did it execution-style. He didn't say that anybody else was present. From the comments he made, I got the impression that he thought Boshell was a grass and I think that's why he shot him.

'The reason I didn't tell the police was that it's none of my business. It had nothing to do with me and I just didn't want to get involved. Damon is someone to be wary of; he's not someone you would want to have turn on you.

'He told me that the gun was in the allotments already plotted up, there and waiting. In a later conversation with Damon, he told me that a man called Greg was his driver that night. He claimed that Greg had been caught driving around with a rope in the back of his car. I found the whole story completely unbelievable and didn't pay much attention to what he said. Damon also changed this story at a later date and said that Ricky Percival was his driver that night.'

It is impossible to know if Michael Brown was telling the truth. After giving his statement to Percival's solicitor, he went on the run because he was wanted by Essex police for two offences. Aged 42, Brown had accumulated no fewer than 90 separate offences, ranging from theft and failing to surrender to bail to possession of class-A drugs and numerous motoring offences.

In the eyes of the law that makes him unreliable as a witness, but Alvin, the man he was accusing of being a liar, was hardly credible himself.

Villains informing on villains always leaves a whiff of conspiracy, but Brown's story was far less damning than one told by one of the prison officers. Aged 54, he is a former soldier and had completed 15 years in the Prison Service when he met Alvin. Throughout those 15 years of service, he had only been disciplined once and that was for hanging his coat on the door of an inmate's cell, which was in breach of prison procedure.

Recalling the arrival of Percival and Alvin at Chelmsford prison in 2004, he said, 'Alvin was very outgoing in comparison to Percival. He was loud, whereas Percival was like a church mouse. During association, when inmates are allowed to mix, Alvin frequently got his case papers out and sat with a crowd of other prisoners. On one occasion, I can recall Alvin saying in front of a number of inmates, "I couldn't have been there, I had to go and turn the tortoise lights on." The other inmates took the piss out of Alvin when he made this comment and said it would never stand up in court.

'Alvin frequently went through the case photographs during association time. He would show the other inmates photographs of the murdered man's post-mortem. I can recall watching Alvin and noticing that whenever he was looking at the photographs he didn't show any remorse; there was absolutely no change in his emotion. I thought that any human being looking at those photographs would have to display some form of emotion.

'One weekday afternoon in September 2005 I was working on landing D3. I had just come out of the legal aid office after making a call and an inmate asked me if I would get him a towel from the kit room. I went to get him a towel but found there were none. Towels are normally exchanged at the weekend and so it's not unusual for the wing to run out by midweek. I left the kit room empty-handed and walked past the showers. The door to the shower room was closed, but I could hear Alvin's voice. I would say that he sounded extremely agitated. I paused outside and heard Alvin say the following: "Fucking hell, mate, at the end of the day I done him. The only thing that has got me in the clear is that the old bill has got the time of death at 11.30 p.m., but I done him in the early hours of the morning." I then saw Alvin's silhouette coming towards me through the frosted glass and so I walked off. I recall thinking, "Fucking hell, he has done it." At the time I didn't want to say anything to anyone, as I really didn't want to get involved. In the course of my job, I do occasionally hear inmates admitting to offences but never anything as serious as this.'

Alvin's boasting and bravado in prison was short-lived. Essex police, despite the late hour, were still actively seeking out evidence to convince him that it would be in his best interest to tell them his version of events. Alvin's choice was simple: risk sitting out a trial for murder and hope that the jury don't convict you, or confirm the police theory about Boshell's murder and blame Ricky Percival.

13

THE BEST LIE

The best lie is always the one closest to the truth

— DS Carter talking to Damon Alvin,
16 April 2003, Gravesend

On 2 September 2005, just ten days before Alvin's trial was due to begin, DC Sharp was dispatched to take a more detailed statement from Gordon Osborne. The police wanted to cement their theory that the telephone call made at 11.48 p.m. from the payphone to Alvin's girlfriend was relevant to Osborne's recollection of hearing a gunshot or, as he later described, gunshots between 11 p.m. and 11.30 p.m. Police believed that Alvin could have murdered Boshell around 11.30 p.m. and then made his way to the telephone box, which was described as being a stone's throw away, to ring his partner Clair for a lift home. Osborne's timings, if correct, combined with the time of the call to Clair, certainly suggested that this might have been the case.

Since the murder, Osborne had left the UK for Spain, where he had started up his own civil engineering business. When DC Sharp arrived in Spain and spoke to Osborne, he explained that he had emigrated because he was 'fed up of life in England'. He said he was never going to return because he was settled where he was. In any event, he said, the weather was far better in Spain than Essex.

DC Sharp noted that during their conversation Osborne appeared relaxed and spoke freely about his business, his plans for the property he was living in and the quality of life that he was enjoying. The mood changed, however, when DC Sharp explained that the contact numbers

Osborne had given to the police were no longer in use and the address he had provided was false.

'Locating your whereabouts,' DC Sharp said, 'has not been easy.'

Osborne explained that he was not trying to avoid the police; he had merely lost his phone and he had only recently become aware of his actual address.

It seems almost incredible that a person does not know his or her home address, but Osborne's explanation was accepted without further comment. DC Sharp asked Osborne if he would be willing to attend court and give evidence about the gunshots that he claims to have heard. Osborne was emphatic when he said no, and he assured DC Sharp that he would never change his mind because he feared reprisals from those who had been charged in connection with the murder.

Disheartened but refusing to concede defeat, DC Sharp asked Osborne to make another statement, which he would submit to the prosecution in the hope it could be read out at the trial in his absence. He felt that if the judge was made aware that Osborne feared for his safety, then this method of hearing his testimony could be ruled as acceptable. Osborne agreed and, despite its being four and a half years since the night Boshell died, he managed to recall even more detail than in his previous statements.

'Dealing first with the house-to-house inquiry form,' he said, 'I recall the details I gave were recorded by a detective who called at my door. I will admit that at the time I didn't really think about the answers I gave to the officer and I was quite vague about what I said. However, by the time an officer called to take a full statement from me I had given it more thought. In this statement, I said that I went to bed about nine o'clock on the night in question. This was probably earlier than the usual time I go, but I'd had a hard day at work. My bedroom was at the rear of the house. I would always have one of the bedroom windows open; the curtains would also have been open because they were never closed. Occasionally I would read in bed, sometimes I would just drift off to sleep. On the night in question, I can't recall what I did or how long I was awake before I went to sleep.

'I woke up about eleven o'clock that same evening. I'd heard two or three shots coming from the allotment. I can't be more specific about the time now, but I had a digital alarm clock by the bed, which I looked at. I immediately recognised the sounds as coming from a handgun: this type of weapon has a distinctive sound, totally different to a shotgun or rifle.

'I have had experience of firearms since I was 11 years of age, when I shot rifles with the Sea Cadets. I remained in the Cadets until the age of 16. At the age of 17, I joined the Royal Marines, staying with them for 18 months. During my time with the Marines, I was trained on the Browning 9 mm semi-automatic pistol, self-loading rifles, Lee Enfield rifles, American M16 rifles, German Mausers and Lugers. Since leaving the Marines, I have not had any dealings with firearms but, like riding a bike, you never forget what you have learned and the sound each weapon makes.

'I can't say how far away these shots were; all I can say is that the sounds definitely came from the back of my house.

'I have been asked if I will return to the United Kingdom and give evidence; I can state that I will not. Whilst living in the Leigh-on-Sea area I would frequent the Woodcutters Arms and I am all too aware of the reputation of the people that use this pub and those charged in connection with the murder. I would fear for not only my safety, but for that of my family should I return as a witness. I have also been asked if I would consider giving evidence by video link; I will not for the reasons already explained.'

Osborne's statement was encouraging for the police. Here was a man with an excellent knowledge of firearms who had not only heard two or three shots around the time Boshell was believed to have died but also had identified them as coming from a handgun. Such knowledge and expertise would surely impress a jury.

When Alvin, Griffiths, Percival and Walsh appeared at Chelmsford Crown Court to stand trial, they all pleaded not guilty to the charges they faced.

During the first week of the proceedings, the jury was sworn in and the opening speeches made, but in the second week, due to legal arguments, the jurors were removed from the room. The prosecution wished to introduce as evidence the notes the police had made when Boshell had been giving information about his associates. These notes would prove extremely damaging to Alvin's defence and so he had instructed his legal team to oppose the application. The defence claimed that Boshell had been a fantasist whose word could not be relied upon. To highlight the fact, a letter written by Boshell whilst in prison was read out, in which he talked about taking a knife from a fellow inmate and repeatedly stabbing him after he had been set upon by a gang. It was proved beyond doubt that no such incident had ever occurred.

Using Boshell's word to help convict a defendant of murder would, the defence argued, be at best unsafe. Another problem with permitting Boshell's evidence to be used was that the defence would not have an opportunity to cross-examine him.

During the course of these legal arguments, the judge invited prosecuting counsel and two police officers involved in the case into his Chambers so that he could be made aware of some of the unused material, which included police intelligence reports regarding the alleged identity of Boshell's killer.

Defence lawyers were not invited to attend this meeting and were therefore unable to make representations on behalf of their clients. It is understood that only intelligence accusing Percival of the murder was put before the judge. Apparently, the judge had given prosecuting counsel his opinion that they might like to reconsider the 'central' direction in which the prosecution were heading. The meaning was clear: the judge thought that it should be Percival facing the murder charge, and not Alvin.

When the judge ruled that Boshell's evidence could be used, Alvin was crestfallen. Fearing he might be convicted of murder, he immediately announced that he wished to talk to his barrister in private.

'At this stage in the proceedings I wasn't happy,' Alvin said. 'I was getting worried about the possible outcome of the trial. I began to realise that my legal team were talking sense. They had informed me that there was a good chance that I would be convicted if I didn't tell the police the full story. They didn't know the truth – all they knew was that I was denying the murder.

'The trial was adjourned and I was given the weekend to contemplate my future. I spent it in my cell with Percival. I don't think he really knew what was happening. He just talked to me about his brother Danny. He said he had identified two jury members involved in our trial that he planned to approach. One of these was a young blonde girl that he believed he knew and the other was a young lad who drove a Citroen C2. Percival said that Danny had followed at least one of these jury members. I don't know what happened in the end, but Percival said that Danny was going to offer them a bribe.'

Despite all the serious allegations that Alvin has made about Danny Percival throughout this story, the police have not spoken to him once. Danny is self-employed, he is in a long-term, stable relationship and has no criminal convictions. He loves his brother Ricky dearly but says there is no way he would have tried to bribe jury members on his behalf.

'Ricky was facing a charge of perverting the course of justice, not murder. If he had been convicted of that offence, which I doubt, he would have been sentenced to two or three years' imprisonment. Ricky had spent a year in prison awaiting trial. That means he would have had to serve about another six months. Am I really going to offer two jurors thousands of pounds and risk going to prison myself to prevent my brother serving just a few more months? Alvin's lies are impressive to people who are denied the facts that may prove or destroy them. That's why so many people believed him in the end. He was allowed to make outrageous allegations about me and the police didn't even bother asking me if they were true. They were just accepted and read out in court as fact.'

Throughout the weekend at Chelmsford prison, Alvin pretended to be his normal self with Percival, but behind the mask he was plotting and scheming against his unsuspecting friend. Alvin had decided that Percival was his get-out-of-jail card, which he could use at any stage of the game he was playing to get him out of trouble.

On Monday morning Alvin discussed his prospects with his legal team in an interview room at court. They advised him that the evidence against him was not favourable and there was every possibility that he would be convicted of murder and sent to prison for life. In a corner and out of ideas, Alvin played his final card. He told his legal team that Percival was responsible for Boshell's murder and, although present, he himself had played no part in the killing.

Alvin's defence team made the prosecution aware that their client wished to make a fresh statement, and when the judge was informed of this development he granted an application by the prosecution to adjourn the case. The jury was discharged and the judge allowed Alvin as much time as he needed to make his new statement in full. Instead of being returned to HMP Chelmsford that evening, Alvin was taken into police custody so that he could give his latest version of events.

In the first of many interviews, DC Sharp told Alvin, 'Through your legal team you served a further defence statement in which you indicated that you were not actually responsible for the murder of Dean. You described in some detail how Mr Percival committed the murder and how a man named Trevor Adams, although not party to this charge at the present time, was asked to assist in some way. I must inform you that you're not viewed as a witness for the prosecution and you must understand that your cooperation does not mean that the case against you will or may be discontinued. Any information you do provide will, together with the results of any subsequent police investigations, be passed to the Crown Prosecution Service for its further consideration of the case against you.'

The police, working quite correctly within the tight restraints of procedure, knew that if the charge against Alvin was not discontinued he could simply say, 'I made the story up so that I would be given a less severe sentence. Percival and I are, in fact, totally innocent.' The case against him and Percival would then collapse.

Alvin breathed an inward sigh of relief because he knew that he was home and dry. The freedom for which he had been prepared to stab himself, steal wreaths from graves and tell continual barefaced lies was ensured.

All Alvin had to do was tell a convincing story that tied in with the evidence that the police had collected and the murder charge against him would be dropped. His was an easy task.

For a year, Alvin had been locked away in a prison cell studying copies of every document, witness statement and crime-scene photograph relating to the murder of Dean Boshell. Any story Alvin eventually came up with indicating Percival's guilt was bound to have a ring of truth about it. In the weeks and months that followed Alvin was interviewed on an almost daily basis. After contradicting himself, 'forgetting things' and then miraculously remembering them, the final draft of his statement concerning Boshell's murder was, he says, the definitive truth of events that night.

'I suppose it started about two weeks before Dean's death,' he said. 'I was invited by Percival to go on a job that involved robbing a large amount of skunk which he said was growing in a barn in the Chelmsford area. He said that the drugs would be worth in the region of £80,000. You don't have to steal the whole skunk plant because it's only the buds that are useful. It was decided that we would wait until the rightful owners had taken the buds off, bagged them up and then left them out to dry. The theft could then take place without us having to do any of the hard graft. We spoke about the job and Ricky told me that it was going to be me, him and one other who were going to do it.'

Alvin claimed that he and Percival had then discussed employing Boshell as the driver for the job. 'I wouldn't want to drive the van around at night with 25 kilos of skunk in it, and neither would Ricky,' Alvin said. 'Skunk has a very distinctive, strong smell. A van being driven in the middle of the night is likely to be stopped by police, therefore I definitely didn't want to be found in the van. I was happy to drive my own car, either in front or behind it en route.'

Percival, according to Alvin, was unsure, but when he was reminded that Boshell was in debt to him he agreed. This debt, Alvin said, had arisen after more than 1,000 Ecstasy pills had supposedly been stolen from Boshell's flat. The pills, which Alvin claimed belonged to Percival, were to have been sold by Boshell, but 'guests' at one of his regular parties had stolen them.

Continuing with his statement, Alvin said, 'The skunk was in a barn on a farm near Chelmsford. The barn was totally separate from the farmhouse. It was intended that we would cross a field to the barn, thereby avoiding the farmhouse and any possible occupants. From the information that Ricky had been given, it was only the barn doors that had been alarmed, so we knew that as long as we didn't enter through the doors we would be OK. The plan was we would just cut our way in through the wooden walls of the building. We would be able to get in and steal the crop without anybody knowing. The only piece of equipment that I was required to provide was bin bags that I used in my building business. They were going to be used to transport the skunk from the barn to the van. It was to be unloaded into a workshop used by Ricky. It would have been easy to sell the drugs, as there was a ready market for the substance.'

Alvin claimed in his statement that the job was cancelled because the crop of skunk had not been harvested. Alvin says that he contacted Boshell and informed him that the theft had been temporarily delayed. 'During the conversation,' Alvin said, 'Dean had mentioned obtaining a gun from Ricky that he was intending to use to rob a drug dealer. I had reservations about Dean robbing a drug dealer on his own. If the intended victim was a soft person, he may well have carried out the robbery, but I don't think he would have been able to go up against somebody who might have caused him problems.'

The following weekend, again according to Alvin, Percival is supposed to have contacted him and said that the crop had finally been harvested. The theft was going to take place three or four days later than planned on the Tuesday. Alvin informed Boshell about the development during a social visit to the White Horse pub in Southchurch.

When reading Alvin's statement, it is clear that he had rehearsed his story numerous times before telling it. His version of events leading up to Boshell's murder is slick, precise and ties in with evidence he had been led to believe was infallible.

'On Tuesday afternoon,' Alvin continued, 'Percival had phoned me and said the job was all ready for us to do: he had the van and that was it; it was ready for that night.

'That day I had been at work with my brother. I got home about two o'clock. I put old clothes, trainers, a hat and a pair of Marigolds in my car. I intended to change into these clothes prior to the theft of the skunk. I didn't want the smell of drugs on my good clothes.

'Two hours later, I drove to Elmsleigh Drive and telephoned Dean and Ricky from a phone kiosk. I wanted Ricky to know that I was in Leigh-on-Sea and I wanted Dean to know that I could pick him up later or he could make his own way to me. After making the calls, I went to Kevin Walsh's flat. I think it was around six o'clock when I arrived. Kevin was home with Sean Buckley. About an hour after I arrived, we were joined by Ricky. I can't recall who suggested it, but we all decided to go up to the Woodcutters Arms.

'The three of them went into the pub whilst I remained in the car park talking to a man I knew. I was with him for about ten minutes before I, too, entered the pub.

'About 8.32 p.m., Dean phoned me from CJ McLaughlin's mobile and said that he was in Southend and had no way of getting down to Leigh-on-Sea. I told him not to worry and said that I would pick him up. Percival and I left the Woodcutters pub just after 9.15 p.m. to go and get the van and sort out anything else that we might need. We left the car park to go to Ricky's house, but I stopped off at the phone kiosk in Elmsleigh Drive to ring Dean to let him know that I was going to come and get him. His phone rang a couple of times, but I hung up before he answered because I thought we should get the van first, get everything sorted and then pick up Dean.

'When I arrived at Ricky's house, he looked out of the window and indicated to me that he would only be a minute, so I waited in the street for him. When he came out of the house, he had changed into dark clothing. He was wearing dark jogging bottoms and a black or dark bomber-type jacket. We spoke about what we were going to do and it was agreed that we should pick up the van and the tools we were going to need. Ricky told me to follow him and he got into his old Sierra.

'Just as we were leaving, Dean telephoned me and said that he needed a lift from Southend. He said that he would wait for me outside Lidl's supermarket in Woodgrange Drive. The time was 9.26 p.m. I told Dean to remain where he was and I would be there soon. I followed Ricky to the end of his road and then up along Elmsleigh Drive. Because of the route we were taking, I assumed we were going to Trevor Adams's house. Trevor had a van and was good friends with Ricky and I, and so it was a reasonable thing for me to assume.

'Ricky turned off the route I was expecting him to take and parked at the top of Randolph Close, which is adjacent to the allotments. He got out of his car and I wound my window down, as he indicated he wanted to talk to me. Ricky said that he was going to pick up the tools. I asked him if the van was at this location and he replied no. He walked down Randolph Close, which borders an allotment area. I got out of my car and followed him.

'Ricky climbed over a three-foot-high fence into the allotments. I remember stopping at a big oak tree to have a piss. Ricky was gone for a few minutes and so I walked back to my car. When he returned, he said that he couldn't find the tools and so I suggested he take another look. I had agreed to pick up Dean and so I told Ricky that I couldn't hang about. He said he would sort the van out and after I had picked Dean up we should all meet at his house. Before we went our separate ways there was a brief conversation about me picking up plastic bags to put the drugs in. We then agreed to meet back at Ricky's house later.

'When I arrived at Woodgrange Drive, I drove past Dean. He was standing outside Lidl's, as arranged. I took the next left into Victoria Drive and pulled up. The general conversation between us centred on the proposed theft of the skunk that night. Dean asked me if I could stop at an off-licence and buy him some cigarettes, as he was out of money as usual. I stopped on West Road, gave Dean some money and he went in and bought cigarettes and two bottles of Lucozade. I then drove to my brother's address to pick up the builder's bags I had stored in his garage. I assumed my brother was not at home when I got there, as his car wasn't on the drive.

'It's standard practice among our group that if we are involved in anything criminal we do not park our vehicles outside the address of the person we are working with. It is common practice to park several streets away, just in case we are under police surveillance. On this particular night, I drove to the road before Ricky's and parked up. We walked along an alleyway. Dean was drinking the Lucozade he had bought; he had left the cigarettes in my car.

'When we reached the end of the alleyway, we were just about to turn into the road where Ricky lives when I heard somebody call my name. It was a call as though they were not sure who I was. I looked towards where the voice had come from and saw Ricky standing near the entrance to the allotments.

'Dean and I started to walk towards him and he began to approach us. We met somewhere in the middle of the drive. He looked proper pissed off. Ricky started firing questions at Dean about a gun going missing. I wasn't sure what he was talking about at first, but it didn't take long for me to work it out. I asked him what the matter was and he said a gun was missing from the allotments. Dean said he hadn't been anywhere near it and repeatedly said he hadn't touched it. Ricky was saying that Dean must have because he was the only one who knew it was there. Dean said something like, "Trevor Adams might have it," but Ricky said he had already spoken to Trevor and he hadn't touched it.

'Dean suggested Ricky might not be looking in the right place but that sent Ricky off on one. He said, "I am not a fucking idiot. I know where I put it and you know where I put it." At this stage, I began to feel uncomfortable because I knew that Boshell had a gun, or at least he had told me that he'd got one. I decided not to say anything, as I didn't want to aggravate the situation.

'Dean was quite worried by this time. Normally, he was a quiet person, but his fear was apparent to me that night. He continued to deny any involvement in the disappearance of the gun and volunteered to go and search for it. Ricky began to mock Dean, saying, "Yeah, well, you're obviously cleverer than me. I'm obviously too much of a fucking idiot to know where I put it. Why don't you go and have a look?" Ricky was getting the proper hump. He was saying, "Well, let's go look, you know you're wasting my time. I know it's not there. I'm not fucking stupid."

'I intervened and said, "Let's just go and have a look. I'll change into my trainers, get the torch out of my car and we can make sure it's not there."

'As I headed towards my car they started to walk towards the gates of the allotments. I changed my shoes, put on an old, dark bomber-style jacket, collected the torch and then made my way back towards Dean and Ricky. I'd been gone for seven or eight minutes, but when I returned I could still hear them shouting. I climbed the gates and started walking along a track to where they were. I could see Dean in front of me and Ricky directly behind him. I just thought, "For fuck's sake," and shouted out for them to shut up. They sounded like a couple of girls bitching.

'At that point, Dean turned to his left to face me. He had both hands up to his face. Because of the darkness and the distance between us I couldn't see if his hands were covering his eyes or not. I immediately assumed that Ricky had punched Dean, although he didn't appear to be moaning or anything like that. Dean started moving towards me, but he'd not taken more than a couple of steps when there was a large bang and a flash from a gun. Dean then crumpled to the ground.

'I saw Ricky walk towards Dean, who remained on the floor. My one thought was that Ricky might be coming for me, so at that point I turned and ran back the way I had come. As I did so, I heard two more bangs and, for some reason, I thought that Ricky was now shooting at me. I sprinted along a track that runs alongside the perimeter fence in the allotments. I can't say how far I ran, but I remember looking behind me and feeling relieved that I couldn't see him any more.

'I climbed over the fence, which is about four feet high, crossed a footpath and leapt down into a brook, which had little, narrow concrete ledges. I can't even say how long I stayed there; at a guess, it was ten, twenty minutes. I was trying to listen out to hear who was coming. I kept hearing loads of noises, but not of anybody approaching.

'I walked along the bank of the brook until it turned into mud banks. After waiting a few more minutes, I climbed out, jogged along the footpath until it reached the road and then I crossed over to a place called Bonchurch Park, which is a recreation ground. I waited around for another 15 or 20 minutes because I was panicking and unsure what to do. I didn't want to walk back to my car because it was near Ricky's, so I decided to telephone Clair. I walked back to Elmsleigh Drive and used a public telephone.

'When I got through to Clair, I tried to act calm. I didn't let on what had happened and arranged to meet her at Kevin Walsh's flat. As I was walking away from the phone kiosk, I saw a car pull up. I didn't take much notice of it at first, but then I realised that it was Ricky's Sierra. As he got out of the car, I immediately looked at his hands and he held them out to indicate that he wasn't carrying anything. I asked him if Dean was dead and he replied that he was. Ricky began to apologise about what had happened and I asked him what the fuck had he done it for. He said that Dean had pulled a gun on him. I knew that was total bullshit because Dean didn't have anything in his hands when he had held them to his face. I didn't mention this to Ricky because I didn't want to provoke him. He seemed to have calmed down and was saying, "Look, it happened, I didn't mean it, you would have done the same if he had pulled a gun on you." I just knew that Ricky was lying. He asked me to get in his car and when I did so he began to say, "I will sort this out, I will sort this out."

'I told him that I couldn't believe he'd done it. "It wasn't needed," I said. "He didn't deserve it." Ricky kept saying, "He pulled a gun! He pulled a gun, what was I supposed to do?" He asked me where I was going and so I told him that I had rung my girlfriend and arranged for her to pick me up from Kevin's. "All right, I'll drive you there," Ricky replied. When we pulled up outside the flat, Ricky repeated that he would sort it out and added, "Nobody needs to know."

'He made me promise that I wouldn't tell my girlfriend, Kevin or anybody else. He kept saying that he would sort it all out. We went into the flat together. I think it was Kevin's girlfriend, Kate Griffiths, that let us in. The conversation in the flat wasn't about anything in particular – Ricky just kept staring at me from the other side of the room. I kept thinking to myself, "For fuck's sake, Clair, come and pick me up." It seemed to take forever, but obviously Clair didn't realise that I just wanted to get out of the area. Ricky left after approximately 15 minutes. He reiterated the fact that he would "sort that thing out, Damon" before walking through the door.

'At about half past midnight, Clair arrived at the flat and we drove home. I didn't say anything to her about what had happened to Dean. She had a Chinese meal waiting for us at home, which I didn't really fancy eating but forced down, otherwise she would have known something was wrong. After eating our meal, we went to bed and slept as normal.

'The following morning, Clair took me back to my car. I can't remember the time – it was probably eight o'clock or eight-thirty – and I could see as we travelled around the corner that there were no police at the allotments. I remember thinking – is he dead? I got in my own car and saw that my phone was in the centre console. I tried to turn it on, but the battery was flat, so I put it on charge and drove to my brother Darren's. On the way, I turned the phone on, as it had charged up a bit. It immediately rang and when I answered I found out that it was Percival. He was panicking, asking, "Why haven't you answered your phone? Why haven't you answered your phone?" I explained that my phone had gone flat after I'd left it in my car overnight, but he continued to complain about not being able to reach me. He said, "I've been trying to ring you all fucking morning. What's the matter?"

'I replied, "Nothing's the matter. I can't turn my fucking phone on if I haven't got it with me." After that Percival calmed down and asked me if everything was OK. I explained that everything was fine, I was on my way to my brother's and then I had some work to sort out. "We need to speak," Percival replied. "I'll meet up with you later." As almost an afterthought, Percival added, "We went back to the body. I've got his phone. Make sure you get a new one."

'I did go and purchase a new telephone; I got it from Argos in Southend. I didn't throw my old phone away. I kept it.

'Despite my promise to Percival, I felt I had to talk to somebody about Dean's murder and so I told my brother when I arrived at his home. He said I had two choices: either tell the police all I knew, which he recommended I do, or never mention the matter again. I can't recall how long I spent with my brother, but I remember seeing Percival later that afternoon. He said, "All you have got to say is where you were between 9 p.m. and 11 p.m." When I asked Percival who he had returned to the murder scene with, he wouldn't say. He said he'd tried to open a manhole cover; he broke the padlock off and said they were going to throw Dean's body down there. He said there was too much blood to move Dean so they just took his phone and left him there.

'I told him that I thought he was shooting at me that night, but he denied doing so. He said he had fired two more shots into Dean because his legs were still moving. I can't remember much about what I did after leaving Percival. I just remember thinking, you are a sick fuck. I did go to the back of the Anne Boleyn pub in Rochford and dump my clothes in the bins. Ricky had suggested I dispose of them because my footprints would be in the allotments. When I pressed Ricky about why he had killed Dean, he would only say that Boshell was a liability and a prick. He said that I needed to get over it. "It's no big deal, what's done is done." That's when I thought bollocks, I am not standing trial for his murder. Ricky didn't give a fuck about Dean at the end of the day, his attitude was: "I am untouchable."

'I have since discussed going on the witness-protection programme with Clair because I wanted to tell the police what had happened. She said, "Tell them all you know," and that is what I have now done.'

When the police contacted Alvin's brother and asked him to corroborate Alvin's claim that he had confessed to him about the murder, Darren said he had no idea what Alvin was talking about. He continues to deny having any knowledge of his brother's allegations. Telephone records prove that Percival did not ring Alvin the morning after Boshell had been murdered, as Alvin claimed. Trevor Adams was arrested and interviewed by the police for allegedly returning to Boshell's body with Percival and removing his phone, but not a shred of evidence was found to even suggest that Adams had done such a thing and he was released without charge. The manhole cover from which Alvin claims Percival snapped off the lock had not been tampered with and the lock had not been broken.

Little wonder that none of these witnesses was required by the police to give evidence in court when Percival eventually stood trial.

14

ONCE UPON A TIME . . .

After signing the agreement to join the witness-protection programme, Alvin was required to reveal everything he knew about crimes that he or others had committed. Whether it was stealing a sweet aged ten or blowing a friend's brains out on an allotment, he was told that he would have to tell the police all the gory details. After blaming Percival for a variety of serious offences, including the Locksley Close shootings, the Wickford snooker club robbery, the murder of Dean Boshell and firearms offences, Alvin rolled up his sleeves and got down to the business of betraying his associates.

Starting with the trivial, Alvin accused former Raquels doorman Martin Hall and his father, Norman, of a whole host of crimes, including running what amounted to a distribution centre for stolen goods from their farm in Benfleet.

Martin and his family have been firm friends of mine since I first moved to Essex in the late 1980s. Martin and I worked together on some of the most violent nights Raquels ever knew and, as the good people of Basildon are aware, it has been the scene of a few. These days Martin runs a very successful clothing company, designing exclusive garments for numerous celebrities throughout the world. He is hardly the type to be mixed up in Alvin's sordid business.

Alvin told police that Malcolm Walsh claimed to have 'found' a 40-foot trailer full of bicycles parked in a layby near Shoeburyness that belonged to Universal Cycles. Malcolm and others had apparently decided to steal a lorry so that they could pull the trailer to an empty industrial unit and access its lucrative cargo using brute force and a sledgehammer. After hooking up the trailer to the lorry, they drove into the industrial unit and secured the premises before going in search of a legally owned van to distribute the bikes. According to Alvin, the entire load ended up being delivered to Norman Hall's farm.

The Halls were allegedly unable to sell the bikes because they were pedal-back cycles that were destined for Holland. As far as I know, a bicycle is a bicycle, whichever country it happens to be in.

My suspicions aroused, I contacted Universal Cycles and gave them a detailed account of Alvin's version of events concerning the theft. I have to admit I was not surprised when the company told me that they have never had a trailerload of bicycles stolen that were 'due to go to Holland'.

When I informed the Halls about the allegations Alvin had made, Martin said, 'I am a friend of Ricky Percival, and Alvin told the police a lot of stories about people who just happened to know Ricky. The police must have known that Alvin was lying because nobody has ever visited our farm to ask about bicycles, guns, stolen lorries or any of the other nonsense he dreamt up to save himself from a prison sentence. I think it is disgusting that so much weight is being attached to an individual who is so transparently false. Apart from saying that my family resides on a farm, not a single word Alvin has said about us is true. He couldn't even get our name right – Alvin told the police that my father and I were Norman and Martin *Hills*. I think that sums up the quality of his information.'

Alvin told the police that Percival believed he was untouchable after getting away with the Locksley Close shootings and the murder of Dean Boshell. Anybody who disrespected, displeased or dared to even dream of crossing him was in grave danger of being beaten, shot or murdered.

Alvin related a story about a dispute over drugs involving three men whom I shall call 'Mickey Davies', 'John Neville' and 'Billy Smith'. Smith was a small-time cocaine dealer who had previously employed Davies and Neville to distribute his drugs. Davies and Neville one day gained entry to Smith's flat using a stolen key. Once inside, they ransacked the premises and took half an ounce of cocaine. When Smith discovered that somebody had burgled his home, he certainly didn't require the services of Sherlock Holmes to work out who had stolen his stash of cocaine. Smith phoned Neville immediately and warned him that he would be requiring an ambulance if the drugs were not returned. Neville blamed his habit for the indiscretion, apologised profusely and repaid Smith what he owed. Davies, on the other hand, was reluctant to hand over the cure for his craving. He ignored all calls to his phone and stayed clear of his usual haunts in an effort to avoid the inevitable confrontation with Smith.

According to Alvin, Smith's older brother became involved at this stage. He thought that Davies and Neville were taking advantage of his younger brother and needed to be taught a lesson. When he saw Davies in the street, he chased after him, but Davies sought refuge in a nearby shop. Fearing he was about to witness a particularly brutal murder, the shopkeeper called the police. Smith's brother made good his escape down the street, leaving Davies cowering under the counter.

Essex police received intelligence that Alvin and Percival had been involved in this incident and pinned letters to both their front doors. The letter informed them that information had been received concerning their intention to harm Davies and so they wished to make them aware that if anything did happen to him they would both be prosecuted.

Alvin told the police that he had no idea why they had pinned the note regarding Davies to his door. 'Where this intelligence came from, I don't know,' he said. 'This was a shock to us both because we didn't have any issues with Davies whatsoever. I remember we both contacted the police about this. I told them that I hadn't made any threats concerning Davies and had no reason to do so. If Davies stayed away from me, I would stay away from him. Percival's approach was slightly different. He told the police that if he was going to do something, a piece of paper would not stop him. He had the raging hump over it – his name had been mentioned, his house had been visited by the police for no legitimate reason and he was being dragged into something that had absolutely nothing to do with him.

'He never mentioned the matter to me again. I presumed the incident had died a death, but when I found myself sharing a cell with a guy named Steve Penfold at HMP Belmarsh in May 2003 he brought the subject up again. Penfold told me that Percival had approached him and asked him to shoot Davies. Penfold didn't say why Percival wanted Davies shot but I did think that whatever the reason was, it was taking things to the extreme. But this is what Percival was like. He knew Penfold was the type of person who would carry out his request. Penfold would not shoot somebody's kneecaps, he would stick a gun in your face and pull the trigger. He has numerous convictions for firearms and violence and this was not the first occasion that Percival had paid him to shoot somebody.

'Penfold told me that he had actually obtained the shotgun that he was going to use in the shooting. On his way to do it he realised that he was being followed by a police car. This was near the A127 arterial road near Southend. As he crossed the junction, there was some sort of accident. I don't know if Percival was directly involved, but he managed to get himself and his vehicle safely away. If Penfold had confronted Davies, wherever he was that night, I am sure that he would have shot him. I know Penfold was expecting some sort of payment from Percival, but whether this was through Smith and his brother I don't know, as the original problem stemmed from them. It's possible that Penfold went into more detail about the incident, but I can't remember. All I remember him saying is that he managed to get back to a friend's house.'

According to Alvin, another occasion when Penfold had been employed to shoot somebody had arisen when Percival had apparently become involved in an altercation at a nightclub in Basildon.

'Percival was looking for somebody who owed him money,' Alvin claimed. 'I assume the money was owed for drugs. He'd been to the club on a couple of previous occasions and on his third visit he found the person he was after. I don't know for sure, it's only what I've been told, but I believe Percival confronted the man. The guy was terrified and he appealed to his friend for help. This friend went to fetch a bouncer that he knew in the club. Before Percival could do anything to the man he was taken into one of the offices by the bouncers and a knife was put to his throat. Percival told the bouncer that he was in the club to collect money that was owed to him. The bouncer turned the tables on Percival and said that he now owed him money for coming into the club and causing problems. Percival eventually obtained a phone number for the bouncer and a week or two later he rang him to say that he had the money that he had demanded from him. Percival suggested that they meet up so he could "give it to him" – he obviously had no intention of paying him.

'By this time, the bouncer had been made aware who Percival was and apologised for his actions. He even made a cash offer to Percival to forget about it, but he declined payment and told the bouncer that any money he gave him would be burned. He told him that he was a dead man walking.

'Penfold told me that Percival had paid him to go and shoot this bouncer. He might have told me his name, but I don't recall it. Penfold explained how he had driven to a club where the bouncer was working and had lain in wait for him to come out. Penfold was in constant contact with Percival whilst he was waiting to shoot the man. After waiting for quite some time, Penfold said he realised that the bouncer wasn't going to appear and so he went home.

'From what Penfold told me, he had the shotgun with him, but he didn't say where he had got it from. The money for the shooting had been paid up front by Percival; I think it was only a couple of hundred quid. Unfortunately, Penfold had spent the cash as soon as he had been given it and because he failed to shoot the bouncer it caused a bit of an atmosphere between him and Percival. The way he was talking to me about Percival, he knew that he wasn't happy with him. Percival has never discussed this incident with me.

'After I was released from HMP Belmarsh, Percival turned up at my home on a motorbike with Ronnie Tretton. Percival told me that he was going to shoot a bouncer who had threatened him. He said that he knew the man had relocated to either Clacton or the Colchester area to avoid him. Tretton was going to take him to the bouncer's house and Percival was going to shoot him. He said that he intended to knock on the bouncer's door and shoot him when he answered it. He wasn't even bothered about having to shoot the man in front of his family. I remember telling him that it wasn't worth it over something so trivial. When I said this, he sort of backed down. He agreed that it was a bit over the top and said he would just shoot him in the leg to teach him a lesson instead. I told him that we already had enough shit to contend with over the murder of Boshell and he should leave it. Percival just couldn't let it go. The shooting never did take place. I cannot say why.'

Despite Alvin having given the police details of what were three separate conspiracies to commit murder, not one of the people named in the plots, including Percival, has ever been questioned in relation to these matters. Either the police did not believe Alvin or conspiracy to commit murder is not deemed a serious crime in Essex.

As well as other people's alleged crimes, Alvin was required to disclose everything relating to his own criminal past to qualify as a protected witness. This included him divulging not only facts about the crimes themselves but also the stories that he had concocted to tell the police or had used in court to defend himself.

One incident of particular interest to the police was Alvin's recent conviction for possessing a kilo of cocaine with intent to supply. Despite there being a substantial amount of evidence pointing towards Alvin being more than just an occasional small-time drug dealer, he had at the time refused to concede that the majority of his income had been earned from supplying drugs. The fact that Alvin had been arrested with large amounts of cash and a kilo of cocaine was, he said, coincidental. When asked to disclose the truth about the offence, Alvin claimed that a couple of his old customers had been 'screaming out for cocaine' and so, reluctantly, he had agreed to supply them one last time.

The man with whom Alvin said he had picked up the cocaine on the morning of his arrest turned out to be yet another character from the original *Essex Boys* story. Dean Power was a one-time friend and later victim of an infamous sadistic Essex gang leader named Jason Vella.

Throughout his short reign, Vella and his men had kidnapped, tortured and humiliated rivals in an attempt to keep their drug-dealing empire, which spanned across south-east Essex, running smoothly. Vella, who is always referred to as the 'Tsar of Essex' in the media, would force his victims to pose for degrading photographs, which would then be distributed amongst his cronies to cause the subject further humiliation.

I met Vella on several occasions when he visited Raquels nightclub in Basildon. He was never involved in any of the regular pitched battles fought at the club and was always polite. To my knowledge, he and his gang never attacked or assaulted people other than those involved in the murky world of drugs. I am not saying that Vella was not a cruel or violent man, but the Tsar of Essex is a title I think he might not be quite qualified to hold. That is only my view; my brother-in-law and Vella's numerous victims may not agree.

I mention my brother-in-law because one evening whilst Vella was fooling around with a loaded handgun he accidentally shot him in the chest. Whilst recovering from life-saving surgery in a private room at Basildon hospital, my brother-in-law was visited by his deeply religious mother. Everybody who knew her, including Vella, was aware of her devout Christian and clean-living views. Because he had been heavily sedated, my brother-in-law was unaware that Vella and his friends had paid him a visit and had left laughing hysterically moments before his mother arrived. Awoken from his deep slumber by cries of anguish, my brother-in-law struggled to sit upright in bed and pleaded with his mother to tell him what was happening.

'This filth! This filth!' she screamed, pointing at the walls, which appeared blurred and smudged to my semi-conscious brother-in-law. 'Why have you put this filth up?' As his eyes began to focus, he saw that whilst he had been asleep Vella and his friends had plastered the walls around his bed with pages from hardcore pornographic magazines.

Explaining to his mother that he wasn't responsible for posting the pictures on his wall turned out to be far more difficult than explaining his gunshot wound to the police.

If nothing else, the incident proves that Vella at least had a sense of humour. When referring to this shooting incident in newspapers, at least one book and several television programmes, police officers have implied that 'the victim' was too scared to make a statement, thus adding to Vella's sinister reputation. The truth is that Vella and my brother-in-law were friends and it was no more than a regrettable accident.

One of several men who genuinely fell foul of Vella was Reggie Nunn, who was invited to his flat and brutally attacked. Nunn had been sent to Scotland to peddle Vella's drugs, but he had been foolish and squandered some of Vella's money on excessive expenses. In a rage, Vella had kicked, punched and finally stabbed Nunn. To escape what he believed was certain death, Nunn had leapt through a closed first-floor window.

Another man named Mark Skeets was invited out for a drink by Vella. Instead of being tied up in social banter, Skeets was tied up with rope and badly beaten. Vella then chopped at Skeets' hair with a knife, shaved his eyebrows off and took photographs of his handiwork. Just as Skeets thought his ordeal was over, Vella jabbed him with knives and burned his body and the soles of his feet with cigarettes. To finish off the evening's entertainment, Skeets was forced to lick LSD-coated paper and snort excessive amounts of cocaine. His crime? He had been judged to have taken a diabolical liberty with Vella by having the audacity to send his girlfriend a Christmas card.

Alvin's friend Dean Power appeared to have upset Vella on two occasions. As punishment for his first misdemeanour, Power was whipped with a metal coat hanger and beaten with a bamboo cane. Twelve months later, Vella and another man arrived unannounced at Power's home and proceeded to attack him. He was overpowered, jabbed with a toasting fork, beaten with lumps of wood, kicked in the head and had his arms and feet stamped on. He was totally disfigured by this barbaric beating.

In 1994, Vella and his gang were rounded up as part of Operation Max, which took three years to complete and resulted in Vella being sentenced to seventeen years behind bars. His gang were given prison sentences ranging from two years to six years and eight months. Operation Max resulted in 21 prosecutions and Essex police introducing their first witness-protection programme. Describing Vella during the trial, Power said, 'He is like Jekyll and Hyde. The bloke is a lunatic. Seemed like a nice bloke at first, but he is just possessed, like he had the devil in him or something. I am living my whole life in fear.'

Nobody quite knows what Dean Power did to deserve the horrific assault that he suffered at the hands of Vella and his accomplice, nor does anybody know what possessed him to become involved with Damon Alvin. According to Alvin, on the morning he was arrested he and Power had collected a kilo of cocaine from a man named Henry Swann. 'At eight-thirty, we drove to a snooker club in Leigh-on-Sea and waited in the car park,' he said. 'After five minutes, a car pulled up. Power walked over to it, spoke to the driver, opened the boot and took a carrier bag out of it. After getting back into my car, we drove back to Power's flat to weigh and check the gear.

'Usually when you buy a kilo of cocaine it is three, four, maybe five grams underweight, but this was half an ounce light. I was due to pay for it later that day so I wasn't concerned; I would just pay for what I had received instead of the full kilo. Once we were satisfied that it was all OK, I left on my own with the cocaine.

'As I was travelling home, I was stopped by armed police and arrested. My first thought was that Power and Swann had grassed me up. Power didn't get arrested, which was odd because the police had obviously been watching me all morning. Henry Swann, a travelling pikey, had originally said that the cocaine was going to be available the night before but had called it off at the last minute. I thought that he could have used this delay to make the phone call and set my arrest up.'

As usual, Alvin was blaming other people for his own failings. I worked alongside 'Big Henry' on the door at Raquels nightclub before Tony Tucker was invited onto the scene. I have not had the pleasure of keeping his company since I left Essex in the late '90s, but I know that in all the time I knew him he was very anti-drugs. Henry made a living travelling the world, salvaging precious metals from crashed aeroplanes and shipwrecks. When he was at home between jobs, he would work on the doors of various pubs and clubs in the Essex area.

He was slashed and stabbed during an infamous battle between members of West Ham United's Inter City Firm and the bouncers at Basildon's Festival Hall. The injuries he received that night were sustained simply because he and another doorman named Nicky Cook refused to run from the baying mob. When the police visited Henry at the hospital, he refused to assist them, despite having been left for dead and sustaining horrific injuries.

One evening whilst working with Henry at Raquels, a fight had broken out which resulted in a customer losing one of his ears and me being arrested. When I was released from the cells the following day, it was Big Henry who contacted me first to offer assistance should I need it. In short, Henry Swann is fearlessly loyal to everybody he knows and most certainly would not dream of informing on either friend or foe to the police.

The worrying thing about Alvin's de-brief account of the cocaine incident is that, by his own admission, it was not Leach or Webber bullying him into selling drugs that had caused him to be arrested, nor was it loan sharks demanding the repayment of a debt from his wife; it was Alvin simply supplying a kilo of cocaine to his own customers for financial gain. I shudder to think what lies Alvin may have told to escape the murder charge he faced.

During the de-brief process, the police paid Alvin £31,917.28 for his expenses. I am not for one moment suggesting that Alvin and his family should not have been subsidised while he was assisting the police with their inquiries; however, some of the items purchased for him and his family would, I imagine, be deemed luxuries by most people, rather than necessities. They included £290 for an educational course, 60 pence for paracetamol, various sums of money for Christmas presents for his family, £44.15 to MOT his vehicle, £3,491 in removal costs, £876.46 for two months' car rental, £468 for a laptop and £49.99 for a carry case, £19.99 for a mouse for his laptop, a 60 pence parking fee and £82.68 for the purchase of an enclosure for his tortoises. It's comforting to know that some of our hard-earned taxes have been used to re-house and relocate Alvin's tortoises on the witness-protection programme.

Beverley Boshell had her claim for compensation for her son's murder turned down by the Criminal Injuries Compensation Board (CICB). She wasn't asking for much. Beverley is registered as disabled and in receipt of state benefits, so she thought the CICB might have assisted her with her son's funeral expenses. After all, he was undoubtedly the victim of a crime, and victims of crime are the reason the CICB came into being.

According to the police, Beverley's son may have been murdered because he was passing on information about his criminal associates to them. I would have thought that the family of somebody murdered for assisting the police would be considered a priority for compensation. Not Beverley Boshell. She was told that because her son had previous convictions compensation could not be paid.

I wonder how she must feel now, knowing that Alvin, his family and their tortoises were financially rewarded for their information? I felt so disgusted by this outrageous display of nauseating double standards that I have used some of the proceeds from this book to pay for Dean Boshell's memorial at Pitsea cemetery myself.

15

THE PIG CIRCUS

In 1644, Matthew Hopkins, a top Essex boy of his time, who went on to become known as the Witchfinder-General, kick-started his bloody career and introduced the supergrass phenomenon to Essex after arresting a lady named Elizabeth Clarke. A toothless, one-legged octogenarian, Elizabeth was accused of being a witch by Hopkins. Initially refusing to admit her guilt, the hapless old lady was incarcerated and subjected to long periods without food, water or sleep. By the time Hopkins had finished with her, Elizabeth had 'grassed up' 31 of her associates and claimed that they were all witches. These unfortunate, innocent women were rounded up and taken to Colchester Castle to await trial.

In July 1645, the women (four of whom had already died) were tried at the County Assizes in Chelmsford under the jurisdiction of Robert Rich, the 2nd Earl of Warwick and Lord Lieutenant of Essex. John Sterne, Hopkins' evil sidekick, who was being paid handsomely by his master, gave evidence against Elizabeth and claimed that he had seen her 'call one of her white Imps, and play with it in her lap'. This Imp was described as having a remarkable resemblance to a dog. 'It was white, had sandy-coloured spots and short legs,' Sterne said. Another of Elizabeth's Imps was said to look like a greyhound.

Saving the best for last, Sterne told the court that Elizabeth had confessed to him that she had indulged in 'carnal copulation with the Devil' four times a week for the past six years. With no legal representation and amidst scenes of total chaos, all but one of the women were found guilty. Elizabeth Clarke and fourteen of the others were hanged in Chelmsford, but four were taken to Manningtree and hanged on the village green. Nine were later reprieved.

Three hundred and sixty-one years later, Chelmsford was once more the setting for another unusual trial. The names had changed, the charges were different, but there were striking similarities.

Desperate after being incarcerated, like Elizabeth, Alvin had accused his friends of wicked crimes in the hope that he would not have to face the ordeal of a trial himself. Like the false testimony of brutal thug John Sterne, the verbal testimony of Alvin, who had nothing to lose and everything to gain, was the only evidence against Percival. And like a dog with sandy spots being described as the Devil's Imp, innocent conversation, meetings or events were portrayed as something far more sinister.

Ricky Percival stood shoulder to shoulder with Damon Alvin when he faced his murder trial 11 months earlier. But when it was Percival's turn to face his murder trial, Alvin was noticeably absent. Everybody present was aware that he was sitting in a local police station waiting to be escorted to the trial. He was then going to face his former friend and accuse him of a whole host of evil crimes, including murder.

Alongside Percival sat Kate Griffiths and Kevin Walsh. The last time they had been in court it had been alleged that along with Percival they had given Alvin a false alibi to cover up the fact that he had been elsewhere committing murder. It was now being said that they had given Percival the same alibi to conceal the fact that he had been elsewhere committing the same evil deed.

After the jury of seven men and five women had been sworn in, the three defendants were asked to stand and plead to each of the charges they faced. The clerk of the court read out one joint charge to Percival, Walsh and Griffiths, which was that 'between the 26th day of February 2001 and the 6th day of March 2001, they had conspired together to pervert the course of public justice'. All pleaded not guilty.

Percival alone faced a further nine charges. It was alleged that he had murdered Dean Fergus Boshell, conspired together with Damon Alvin and another to pervert the course of justice by preventing CJ McLaughlin from attending court, conspired together with Damon Alvin and Dean Boshell to steal cannabis of a value unknown belonging to a person unknown, robbed the manager of the Wickford snooker club of £2,000, had with him a firearm or imitation firearm, namely a silver handgun, with the intent to commit robbery, had in his possession a firearm, namely a 'Savage Stevens' pump-action 12-bore shortened shotgun, with the intent to endanger life, and had attempted to murder Raymond Tretton, Stuart Tretton and Jenny Dickinson.

Staring straight ahead with his hands clasped firmly in front of him, Percival answered not guilty to each charge. As the proceedings got under way, Alvin arrived at the court in an armoured car escorted by police vehicles with flashing lights and sirens. The entrance to the court was guarded by a number of armed policemen brandishing machine guns. More armed officers guarded the door to the room where the trial was taking place. During the course of the proceedings, these officers would often walk across or stand in front of the glass panes in the door immediately opposite the jury, creating the false impression that an extremely dangerous criminal was on trial and everybody present was under threat. Such an impression could of course sway the jury into thinking that the defendant was more than capable of carrying out the crimes he was alleged to have committed before they had even considered the evidence.

Percival by this time had been travelling back and forth to the same court for nearly two years, but such measures had never been deemed necessary before. In my opinion, it was an unnecessary and unsavoury spectacle for jurors to be greeted with upon their arrival at court each morning. I certainly felt that the presence of so many heavily armed men created a distinct atmosphere of menace.

If the jury were not convinced of just how dangerous Percival was by this show of arms, they most certainly were by the time Alvin had finished giving his evidence. Alvin told them that Percival and his brother Danny had tried to bribe and/or physically harm jurors at the first trial. Despite the fact the police hadn't bothered to question the Percival brothers about this serious crime, they permitted Alvin to make his allegation in open court.

Alvin also accused the Percival brothers of trying to bribe a prosecution witness so that he would not testify. CJ McLaughlin had told the police that Boshell had used his phone to call Alvin on the night of the killing. According to Alvin, the Percival brothers wanted CJ to withdraw his statement. Danny was alleged to have gone to talk to CJ's uncle, who happens to be Trevor Adams. This is the man Alvin claimed had returned to Boshell's body with Percival to remove his phone.

Alvin testified that when Danny visited Adams, he had said that he didn't want to get involved and this really upset Danny. 'After that Danny was sent to go and offer £4,000 to CJ's father,' Alvin said. 'In return for the money, he was required to take his son away to a coastal caravan park so that he wouldn't be around to give evidence.

Danny had been told to give him the cash, a clean mobile phone and to make sure they disappeared until they received a call telling them to come home.

'Before leaving, CJ was to contact the police and inform them that he wasn't prepared to give evidence and that his decision had been made of his own free will. CJ's father went and spoke to his ex-wife and she refused to allow her son to be party to this. She said that her son had done no wrong and therefore he was going to attend court. Percival was really upset by this news and said that he was going to have nothing to do with the family again.'

When the police questioned CJ and his family about Alvin's story, they denied any knowledge of such a plot. As far as they were concerned, Boshell had used CJ's mobile phone as a favour to make a call. That call was an indisputable fact because phone records show that it was made. CJ, therefore, couldn't possibly deny it, even if he wanted to. His family were adamant that he had no reason to hide anything and so he would be attending court. In any event, a call made by Boshell to Alvin using CJ's phone had no bearing on the innocence or guilt of Ricky Percival whatsoever, so why would he ask his brother to bribe the family? Furthermore, why would Trevor Adams refuse to assist a man with such a relatively minor crime if, as Alvin alleged, he had already assisted the same man after a murder? It was ludicrous, but nevertheless the denials made by McLaughlin and his family were disbelieved.

Whilst trying to prove Percival's guilt in regard to the Locksley Close shootings, the prosecution had called Carla Evans, in whose home the incident had occurred. Evans had made a detailed statement to the police at the time of the shootings in which she claimed that after the death of Malcolm Walsh she'd had an altercation with Percival. During this incident, Percival had allegedly shouted and sworn at her and threatened to rape her. I cannot say if this is what actually happened, but this is what Evans said occurred, so I am fairly certain that she doesn't think a great deal of Percival.

Whilst giving her evidence at the trial, Evans happened to mention that the man who had burst into her home with a shotgun had blue eyes. Percival has brown eyes. This is an extremely important point. The gunman was wearing a balaclava and so his eyes would be the focal point of the witness's attention. If the jury had believed that Evans was absolutely certain about the colour of the gunman's eyes, it was more than likely that they would have acquitted Percival of all charges relating to the Locksley Close shootings. Unfortunately, the task of deciding themselves was taken away when the judge intervened and permitted the prosecution to treat Evans as a hostile witness. This meant that Evans was deemed as a witness who was deliberately giving false evidence that would assist Percival. Evans and her evidence were discharged from the proceedings forthwith.

She had given no indication that she was going to vary her account of the shootings from her original statement; it just seemed like she had simply given an answer that didn't suit the prosecution's case. The prosecution even asked Evans if she was expecting to be invited to Percival's victory party and the judge chose to repeat the same rather florid phrase in his summing up of the case.

Unfortunately for Percival and justice, the trial trundled on in much the same vein throughout. Numerous allegations made by Alvin concerning third parties (most of whom were absent) were presented to the jury and, without the presence of important witnesses to challenge them, they were left hanging in the air like a bad smell.

Steven and Raymond Tretton had unfortunately died from alcohol-related illnesses approximately two years after the shootings. There was material to suggest that at least one of them might have given evidence that Percival was not the gunman. The other had made a statement but only part of it had survived. The police claimed that they had somehow lost the crucial page that would have assisted Percival's defence. It was obviously impossible for fresh statements to be taken.

I doubt that Essex police would have deliberately lost or destroyed evidence in a murder case, but it does seem an unfortunate coincidence that it was the one page that could have proved Percival's innocence that vanished.

When Alvin was cross-examined about the shootings, he denied that he had set foot in Carla Evans' house. As far as he was concerned, Percival had been the only one with a gun and the only one who had burst into the house and opened fire. Three of the people present in the house that night, however, were adamant that there were two gunmen. When the police had appealed for witnesses after the incident, even they were claiming that 'two masked men armed with pump-action shotguns had burst in on the party'. When Alvin was asked to explain why so many people thought they had seen two masked men, he said that they must have mistaken a coat that was hanging on the banister at the bottom of the stairs for a gunman. Percival's barrister asked Alvin if that coat also appeared to be wearing a balaclava, to which he meekly replied, 'No.'

Although deceased and having a zero credibility rating, Dean Boshell was given a voice at his own murder trial. He had informed his police handler that Percival and a 'doorman named Dave' had carried out the Locksley Close shootings, though nobody doubted that he was lying. No such person was ever identified by the police or mentioned by any other witness. Boshell had simply invented this name to protect the true identities of the gunmen.

Putting Percival's name alongside Dave the Doorman's was an obvious choice because Percival had been arrested for the shootings and had revelled in the rumours that he had been one of the gunmen. The interesting thing about the information that Boshell gave to the police is that he too was claiming that two gunmen were involved. When asked why Boshell would say this, Alvin replied, 'Boshell lied about the Locksley Close shootings. He said the shotgun was a double-barrelled shotgun and that Dave the Doorman was involved. If Doorman Dave does exist, I don't know him.'

The reason Alvin was so keen to point out that Boshell was lying about the weapon used in the shootings failed to register with all concerned at the time. If the police had accepted what the witnesses and their informant Boshell had told them about there being two gunmen, they would never have been able to charge Percival with three attempted murders and firearms offences unless they charged Alvin too. They couldn't charge Alvin with such serious crimes because the likelihood was he would have then refused to cooperate with them. Without Alvin, there was no case against Percival.

Alvin was forced to say that only three shots were fired during the attack because the pump-action shotgun, which was recovered by police from the drain in Burgess Close, still had four live cartridges in it. Normally, such a weapon can hold only six cartridges, but it is possible for it to be loaded with seven. Three shots fired and four found in the weapon equals seven. Because Alvin had said that only three shots had been fired, the mathematics indicated that he was being truthful. The fact that only three people had been shot also supported Alvin's story.

If there had been any more cartridges found in the gun, it wouldn't have taken a super sleuth to work out that another gun had been used in the attack. As a result of this evidence, the police chose to ignore their own initial claim that two gunmen had burst into Carla Evans' home. They also disregarded Boshell's evidence about a double-barrelled shotgun being taken to the scene that night, and the victims' evidence that up to six shots were fired.

THE PIG CIRCUS

Unlike a pump-action shotgun, a double-barrelled shotgun only holds two cartridges. When fired, the cartridges are not ejected from the weapon and therefore they wouldn't have been found at the scene. The fact that an 'arc of pellets' were in a wall (one shot), the top of the settee had been blown away (two shots) and three people had received serious gunshot wounds (five shots) indicates that the victims and Boshell were telling the truth about a second gunman. Three shots fired by the pump-action shotgun and two by the double-barrelled shotgun tallies up with the physical evidence and statements by Boshell and the victims. The most convincing evidence to support this scenario came from a man called Jay Tolfree, who was in the house when the shootings occurred. He had been upstairs checking that the children were in bed when he heard a loud bang. Tolfree then heard gunshots and, after peering through the banisters towards the lounge, he said he saw two figures run along the hallway towards the front door.

This man had no reason to lie – he was not in shock or in danger and had an unobstructed bird's-eye view of the gunmen that night – yet he was not believed. If Alvin was carrying a shotgun, as the evidence suggests, the police were wrong to offer him any sort of deal and he certainly should not have been allowed to plead innocent whilst blaming Percival.

One of the many disconcerting factors during the trial was the prosecution's efforts to establish that Boshell had been murdered between 11 p.m. and 11.30 p.m. This was absolutely crucial to their case. Their version of events was that Gordon Osborne had heard Boshell being shot three times at approximately 11.30 p.m. and Damon Alvin had then run to the telephone kiosk, where he had telephoned his wife approximately eighteen minutes later. It was a credible theory supported by the fact that Osborne had intimate knowledge of firearms and the sounds they made when fired. Furthermore, he had no way of knowing that Boshell had indeed been shot three times. If Osborne could have been shown to be mistaken, the case against all three defendants would have collapsed.

Telephone records proved that a call had been made to Clair's mobile phone at the time and from the location that Alvin had claimed. Griffiths, Percival and Walsh said that they had all been with Alvin at Walsh's flat at the time the call was made to Clair and the time the murder is said to have taken place. The trio's statements had only been challenged because Kevin Walsh had rung Alvin's mobile at 11.17 p.m.

and 11.47 p.m. Understandably, the police wanted to know why Walsh had to ring Alvin if he was in the same room as him.

Phone records have since proved that both calls only lasted a second or two and were not answered. This indicates that Alvin was initially telling the truth when he told the police that he had mislaid his phone. These two extremely brief calls had been Walsh, at Alvin's request, ringing Alvin's phone in the hope that he would hear and then be able to find it. On both occasions, the calls had gone directly to Alvin's answering machine and so Walsh had immediately terminated the call. If Alvin had been at the allotments, as the prosecution claim, and Walsh had been ringing him from his flat, surely Walsh would have tried calling Alvin for longer than a second or two and again shortly afterwards. If a call goes directly to an answering machine, it often indicates that the person is currently on another call and might be free momentarily.

Clair and several others had also tried ringing Alvin numerous times that night without success. Alvin has since admitted that Clair had been sulking when she arrived at Walsh's flat because he had not answered his phone. 'I explained to her that I did not realise it was off,' Alvin had said.

Alvin claimed that he had mislaid his phone and to prove that fact he had called his own phone twice using Clair's, just as Walsh had done earlier. These two calls to Alvin's mobile are recorded as being made from Clair's phone at approximately 12.32 a.m. and the other a few seconds later.

Between 9.17 p.m. and 12.37 a.m. a total of 70 incoming calls were either diverted or forwarded to Alvin's voicemail. This proves beyond doubt that Alvin had either mislaid or switched off his phone between the time he picked Boshell up and the time his wife arrived at Walsh's flat. Walsh's explanation, therefore, should have been accepted.

When Alvin faced the charge of murdering Boshell, he had denied being the one who had called his wife at 11.48 p.m. from the public telephone box. He said that he had been in Walsh's flat at the time. One of Walsh's calls to Alvin's mobile had been made at 11.47 p.m. That is just one minute before the call that was made from the public telephone box. Everyone accepts that Alvin could not possibly have been in two places at once.

Alvin went on to accuse Percival of the murder and changed his story to say that it was he who had made the call to his wife. This version of events tied in nicely with Osborne's evidence and so it was never scrutinised or challenged by the authorities. The fact that Clair had previously refused to sign her statement, in which she said that Alvin was the one who had made the call, should have set alarm bells ringing loud and clear.

Unable to reach Alvin because his mobile phone was being ignored or was mislaid or switched off, could it possibly have been Boshell who had telephoned Clair to ask where her husband had got to because he was waiting for him? What possible motive would a young girl of good character like Kate Griffiths have for lying about Alvin being at her flat? Clair, on the other hand, had assisted her husband in the past by claiming she had received death threats from fictional loan sharks. She also said that she had been frogmarched to a cash machine by a gang and was forced to withdraw large amounts of cash. Is it beyond comprehension that she may have lied for him on this occasion also?

It was cold, wet and windy the night Boshell died. They were certainly not ideal conditions for hanging around in the dark, waiting for a partner in crime to turn up. If it had been Boshell who had telephoned Clair, Alvin could have been picked up by his wife from Walsh's flat shortly afterwards and then dropped off to meet Boshell at the allotments. It is a perfectly valid theory: unless, of course, Gordon Osborne is to be believed. According to his evidence, Boshell was already dead when the call to Clair was made. It was quite a shock, therefore, when the jury was informed that Osborne, one of the star witnesses, would not be attending the trial.

The prosecution explained that he was now living in Spain in fear of the defendant and his associates and had therefore refused to return to Britain. His fear was such that he had even declined to give his evidence via a video link.

Percival's defence team seemed to think that Osborne might have had another reason for not wishing to return to the UK. Essex police had issued a warrant for his arrest in relation to an allegation involving a sex offence. When they had visited Osborne in Spain prior to Alvin's trial, he had told them that he was aware of this allegation but refused to comment on it further. He insisted that this was not the reason he would not attend the trial, and this was, surprisingly, accepted by the court.

In June 2001, Osborne had made and signed a statement which included a declaration that he had done so of his own free will and was willing to attend court if required. He was, therefore, under no illusions about his obligation to attend court and give evidence. I say he was under no illusions because Gordon Osborne is no stranger to the workings of the legal system. Osborne has in fact been convicted of 65 offences, including theft, deception, burglary, assault and impersonating a police officer. I would suggest that the only reason Osborne did not want to return to England was that he did not want to risk exchanging his Spanish villa for a prison cell. He must have known that he would be arrested as soon as he set foot in the country in relation to the sex offence. As a result of the court accepting Osborne's claim that he 'feared for his safety' and therefore wouldn't attend the trial, his statement was read out to the jury and the defence were denied an opportunity to cross-examine him.

It was argued in court that Osborne had been mistaken about the shots he claimed to have heard and it was suggested that the murder had taken place much later that night. In an effort to substantiate this, the defence summoned Hansel Andrayas to tell her story. Like Osborne, Andrayas had spoken to the police during their house-to-house inquiries. She had told them that around 2 a.m. on the night of the murder she had heard a loud bang, a noise like an echo, and then further noises, like a fence being climbed or broken. She added that the noises had awoken her youngest daughter. Andrayas then described hearing a van driving fast along the road. The vehicle had made 'skidding noises' as it left the scene. The time given by Andrayas did not suit the prosecution's version of events, and the judge appeared to agree that her evidence was irrelevant to the case. He suggested the noises Andrayas had heard were simply 'things that go bump in the night'.

Andrayas's home is one of the nearest buildings to the spot where Boshell met his death. If anybody near the scene of the crime was ever going to hear anything that occurred that night, it was the occupants of her home or a neighbour. It is also worth noting that her account is supported by the fact that her youngest daughter also heard the noises because she was actually woken up by them. The initial loud bang that Andrayas says she heard may well have been the first shot being fired. It is agreed by all parties that Boshell was standing a few feet away from the gunman when this shot was fired, therefore this sound would have been loud and clear. The muzzle was put to Boshell's head when the second and third shots were fired into him, so his head would have acted somewhat like a silencer, muffling the sound of the last two shots. These noises could well have been the echo sounds that Andrayas described.

Another interesting point about Andrayas's evidence is that Alvin appears to agree with some of it in his account of the murder. Her statement supported Alvin's story that he had clambered over a fence in the dark, because she reported hearing sounds like 'a fence being climbed or broken'. Likewise, Osborne's evidence supports Alvin's story that he fled to the telephone box after the murder and rang his wife. Is it merely a coincidence that after spending a year on remand, reading all the case papers, Alvin's account of the murder just happens to be supported by the independent evidence of both parties? Some believe that he had incorporated every possible version of events into his story to ensure it sounded credible. Alvin certainly convinced a lot of the people present at Chelmsford Crown Court that his story was honest and true.

The jury took nearly 25 hours to reach its verdict. Kate Griffiths was found not guilty of conspiring to pervert the course of justice. Kevin Walsh, who faced the same charge, based on the same evidence as Griffiths, was found guilty and sentenced to three and a half years.

Ricky Percival was found guilty of all ten charges that he faced. Judge Christopher Ball QC told him: 'You have been convicted of what I judge to be the brutal and cruel killing of Dean Boshell, one of your criminal associates, who had the misfortune that night to cross you. The manner of his killing has not surprisingly been described as an execution. This was the most wicked of murders by a man who plainly suffers from no psychiatric disorders, but simply a man with a grave and aggressive violent streak running through him. You are an unstable and volatile young man with a cold and ruthless streak. Anyone that crosses you, however slightly, is at great risk of harm.'

Rooted to the floor of the dock and staring directly at the judge, Percival listened in total disbelief as he was sentenced to life imprisonment, with a recommendation that he should serve at least 28 years.

The following morning it was refreshing to read in the local newspaper that Essex police had announced that they would be 'reviewing evidence' of criminal matters raised in the trial.

Surely now, I thought, the silent witnesses would be contacted and questioned and the truth regarding some of Alvin's rather more bizarre claims would begin to emerge?

16

SILENCE IN COURT

The Wickford Robbery

As I read through the documentation that had convicted Ricky Percival, I was astounded by the number of witnesses to crimes who had not been interviewed by police or called to give evidence at the trial. Former Detective Sergeant Moran, Nipper Ellis, Steve Penfold, Carla Shipton, Clayton Shipton, Stacie Harris, Trevor Adams and Ronnie Tretton to name but a few were all central figures in Alvin's stories, but none of them were required to attend court.

It didn't make sense to me at first. Surely, if Alvin was a witness of truth, DS Moran should have been charged with offences relating to corruption and Carla Shipton should have been charged with armed robbery. Trevor Adams should have been charged with assisting an offender and Ronnie Tretton, Nipper Ellis and Steve Penfold with serious conspiracy offences. As I began to think of more names that fell into this category, such as Danny Percival, Gavin Spicer, Martin Hall, Norman Hall, Henry Swann and Carlton Leach, the reason for their omission suddenly dawned on me. If the police had taken Alvin at his word and charged everybody he claimed was guilty, the trial would have consisted of more than 20 or 30 defendants calling Alvin a liar and Alvin alone pointing his accusing finger back, claiming that everybody but him was mistaken. No jury would realistically take the word of one man over that of twenty or thirty-plus people.

The decision by the police not to interview so many important witnesses is a concern. Surely it is their job to gather all the available evidence and then present it to the courts so that a jury can decide who is guilty and who is not. They would be failing the public if they cherry-picked whom they interviewed so that the evidence would fit their often misguided beliefs.

Rather than wait for the findings of the review that was allegedly being conducted by Essex police, I decided to make my own enquiries so that I could discover what evidence the jury had been deprived of hearing. The most important but absent witness from the trial in relation to the Wickford snooker club robbery was the assistant manager and Boshell's ex-girlfriend, Carla Shipton.

Alvin claimed that Carla not only conspired with him to rob the premises but also actually assisted him. According to Alvin, Carla sat in his vehicle before the robbery. They had agreed, according to Alvin, that Carla would leave the snooker club door open when she was leaving the premises at the end of her shift.

Alvin went on to say that Carla might actually have rung him to reassure him that everything was OK before she had finished her shift that night. In my opinion, these claims were blatantly untrue because Carla was not at work at the snooker club that night. She couldn't, therefore, have telephoned Alvin to advise him if any problems had arisen there. I decided to try and contact Carla to discuss Alvin's allegations with her. It was no easy task.

I spent three days in Essex visiting her old acquaintances, several addresses I had been given and all her known haunts. Eventually, one of the numerous 'please call me' notes of which I had left a trail throughout Essex yielded a result. We arranged to meet at a quiet pub on the outskirts of Basildon one Saturday night. Twenty minutes after the agreed time, I had resigned myself to the fact that Carla had changed her mind and wasn't going to appear. I was not relishing the long drive back to Birmingham knowing that my journey had been in vain, so I decided to ring her in the hope that she was simply running late.

'Is everything OK?' I asked when Carla eventually answered her phone.

'Sure,' she replied. 'I don't want to go into the main bar. I'm in the small room at the back of the pub. Where are you?'

Moments later, I was introducing myself to a tall, attractive girl whose eyes darted around the room nervously.

'Promise me that Damon won't ever find me,' she said, whilst looking over at the door to check that I hadn't brought company. 'That's all I'm bothered about. I'm really worried that he's going to find me.'

I bought Carla a drink, found us both a seat and set about trying to calm her and reassure her. 'Damon Alvin doesn't exist any more,' I told her. 'He has a new identity and is subject to the rules and regulations of the witness-protection programme. If he was to contact, threaten or assault you or anybody else, the protection he and his family enjoy would be revoked and he would probably be returned to prison.'

'You don't understand what he is like,' Carla replied. 'Somebody upset him before – he saw them making a call in a phone box, he opened the door, squirted them with ammonia and set fire to them. I don't know for sure if that's true, but it's what he used to tell me. Perhaps he was just trying to scare me into keeping quiet about matters that related to him, I really don't know. But if he was just trying to scare me, it certainly worked.'

Once she had relaxed, which took quite some time, I asked Carla to tell me about the night of the robbery and the events surrounding it. Despite the passage of time, she remembered all that had happened quite clearly. Her fear no doubt ensures that her memories of Damon Alvin will never leave her.

'On 20 August 1999, the snooker hall where I worked was robbed by two men,' Carla began. 'I wasn't working that particular night, but I'd gone to the club to pick my brother up. He wasn't employed there full-time, but he did work the occasional shift. When my brother and I were leaving that night, we saw a couple of guys hanging around outside, but that's not unusual. The club was in an area that was regularly in the local newspapers at that time because of the problems caused by young lads hanging around there.

'A few days after the robbery, the police interviewed all members of staff, including myself. Having assisted the police, I heard no more about it and considered the matter to be closed. The police contacted me again a few months after Dean's murder and said they wished to talk to me. My life had moved on since my relationship with Dean had ended and I didn't really wish to get involved, but they were insistent. They agreed that they wouldn't come to my home and we could meet at a location of my choosing for an informal chat. I eventually arranged to meet them at a pub called the Shepherd and Dog, which is on the outskirts of Basildon.

'Two officers came to see me, one was male, the other female. They didn't ask, they told me that they knew Damon Alvin and Ricky Percival had carried out the robbery two years earlier at the snooker club. Whilst we were talking, the female officer received a call on her mobile phone during which Dean's murder was discussed. I cannot say for sure, but it appeared to me that the call had been pre-planned. The female officer, who was sat directly in front of me, accidentally "let slip" that Damon had murdered Dean. The call, as far as I know, was from someone at police headquarters. I obviously couldn't hear everything that was being said. After I had "overheard" that Damon had murdered Dean, the female officer feigned shock and said to me, "Oh, I am so sorry, you were not meant to hear that." She then turned away from me and cupped her hand over the phone.

'When the call had finished, the officers told me that I would have to make a statement saying that Damon and Percival had carried out the robbery. They said that if I refused to do so, I would be arrested for armed robbery. I told the officers that I had no idea who had robbed the snooker club and therefore, regardless of the consequences, I was unable to help them. Despite their threat to arrest me, the officers asked no further questions and left.

'Approximately five years later, I received a phone call out of the blue and a detective informed me that they had now decided to arrest me for armed robbery. I was absolutely terrified. "I'm not in Essex," I replied. "I have a new life in London, I don't need this." Despite my pleas for the matter to remain firmly in my past, the detective insisted that I should hand myself in.

'I met the detective at a police station in Essex, where I was formally arrested for the snooker club robbery. I was told that the renewed interest in the robbery had arisen following Damon Alvin's decision to turn supergrass. I was questioned at length, photographed, fingerprinted and bailed to reappear at the police station, pending further inquiries.

'The police told me that Dean had used me to glean information about the snooker club so that they could rob it. I know that isn't true. Damon controlled Dean. If anybody was using me, it was Damon. Dean didn't have the brains to plan a robbery.

'Because I was so frightened, I told the police that I saw Percival and Damon when I walked out of the snooker club on the night of the robbery. I said they were just standing there. I had walked past them and gone home. A few days before I was due to answer my bail, I received a phone call from the police, who advised me that there was no reason for me to attend the police station as no decision regarding charging me had yet been made. As far as I know, I am still on bail for armed robbery. It's not a nice thing to have hanging over your head. My life is in limbo.'

I was already aware from reading Carla's statement that she had named Percival as one of the men she had seen outside the snooker club. Carla had also said that she had known it was Percival because Alvin and Boshell had once taken her to his home. She had described Percival and his home in great detail and this appeared to be conclusive evidence of Percival's involvement in the crime. But I spoke to Percival and his family and they were all adamant that neither Carla nor Boshell had ever set foot in their home. As I was to find out, like most of the evidence in this case, if it looked like it was true and sounded like it was true, then generally it wasn't.

When I asked Carla to describe the night she had first met Percival, she said, 'Damon was giving Dean and me a lift home from his house one night. He said he had to stop off somewhere. We were in Southend when he pulled up outside a house and said, "This is where Ricky lives." We got out of the car and, after a few moments, the door of the house opened and we all went inside. When we walked in, there was a long hallway, which led into the kitchen. Adjacent to the kitchen was a conservatory. I was told to sit in the kitchen and not move. They all went into the conservatory and I was left alone. I would describe Ricky Percival as follows: six feet tall, muscular, shaved head, tattooed, staring eyes and a very deep voice.'

The house Carla had described does not resemble Percival's in any shape or form, and her description of him is totally inaccurate. He is muscular, but he is not six feet tall. He doesn't have 'staring eyes', he doesn't have any tattoos and anybody who has ever heard him talk will tell you that his voice is the exact opposite of 'very deep'. Whoever's home Alvin and Boshell had taken Carla to that night, it certainly wasn't Percival's.

To confirm what I now assumed, I showed Carla a photograph of Percival taken around the time of the robbery. With a look of total disbelief on her face, Carla exclaimed, 'I can say with one million per cent certainty that the guy I met with Alvin and Dean was not Ricky Percival. It's just what they told me. I was led to believe that the person I met was Percival, but after seeing the photo I know it was not him. I did name Percival, but only because I was told it was him. I only had Damon's word that it was true.'

The police should have arranged an identity parade or what is known as a 'Viper identity parade', which is a similar process using photographs or video images instead of people. I say that because in Alvin's account of the robbery he says that the only time Percival and Carla ever met was in the car outside the snooker club. I find it odd that the police did not go back to Alvin and ask him about Carla's alleged visit to Percival's home. It is equally surprising that after Carla named Percival and Alvin as the people she saw outside the club that night, the police did not require her to attend the trial. There was certainly no other witness who identified the robbers.

I have no idea if Carla Shipton is being honest about whether she has met Percival or not – that should have been something for the jury to decide. I am in no doubt, however, that Damon Alvin lied throughout his account of the robbery. For instance, he has said that he punched the manager once, and, after securing his hands with cable ties, Percival stood guard over him with a gun. Alvin's claim that he only struck the manager once is a far cry from his victim's recollection of the attack.

The manager told the police, 'I was squirted in the face with a substance which burned my eyes and made me lose my breath. One of the males then started to punch me in the face, which caused me pain and made me fall to the floor. The same male then started to shout at me, "Where's the keys, where's the fucking keys?" He continued to punch me as he shouted. I told them that I didn't want any hassle and I would get them the keys. The male continued to shout at me and hit me. Whilst I was on the floor, I told the male that there was no point hitting me as I couldn't show him where the keys were if he did. At some point, I noticed the other male was standing over me and appeared to be holding a silver-grey handgun. As a result of this incident, I have a black left eye, which is swollen. I have a number of red marks around my right eye and an eight-inch weal mark from my left eye to the top of my head.'

If Alvin could inflict so much damage with a single punch, he should have given up drug dealing and robbery and taken up boxing. It is my view that Alvin was being at best liberal with the truth during his account of the robbery. Boshell's informant evidence regarding the incident raises more questions than it answers because of his lack of credibility. The victim's testimony contradicts that of the prosecution's star witness, and an extremely important witness was not required to attend the trial. How could a jury say with any degree of certainty that Percival was guilty of that robbery? Apart from Alvin, there is nobody who can say that Percival was even in Wickford that night.

The day Percival was convicted of these crimes on the strength of such shoddy evidence marked a very sad and embarrassing day for the British judicial system.

As I was preparing to leave, Carla begged me not to reveal her whereabouts to anybody who might be associated with Alvin. 'I'm worried that Damon is going to come and find me,' she said. 'He really does scare me. It's a shame about Dean. He really didn't deserve to die like that. He wasn't a physical threat to anybody. Dean knew everything about Damon and his family, they were really close, and that's probably what got him killed. If anybody would have wanted Dean dead, it would have been Damon. If he didn't pull the trigger himself, I am certain that he would have been involved in the planning of it. Damon was definitely the sort of person who would do that sort of thing. Whatever you say or do, please don't let him find me.'

I tried to reassure Carla that Alvin could not and would not harm her, but my words fell on deaf ears. She remains absolutely terrified of him. The loveable rogue that the jury saw performing in the witness box at Chelmsford Crown Court is certainly not the same man whose name when mentioned strikes terror into the heart of Carla Shipton.

The Locksley Close Shootings

The death of Malcolm Walsh and the Locksley Close shootings were the catalyst for all Ricky Percival's current problems. Despite being arrested within hours of the shootings and undergoing a whole range of forensic tests, not a shred of evidence was found to link Percival to the crime. It was only when Alvin accused Percival of being the gunman did Essex police decide to charge him. They may have had faith in Alvin's stories, but nobody else who gave evidence, including the victims, appeared to agree with his account.

Carla Evans, who had told the jury that the gunman had blue eyes, was treated like a pariah and removed from the court. Victims who recalled seeing two gunmen and hearing up to six gunshots were disbelieved. The most important page of one of the victim's statements, who has since died, was inexplicably 'lost'. Christine Tretton, one of those injured that night, was openly hostile to Percival during the trial. She told the jury: 'Until the day I die, I say 100 per cent that it was Ricky Percival who shot my family. If somebody put a shotgun to your face, you would know who they were.' She added that he should be brought to justice for destroying her family; however, when asked by

Percival's barrister why she did not say anything like that in her original statement, Christine claimed that she had but the police had failed to write Percival's name down.

The Tretton family, like Alvin, have disappeared into the witness-protection programme, but I did manage to get a letter to them in which I invited them all to meet me so that they could have their say in this book. Unfortunately, they declined my offer. In their reply, they told me that they would have liked to have helped me, but they had endured enough traumas since the shootings. One member of the Tretton family, however, who had not been called as a witness at the trial, did break ranks and say that he would meet me.

My early morning journeys down to Essex had become something of a routine over the previous year. Rise before the sun to avoid the rush-hour traffic. Take a leisurely drive down the motorway. Then, to kill time, like a ghoulish tourist, stroll around an area associated with a particularly despicable crime before meeting one of the unfortunate characters who have had the misfortune to be involved in this story. Most of these people had left me feeling sorry for the terrible things that had happened to them; few had made me laugh. Ronnie Tretton, for all of his numerous faults, was an exception to that rule.

A young man in a constant state of war with all that surrounds him, some of Ronnie's rebellious behaviour reminded me of myself in times I have since tried hard to forget. We had agreed to meet on Leigh-on-Sea Broadway, but Ronnie had failed to appear at the agreed time. I rang him several times on his mobile and each time he told me that he was just a couple of minutes away. After half an hour, I gave up hope and began to walk to my car.

I don't know why, but I had a gut feeling that the tall, slim guy crossing the road towards me was Ronnie Tretton. 'Who are you?' he asked after I had called out his name. Once I had introduced myself, he ceased scowling, forced a smile and suggested we go for a drink together. Going for a drink with Ronnie turned out to be a lot more complicated than one would imagine.

We were turned away from one pub apparently because I had a small Celtic FC badge embroidered on my jacket. Ronnie didn't want to go in the Grand Hotel because he said he didn't like the noise and, in the same breath, he informed me that the Carlton public house was off-limits because of a recent 'massive free-for-all' that he had been accused of starting. Eventually, we gave up hope of finding a suitable pub on Leigh Broadway and drove instead to the Woodcutters Arms.

Chaotic is one way of describing Ronnie Tretton's life to date. He and his family have never seen eye to eye with the law. Neighbourly disputes, high-speed car and motorbike pursuits, manslaughter and the attempt to murder family members all feature in their chequered history. Described in a local newspaper as one of Southend's most notorious young criminals and a thug, Ronnie's most recent encounter with the authorities when I met him had quite rightly resulted in him being banned from entering Southend hospital.

Whilst having an X-ray on a particularly painful broken arm, Ronnie had shouted and sworn at a radiographer. All appeals for him to calm down had been ignored and he ended up throwing an X-ray cassette across the room and kicking a temporary barrier across the corridor. He and a friend had then moved the CCTV camera in the waiting room in an attempt to avoid being identified. The camera had already recorded their images, however, and Ronnie was arrested. It was when he appeared in court that the ban on him setting foot in the hospital had been imposed. A hospital spokesman told the Southend *Evening Echo*: 'He will now have to seek treatment elsewhere unless his condition is so serious staff decide to make an exception.'

At the not-so-tender age of 17, Ronnie had been given the rather dubious honour of being the first person in Southend to be the subject of an antisocial behaviour order. ASBOs, as they are commonly known, are given to individuals with a significant history of causing alarm, distress or harassment to others. A catalogue of incidents including driving whilst disqualified, making threats, assault, criminal damage and harassment had led to Ronnie's order being imposed.

Aged 24, Ronnie had nearly met his death in a horrific motorcycle accident. Tearing along a dual carriageway at more than 100 mph, Ronnie hadn't noticed a white Renault van in front of him. After slamming into the back of the van, Ronnie was catapulted through its doors and into the front passenger seat. The driver of the van was uninjured and continued driving along the road at 60 mph. The passenger received whiplash injuries and Ronnie broke both his arms, his left wrist, his pelvis and right leg. When the van eventually stopped, Ronnie was rushed to Southend hospital by ambulance, where he underwent emergency surgery.

My head was full of questions that I wanted to ask Ronnie about the shootings at his family home, but I couldn't help first asking where the fuck he was going to go after his next accident. It was a reasonable question: the likelihood of Ronnie Tretton going through life unscathed was zero and the local hospital had now banned him from receiving treatment there.

'Perhaps I will move,' replied Ronnie. 'But then again, that would please too many people around here.'

I could have spent all day listening to Ronnie's exploits, but it was his knowledge of Percival and the Locksley Close shootings that I had come to hear about.

'Tell me what you know about Percival and the attack on your family,' I asked. 'I know Percival has been convicted but I am not sure that he is guilty.'

'Neither am I,' Ronnie replied. 'My family are not going to like this, but I know that Percival did not do it. I first met Percival about 13 years ago. My brother Steve was good friends with Percival and he introduced me to him. When my brothers Stuart and Steve were in their early 20s, somebody in our road accused them of damaging a car that was owned by a local hard man named Malcolm Walsh. He was friends with a man named Damon Alvin. My family didn't know Alvin, but we knew of him. I think everybody in Southend has heard of Damon Alvin.

'We knew Walsh and we knew he wasn't a man you ought to cross. Walsh was rightly upset about his car being damaged but wrong to accuse Stuart and Steve of doing it. He was also wrong to threaten to hurt them if they didn't have his car repaired. When Percival heard what had happened, he went to see Walsh because he was friends with him. He said that Stuart and Steve were innocent and Walsh should ignore local gossip, that it was just some fool trying to cause trouble. Unfortunately, Walsh wouldn't listen. He had it in his head that Stuart and Steve were guilty. The threats and abuse continued, and the rest is history now. Walsh ended up dead.

'I used to visit Terry Watkins in HMP Chelmsford after he was charged with Walsh's murder. Everybody in our family felt sorry for Terry because he had been dragged into an incident that had nothing to do with him or us.

'It's fair to say that Percival didn't see it that way. He was annoyed with Terry because he thought there was no need for Walsh to have died over something so trivial. Alvin, too, was also really upset about Walsh's death. I was warned to watch my back by several people because Alvin was apparently out to get a Tretton.

'Walsh and Alvin had been partners in crime and had even lived together at one stage. Alvin started telling people that he hated me for some reason. I don't know why because I had never even spoken to him. He told people that I wasn't to be trusted because I was a Tretton. I used to see him occasionally in the Woodcutters pub. He would be holding court with his little gang of drug runners. His latest bit on the side would be sitting there, gazing at him in awe, and he would be staring straight at me, trying to intimidate me. He was twice my age and size and so there wasn't a lot I could do about it. I would just look the other way and pretend he wasn't there.

'His drug runners and whichever girl he was seeing behind his wife's back that week would all find his antics highly amusing. As soon as I heard that my family had been shot I thought of Alvin. He was the only person I could think of who had a grudge and was mad enough to do such a thing.

'Stuart, my uncle Raymond and a neighbour named Jenny Dickinson lost fingers and parts of their hands in the attack. Two years later, Raymond and Steven were dead because of alcohol. Some say they drank themselves to death because of the shootings, but that's not true. My auntie Christine, Steve and Raymond all had problems with alcohol long before the attack. I'm not saying that the ordeal they went through didn't affect them, of course it did, it affected all of our family. Steve had gone to somebody else's house before the gunman burst in and so he blames himself for not being there and possibly being able to protect the others. Thankfully, Auntie Christine doesn't drink any more. Steve's and Raymond's deaths were a wake-up call for her.

'I went to the hospital as soon as I heard about the shootings and every day thereafter. Not one member of my family even suggested that Percival might have been responsible for the attack. To be fair, nobody mentioned Alvin's name either, although, as I have said, I thought he may have done it. We all guessed that the shootings were something to do with Walsh's death, but beyond that we were clueless.

'The police didn't appear to have much idea either. They fitted panic alarms in our home and we were given personal panic alarms to carry around with us in case of another attack. These alarms were linked to the local police station and if activated would bring armed officers to our location within minutes.

'Two months after the attack, there was a party at the house where the shootings had taken place. Steve, Stuart, Raymond, Auntie Christine and I were all there. Also in attendance was Ricky Percival. Everybody shook his hand when he arrived and talked to him as normal. Nobody even hinted that they thought he might have been responsible for the shootings. Alvin, who was good friends with Percival at the time, didn't attend the party. Percival even slept over that night because we were worried about him driving home after having a drink.

'I don't think any rational person would believe that Percival would have had the audacity to attend the party and stay the night if he was guilty. I heard that Percival was arrested on the morning of the shootings, but forensic tests ruled him out as a suspect. Whenever there is a major crime committed, such as a triple shooting, lots of people are questioned. It doesn't mean they are guilty.

'I continued to associate with Percival after the shootings and he regularly came to my house. Nobody ever passed as much as a comment about him being in our home. When my auntie Christine made her statement, she didn't name Percival; however, by the time she got to court, she had changed her mind and said it was definitely him. I don't know why she changed her story or why she now believes it was Percival. My auntie is well known for getting confused over people's identities.

'I have always been fanatical about motorbikes. I have had one since I was about 13 or 14. Quite a few of the lads my age around Locksley Close also had them and we used to go scrambling over the fields together. The police couldn't really do anything unless we rode them on the road. A few kids used to ride them on the road to get to and from the fields, but I would always push mine. A boy named Shane, who lived near me, would always ride his on the road. My auntie Christine was convinced that Shane was me and would ring my mother to tell her what I was supposedly up to. It caused me loads of grief at home even though I was entirely innocent.

'My auntie has always been like that, she thinks she has seen something or someone and nothing will make her believe any different to what she has in her head. At the time of the shootings, Auntie Christine had a serious drink problem, so much so she was prescribed tablets. Her memory and state of mind was not what I would describe as good. I don't and won't ever believe that she is right when she says Percival shot members of our family. She might believe it in her own mind, but she also believes I was always riding my motorbike around the street when I wasn't.

'At the trial, Auntie Christine said she recalled Percival being at our house party after the shootings because he had shoved toothpaste up her nose. This is just another example of Auntie Christine getting things totally wrong. She was still drinking heavily at that time and it was me messing about with the toothpaste with her, not Percival.

'People in our family only started to talk about Percival as a suspect after his arrest. I guess he fell foul of the "no smoke without fire" mindset. Now he has been convicted, they have absolutely no doubt in their minds that he is responsible. All I can say to that is, apart from lying Alvin's story, where is the evidence? Alvin has admitted being there and lied about how many gunmen entered the house. He says only one entered and fired the shots. All three victims, who had absolutely no reason to tell lies about that night, informed the police that two gunmen had entered the house.

'I believe the other gunman was Boshell because his fingerprint was found on the car used in the attack. Boshell and Alvin were also the two who acquired the gun and went to retrieve it after the shootings. I think Boshell blamed Percival and a doorman named Dave to cover up Alvin's and his own involvement. I think Alvin took elements of truth from that night and added Boshell's bullshit informant evidence. He then spiced the whole story up with lies about Percival so that he could do a deal with the police to escape a lengthy prison sentence.

'My uncle Raymond, who suffered terrible injuries in the shootings, went to the Woodcutters pub when he heard that Percival had been arrested. He wanted to make peace with the Walsh family and show them that he didn't believe Percival was involved. He was adamant that the man who shot him had blue eyes. Unfortunately, Kevin Walsh got upset when he saw him and so Raymond left the pub. I visited Terry Watkins in prison after he stabbed Malcolm Walsh to death. I visited my family in hospital after they were shot. I saw the terrible injuries that the gunmen inflicted on them that night. I spent months of nerve-wracking uncertainty under police protection because of the attack on my family. I helped to carry my uncle Raymond's coffin to his grave. Does anybody in their right mind think for one moment that I would befriend and visit the man in prison who was responsible for all of this?

'I know for sure that Alvin is a liar because he told the police that me and Percival were going to shoot a bouncer. The very thought of pointing a gun at another human being after what happened to members of my family horrifies me. Could anybody honestly believe that I would consider for one moment shooting a complete stranger as a favour for the guy who is supposed to have shot members of my family?

'Alvin is a lying piece of shit. He isn't even capable of being honest with his own wife. As soon as the pressure is on, he says and does everything that will ensure his own skin is saved. If the police genuinely believed that I was conspiring to shoot or murder a bouncer for Percival, why didn't they at least come and ask me about it? They have never been near my door in relation to this ridiculous allegation and, for me, that says it all.'

As Ronnie and I sat talking on a bench outside the Woodcutters Arms, a powerful Honda Fireblade motorcycle roared into the car park. 'Oh, yes,' Ronnie called out, as he jumped to his feet. 'I have got to go now, Bernie. Good luck with the book.'

Moments later Ronnie was sitting astride his friend's bike. His face was glowing with excitement as he called out to me, 'One hundred and four miles per hour in first gear, mate. It'll piss a hundred and eighty flat out.'

Before I could answer, Ronnie was disappearing from view down Eastwood Road North like a blurred flash of blue lightning.

The Hit Man Allegation

The other person Alvin claimed Percival had solicited to shoot people was the guy Alvin had referred to as Steve Penfold. It's not his real name – Penfold is a nickname that his friends use because of his uncanny resemblance to the character of the same name in the *DangerMouse* cartoons. Like Ronnie Tretton, Penfold was accused by Alvin of plotting to shoot people on Percival's behalf. Penfold was not required to attend Percival's trial, nor was he questioned about the allegations.

The house in Southend where I was told Penfold lived hadn't been inhabited for some time when I visited it. After speaking to neighbours, I learned that he had left Essex five or six years earlier. Fortunately, they had a forwarding address for him and so I wrote to Penfold, outlining the matters that I wished to discuss with him. At first I heard nothing, but after two or three weeks he did contact me by telephone.

'I wasn't being rude, Bernie,' he said, 'but I needed to have you checked out before I could speak to you. My mate who runs a few doors around Southend knows you, he said you're OK, and so that's good enough for me.'

Meeting many of the characters in this story whilst researching this book has transported me back to my own darker times in the Essex underworld. Suspicion, doubt and secrecy used to be controlling factors in the most innocent of situations. A person leaving a group to simply go for a piss would result in somebody asking, 'Where's he going?' or 'What's he up to?' Without exception, everybody trusted nobody and conspiracy theories were spawned each time anyone opened their mouth.

Penfold had left the battlefields of Essex to take up residence near the picturesque village of Market Harborough in Leicestershire. It is a mere 60 miles from my home in Birmingham and so I was pleased to be spared the hassle of yet another early morning trek down the motorway network to Essex. His new home is a very large detached property situated down a deserted road on the outskirts of the village. Built in the 1960s, it is guarded by high-tech security cameras and high walls, which hide Penfold from the outside world. Bleak and depressing are the two words that best describe his home, HMP Gartree.

Arriving at 1.45 p.m., the time I was advised to attend, I was told to sit in the prison visitors' waiting room until my name was called. I waited and waited and waited. At three o'clock, I was still waiting in the aptly named waiting room. A large notice directly in front of me stated that visiting time ended at four o'clock, so I began to wonder if I was ever going to be called in. I tried hard not to complain – after being banned from visiting Percival for no rational reason, I certainly didn't wish to be turned away from HMP Gartree for merely highlighting their ignorance.

As I sat biting my tongue, bored out of my brains, two families from Manchester talked about their sons' recent portrayal in the press. They failed to mention why their 'lads' were serving life sentences, but they repeatedly referred to the journalists who had written about them as 'bastards, scum and parasites'.

After handing in my visiting order, my passport was checked to confirm my identity and I was then subjected to the most rigorous of searches. This involved having to remove my shoes and my coat, then opening my mouth, putting out my tongue and finally standing on a designated spot whilst a dog trained to seek out drugs sniffed my legs and groin. When I was eventually let into the visiting room, I had to produce my passport and visiting order once more before being told to sit at table number five and wait.

At 3.35 p.m., Penfold was finally allowed into the room via a heavily fortified steel door. We shook hands and laughed together about the ridiculous lengths visitors have to go to in order to enter a prison compared to the relative ease with which prisoners are currently admitted.

By his own frank and honest admissions, Penfold has been involved in crime for most of his 50 years. After being abandoned and then raised in an orphanage, there seemed to be a certain inevitability about the path his life would take. He has been sentenced to serve more years in prison than he cares to remember. Ten years for an armed robbery during which he pistol-whipped a man; four years for possessing a shotgun; two cases of actual bodily harm; a section 18 wounding with intent conviction, which he earned after hacking off somebody's ear with a machete. Then, of course, there is his current sentence: life imprisonment.

Alvin claimed Penfold had been given this life sentence for murdering somebody, but when I asked Penfold who he had murdered and why he said he didn't know what I was talking about. Penfold explained that in 2003, when he had been sentenced, a new 'two strikes and you're out' law was brought into being by the Labour government. This legislation requires judges to presume that a criminal who commits a second violent or dangerous offence deserves a life sentence unless the judge can be satisfied that the defendant is not a danger to the public. Penfold had already been convicted of hacking somebody's ear off and so a second conviction for a serious violent offence resulted in him being given a mandatory life sentence under the new legislation.

'Armed robbery had become a crime of the past,' Penfold told me. 'Banks and building societies no longer hold much hard cash on the premises and security is so sophisticated these days that even if you did try to rob somewhere, the likelihood of getting away with it is almost zero.

'I didn't fancy getting involved in the drug scene because it attracts too many arseholes and so I decided to try something totally different to everybody else I knew. I decided to enrol on a computer course in the hope that I could get myself a proper job and go straight. I couldn't read or write and so getting my head around something as complex as computers was never going to be easy for me, but I really wanted to give it my best shot.

'Everything was going fine at first. My life revolved around attending Southend College, getting on with my work, going home and keeping my head down. After a few weeks, I noticed that one of my fellow students was being unnecessarily hostile and rude whenever I happened to be around. I chose to ignore him, but one day I went into class and found that he had deleted all of my coursework off my computer. I'd put my heart and soul into my studies and he had erased it all at the push of a button. I cannot deny that I was a little more than angry.

'I had a heated argument with the man before leaving the building to avoid doing something I would later regret. I got into my car and drove away from the college because I knew that I needed to calm down. After an hour or so, I decided to go back and apologise to my tutor and fellow students for my outburst. As I went to get out of my car, the man who had deleted my work walked across the car park towards me. We stood facing one another and then he began mouthing off at me and shouting, "Do you want some?" Before I could reply, he had head-butted me full in the face. I'm not proud of what happened next, but I just lost it.

'This guy had deleted all of my hard work. He had been constantly rude to me for no apparent reason and he had head-butted me in the face. I was fucking livid. I shouted, "Violence! Fucking violence! You want some violence? I'll give you violence." I punched him to the ground, and then went to the boot of my car and took out a long steel spike that is for use with a Kango heavy-duty concrete breaker. As the man was getting to his feet, I hit him over the head with the spike and then clubbed him a few times with it as he lay on the ground. I didn't deny what I had done to the police nor did I offer any excuses. All of the effort I had put into bettering myself so that I could go straight had been wasted.

'My victim was given 19 stitches for the head wounds he suffered and spent a short period of time in hospital, but I'm pleased to say that he has now made a full recovery. As for me, I've spent seven years in prison so far for doing it. Seven long years for a moment's madness. It's sickening. I have no idea when, if ever, I will be allowed out.'

Turning to the purpose of my visit, I asked Penfold about his knowledge of Ricky Percival, his dealings, if any, with him and his thoughts on Alvin's allegations.

'Ricky Percival is a nice enough kid,' he said. 'He's half my age and so I've not had a great deal to do with him. I know his brother Danny better, but only because he works on the pub and club doors around Southend.

'As for Ricky employing me to shoot people, I think I'm capable of causing enough trouble for myself without getting involved in his shit, don't you? I had never met or even heard of Percival's mate Alvin until he washed up in one of the numerous prisons that I have had the misfortune to be housed in. It was in HMP Belmarsh that we first met.

'Prison officers from the internal security unit had turned up at my cell one day and announced without warning that I was being taken to the punishment block. It's not uncommon for inmates to be searched or for them to be subjected to some form of special scrutiny, but I had done no wrong and couldn't understand why this was happening. I was taken to the punishment block, where it was explained to me that the prison had received intelligence from the police that I was planning to escape from the prison van on my next trip out to court. This allegation was totally untrue and the thorough search of my cell, clothing and property that was carried out proved that fact. However, the mere allegation that I was planning to escape ensured that I was put on the 'escapers list' and I was then required to wear patches. This is the name given to a hideous set of clothing potential escapees have to wear which is covered in huge luminous-yellow squares. The patches make you stand out from the crowd so that the prison staff can monitor you more closely. When you're no longer deemed a threat to security, you can return to wearing the normal prison garb, but you have to move to another wing in the prison so all contact with previous associates is severed.

'The cell I was moved to already had two occupants. I acknowledged them when I walked in and set about sorting out my bedding and personal effects. As I was pinning up a few photographs of friends and family, one of the guys pointed at my photos and said, "I know him, and him, and him. You must be Penfold. I've been waiting for you. Damon Alvin is the name, I'm Ricky Percival's partner." I have to admit I was a bit wary of him at first, but when he started reeling off the names of lots of other people I knew I thought he must be on the level.

'I rang my friend Pete that evening – he lives in Southend and knows most of the faces around there. I told him about this guy Alvin who seemed to know everybody that I knew. I said that I was suspicious of him, but Pete said he knew him and assured me that he was "100 per cent".

'Alvin told me that he was on remand for possessing a kilo of cocaine with intent to supply. He asked me what I was in for and I explained that I'd had a difference of opinion with one of my fellow students at Southend College. This type of conversation is pretty standard in prison – the only thing you have in common with most of the guys you talk to is your criminality, so it's inevitable you discuss the offences you're locked up for. Alvin unnerved me, though. He questioned me about my involvement in crimes that I had never even heard about. He claimed that he'd heard about me through "the boys" and they had said that I was a fucking hit man! It's not funny to be called such a thing, but I really laughed when he said it. Who has ever heard of a hit man residing and operating in a little seaside town like Southend? I think the only small residential areas that have regular unsolved assassinations are Emmerdale Farm, Albert Square and Coronation Street.

'I asked Alvin if the person who had told him such bollocks happened to have been sniffing his kilo of cocaine. Alvin kept saying things to me like, "It's OK, you can tell me, mate. Are you sure you didn't try to shoot this person because Percival told me that you did?" In the end I told him to change the record because I had no idea what he was talking about.

'Alvin also talked to me about the murder of a kid named Dean Boshell, who had been shot dead on the allotments in Leigh-on-Sea. I had read about the incident in the newspaper at the time, but I didn't know who Boshell was or why he might have been shot. I guessed that he hadn't been murdered because of some horticultural dispute. Alvin told me that the police were blaming Percival for the murder, but it was him who had done it. He didn't seem worried and when I mentioned this to him he claimed that he didn't need to be because the police didn't have a shred of evidence against him. He was desperate to tell me more, but it's not the done thing. I think that it's unreasonable and disrespectful to burden a guy unnecessarily with that sort of information. I raised my hand, as if to say stop, and told Alvin that whatever he was planning to tell me I really didn't want to hear it.

'Over the next few weeks, Alvin told me that the police were taking him out of the prison to attend identity parades. Almost every day he would get up, have his breakfast and then disappear until later that evening. A sixth sense told me that something was not quite right about this. He would say, "Today, they took me to Birmingham for an identity parade, tomorrow I have to go to Colchester and Ipswich," and another day he would say London. A prisoner might be required to attend a few identity parades, but Alvin made it sound like Essex police were trying to pin every unsolved crime in the country on him. Everybody knows that they wouldn't dream of doing that to somebody.'

When Penfold had finished laughing, he told me that he had later learned that these outings Alvin was making were not to identity parades; Alvin was, in fact, attending de-briefing interviews at Gravesend police station.

'Each night when he returned to the cell, it seemed as if he had been tasked to ask me specific questions about Percival's alleged involvement in serious crime,' Penfold said. 'I became so concerned about the nature of these questions that I rang my friend Pete and asked him if he was sure about this Alvin. "He is fucking up to no good," I said, but Pete wouldn't have it. He kept telling me that Alvin was safe to mix with. I normally respect my friend's judgement, but I just knew that Alvin was conspiring against me, Percival or both of us. The guy freaked me out so much I requested and was granted a move to a single occupancy cell. Alvin almost begged me to stay with him, but I told him straight I wanted to be on my own and I didn't want to discuss anybody or their business any more.

'About a week or two later, Alvin was moved to another location and I never saw him again. Nobody will ever convince me that the escape story wasn't invented so that I could be moved into a cell with Alvin. It never did feel right. I don't believe Alvin even knew the specifics of some of the crimes he was asking me about. It seemed as if he was thinking, "I'll ask Penfold about shooting somebody, he must have done one of those." When I was quite rightly denying any involvement in such a crime, he would say, "Well, some bouncer or villain must have upset you. What about so-and-so? Surely you must have wanted to do him?"

'It's not in dispute that after questioning me all evening he was being taken out of the prison by the police the following morning to be de-briefed. I'm not suggesting that the officers dealing with Alvin were involved in any sort of conspiracy with him. What I would say is that Alvin was trying to get me to admit to crimes or to implicate others so that he could give the officers information in the hope that he would be given some sort of reward. Considering the allegations he has made about me, it appears he wasn't too bothered if the information he gave to the police was true or bloody fantasy.'

Thirty minutes after sitting down with Penfold, a bell rang to announce the end of visiting time. I shook hands with him and wished him well before we went our separate ways. Penfold returned to his prison hell and I made my way out into the car park. The two families from Manchester whom I had seen in the waiting room were trading insults as I walked to my car. From the little I could make out, it was apparent that one of them had been exposed as the source of the newspaper story they had been discussing earlier. I heard one man shout, 'How could you do it to our kid?' before the air was filled with screams.

As I drove away, I could see the males writhing on the floor and punching one another. The females were running around aimlessly, screaming at the top of their voices. A steady stream of prison officers were running towards the melee to break it up.

Honour amongst thieves? I doubt if such a thing has ever existed. It is survival of the fittest and fuck all the rest in their world. Damon Alvin is proof of that.

Jason Spendiff-Smith

In the summer of 2007, a girl named Stacie Harris contacted me, claiming to be the estranged daughter of John Marshall, whom I had known during my days with the Essex Boys firm. Stacie had seen photographs and newspaper articles relating to Marshall on my website. She had no idea that I was writing this book; she was simply trying to trace and contact people who had known her father.

Marshall was a close friend of Pat Tate and, in the days leading up to the Rettendon murders, he had agreed to look after a large amount of money for him. Five months after the murders, Marshall was found dead in the back of his Range Rover. Nobody has been charged in connection with the shooting.

The name Stacie Harris appeared familiar to me, but I couldn't think where I knew her from. I gave her all the contact details I had and thought no more about it. Then one day, whilst trawling through Percival's case papers, it dawned on me: Stacie Harris had been Jason Spendiff-Smith's girlfriend and had spent what turned out to be Boshell's last day alive in his company. I knew there was a possibility that Stacie might have shared her name with another girl from Southend; however, if this was the Stacie Harris from the Boshell case, there were numerous questions I wanted to ask her about her former boyfriend. I had been to Spendiff-Smith's family home, written to him and telephoned him, but he had refused to acknowledge me.

I rang Stacie immediately. 'Do you have an ex-boyfriend called Jason Spendiff-Smith?' I asked when she answered the phone.

'How do you know about that idiot?' she replied.

Lady Luck had smiled on me, but my good fortune didn't end there.

Stacie explained that it would be unlikely that we would be able to meet because she had left Essex and was now living far away in a town called Bilston. Yet another trek to Essex had been avoided – Bilston happens to be a mere ten miles from my home in Birmingham.

The following morning I met Stacie at a café on Bilston High Street. I didn't know what Stacie thought of the town, but I was confident that the virtuous Mary Ellis, a fellow and former Leigh-on-Sea resident, wouldn't have approved. In every direction I looked, all I could see were industrial buildings and more industrial buildings. Stacie and I talked about her father and I promised to include her story in this book in the hope that his family and friends would read it and contact her.

Stacie told me that her mother had been 'well developed' and looked much older than she actually was when she had met a handsome Essex Boy named John Marshall. 'John was a bit of a ladies' man, so I have been told,' she said. 'He had previously courted my mum's sister. It sounds pretty awful now, but when Mum was just 13 or 14 she slept with John and fell pregnant with me. My grandmother was outraged and insisted that my mum leave Essex to go and live in Kent with some of our other family members. When I was growing up, Mum told me all about my dad and I always wanted to meet him. Unfortunately, there never seemed to be a right time. Dad had met another girl named Toni and had married and had three children with her. Mum said it would be wrong to disrupt their lives and I should wait until everyone concerned was older.

'When I was 16, I fell pregnant and said to my mum that I wanted to contact my dad to tell him that he was going to be a granddad. I was, if I am being honest, fed up of being the "daughter in the dark", as I called myself. Sadly, about two weeks later, any chance I ever had of meeting my dad was snatched away from me.

'At about ten o'clock on 15 May 1996, Dad left his home in Billericay to finalise a business deal in Kent. His black Range Rover is believed to have crossed the Queen Elizabeth II Bridge from Essex into Kent at about midday on the same day. He didn't return home and failed to keep other appointments that he had made that day. He was reported missing that night by his wife Toni. She told the police that she was worried because she had not heard from him and he would normally contact her regularly throughout the day. On 18 May, my dad should have celebrated his 35th birthday. My stepsisters, who were then aged thirteen and three, and my stepbrother, aged six, had bought him presents, but he never contacted them. Then, on 22 May, Dad's body was found hidden beneath a bale of straw in the unlocked boot of his Range Rover. A police officer had discovered the vehicle parked in a residential street at Round Hill, Sydenham, in south London. Inquiries revealed that his car had been abandoned in that location the morning after his disappearance.

'Dad had been shot once in the head and once in the chest in an execution-type murder. The only thing clear about the weapon used is that it was not a shotgun. His Range Rover keys, a grey Head sports bag, two mobile phones and a Patek Philippe 18-carat gold watch with a blue face were missing; however, £5,000 cash that he had taken with him the morning he disappeared was still in the glove compartment.

'I had no idea Dad was even missing. I just remember Mum crying and refusing to let me turn on the television or radio. Mum didn't want me finding out that he had been murdered because she was frightened that I would lose my unborn baby. I eventually found out about Dad when Mum was out shopping one day. I heard his name and saw his photo on the television news. Police officers were appealing for information about his murder. I had never met him, but he was still my dad and it broke my heart.

'It saddens me that my brother and sisters don't even know that I exist. I wanted to come forward at that time and tell his family about me, but Mum told me that I had to think of their feelings at such a difficult time. Mum did take me to the funeral, but we walked around the church whilst the service was going on because she didn't want Dad's family to see us and wonder who we were. When everybody had left the cemetery after Dad had been laid to rest, Mum and I went to his grave. That is one of the only memories I have of my father: his funeral, where I had to hide as if I were some sort of embarrassment. I would love to meet my brother and sisters. If they ever do read this, I hope they will get in touch with me.'

Stacie became quite emotional whilst telling me her story. I could not help but feel for her. In order to change the subject, I asked her what she could recall about Jason Spendiff-Smith because his credibility, or lack of it, had been an important factor during Percival's trial. Despite retracting the allegation in his final statement, when he gave his evidence at the trial, Spendiff-Smith had once more alleged that he had received a threatening call from 'Rick', warning him to 'keep his big mouth shut', following the murder.

Stacie told me that she had first met Spendiff-Smith at Tots nightclub in Southend. 'He was the jester amongst our crowd,' she said. 'He was always laughing and joking. He was funny, but a bit of a geeky dreamer, really. Like a lot of young men around Southend, he fancied himself as a bit of a gangster. He told me that his family were really wealthy, but they didn't want anything to do with him. Everybody who went to Tots nightclub who knew Jason used to call him "the Ponce" because that's all he did: ponce money and ponce drinks. He always used to wear a great big white coat to try to make himself look stocky, but everybody used to ridicule him, saying he looked more like the Michelin tyre man.

'When I first got to know Jason, he was boasting about how much cannabis he smoked and how desperate he was for some. I bought him £5 worth off a friend and gave it to him. He made a really crap spliff and, after lighting it, inhaled. After a second or two his face went off-white, then red, then green. He stood up and dashed to the bathroom, where he kept throwing up in the toilet. He's such an idiot. I couldn't stop laughing. Jason hardly left my side for the few weeks that I was in a relationship with him; he was really clingy and always following me around. I thought he had only met Boshell the day he had died, but he has told the police that he had known him for a week or two. If they had met earlier and had discussed committing a crime, or if Boshell had ever shown him a gun, as Jason claims, I would bet my life that he would have told me about it. He didn't.

'Jason was the ultimate wannabe gangster. He loved talking himself up and wouldn't have been able to keep his mouth shut if he had seen a real gun or was planning to commit a crime. When I first saw Boshell, I thought he had messed his trousers because he was walking with his legs apart. I asked him what was wrong and he said, "I've just come out of hospital. I've got lots of bruises, don't worry about it." I got the impression he was too embarrassed to talk about whatever had happened to him. Whatever it was, he had been hurt bad. Everywhere I went that day, Boshell and Jason followed me. Boshell was being really weird, he was racing around the flat like he was on something. I genuinely thought he was some sort of lunatic. He was pacing up and down and appeared extremely agitated. He was saying that he needed dark clothing because he was going to do a job. He kept saying, "I've got a job on, I've got a job on." My brother, CJ, was with me and when I looked over at him, we both said in unison, "Curly, whirly cuckoo", which is a saying we've used since we were kids. It means that the person we are referring to is a nutter.

'I'll never forget Boshell saying, "They won't see me coming tonight if I have dark clothing. They won't see me coming." I remember him saying that because when I heard that he was dead my first thought was: "You were wrong, they did see you coming."

'Whatever happened to him that night and whoever did it, make no mistake, Dean Boshell knew that it was coming. He was acting so strange. I kept looking at CJ and mouthing, "Oh my God, who is this fucking lunatic?" When Boshell went to the toilet, I said to CJ, "You're not going to do anything with him, are you?" He replied, "No, no way." When he came out of the toilet, he asked CJ if he could borrow his phone. CJ looked at me as if to say, bloody cheek, but I indicated that he should let him have it so he would ring whoever he had to ring and hopefully leave.

'Boshell knew the number he wanted to ring off the top of his head. He didn't get a phone out of his pocket to look for a number, he just tapped it in and then walked out onto the balcony to speak to whoever it was, out of earshot. Looking back on that night, I'm not sure Boshell even had a phone on him. CJ thought Boshell was going to steal his because he said to me, "If he nicks that, I will fucking kill him."

'When Boshell had finished his conversation and came back into the room, he looked even more agitated. He said, "If my brother calls me back, will you give me the phone?" Boshell continued to act weird. He was really on edge. He asked me and CJ where we were from, and we replied Leigh-on-Sea. As soon as we said that, Boshell went into the toilet. I asked Jason where Boshell was from and he said that he was also from Leigh-on-Sea. CJ and I were saying, "No way is he from Leigh. He would know Ricky Percival, Ronnie Tretton and all that lot, if he was." Ronnie had been in the newspapers after doing something really stupid around that time and we began talking about him. We said that Ronnie was like a younger version of Ricky Percival, meaning he had a bit of a reputation and took no shit off people.

'That evening is the only time Ricky Percival's name was ever mentioned in Jason's company. Because we were saying Percival was hard and stuff like that, Jason obviously remembered his name and told the police later that it was Percival threatening him. It just shows what a fantasist he is. Jason's story about him receiving threatening phone calls the following morning is complete and utter rubbish. I was sleeping with him at that time and he wouldn't get out of bed to sign on the dole, never mind answer the phone. He's just a nobody who desperately wants to be thought of as a somebody. If he had received threatening calls, the whole of Southend would have heard about it by lunchtime. It would have made his day; he would finally have become the big villain he always wanted to be.

'I genuinely cannot believe that the police or anybody else, for that matter, would consider using Jason Spendiff-Smith as a witness and expect him to tell the truth. He lives in a world of his own that he has created to promote himself as something he is not.

'My relationship with Jason wasn't serious. It was just a casual fling. I cannot even remember how we finished. I think I just left him at my friend's flat one day and she kicked him out. I would have had no objections to giving evidence in court, but nobody contacted me. I find that very strange because I know that Jason was lying about the threatening phone calls. It's shocking that a man has been sent to prison for life on Jason Spendiff-Smith's say-so.'

The Time of Death

Despite his absence from Chelmsford Crown Court, Gordon Osborne's evidence was probably the most crucial independent evidence produced in the murder trial that the jury was asked to consider. A police memo written by Detective Chief Superintendent Reynolds describes Osborne's evidence as being 'particularly important, given his army background'. Without Osborne's evidence being heard, the prosecution would have struggled and probably floundered in proving their case. Had the jury accepted Hansel Andrayas's evidence over Osborne's, Ricky Percival would not have been charged with Boshell's murder.

Andrayas said that she had heard significant noises around 2 a.m. Not only had she heard them but they had also awoken her daughter. Percival had parted company with Alvin long before this time and was sleeping soundly in his own bed. Unfortunately, Osborne's time as a Royal Marine and his boasts about his knowledge of firearms had convinced the jury that such a man couldn't possibly be wrong.

Reading the seven pages' worth of Osborne's previous convictions, alarm bells regarding his credibility and his reluctance to return to the UK should have been ringing in the ears of everybody connected with the case. Despite the significant changes made by Osborne in his statements and knowing that he was a fugitive from this country, no one delved further into his background. Simply by contacting the Royal Marines I have discovered that despite signing a declaration on each of the statements he made – 'I shall be liable to prosecution if I have wilfully stated anything which I know to be false or do not believe to be true' – Gordon Osborne deliberately lied.

When he was visited by the police on the first occasion, Osborne had told them, 'Half of me thinks that I may have heard a bang, but I couldn't be sure. I don't know what time I may have heard this bang, but it was possibly between 11 p.m. and 11.30 p.m.'

Three and a half months later, Osborne suddenly had vivid memories of the night Boshell died. He told the police that at about 11 p.m. he was awoken by the sound of 'two or three gunshots, coming from the direction of the allotments. My bedroom window is always open and I got up to look out of the window towards the allotments but could not see anything, as it was pitch-black. I can say from my experience in the Armed Forces that the shots I heard were from a handgun and not a shotgun.'

Four and a half years later, Osborne's memory had continued to improve. When the police visited him in his new home in Spain, he told them: 'I woke up about 11 p.m. that evening. I had heard two or three gunshots coming from the allotment. I can't be more specific about the time, but I had a digital alarm clock by the bed, which I did look at. I immediately recognised the sounds as coming from a handgun. This type of weapon has a distinctive sound, totally different to a shotgun or rifle. I have had experience of firearms since I was 11 years of age, when I shot rifles with the Sea Cadets. I remained in the Cadets until the age of 16. At the age of 17, I joined the Royal Marines, staying with them for 18 months. I had training on the Browning 9 mm semi-automatic pistol, self-loading rifles, Lee Enfield Rifles, American M16 rifles, German Mausers and Lugers. Since leaving the Marines, I have not had any dealings with firearms, but like riding a bike you never forget what you have learned and the sound each weapon makes.

'I can't say how far away these shots were, all I can say is that the sounds definitely came from the back of my house.'

The reason I say Osborne deliberately lied is simple: he has never been in the Royal Marines. He has never undergone the weapons training that he boasted about and therefore his claim that he can distinguish the sounds of these various weapons being fired is also a lie.

Acting Steward Gordon Osborne, service number P100762, enlisted in the Royal Navy on 30 January 1967. He was discharged less than five months later on 24 June 1967 because he was deemed to be 'unsuitable'.

According to the Royal Navy, as an Acting Steward Osborne's duties would have been providing hospitality services and learning 'core skills in the hotel trade' aboard ship. If Acting Stewards are on board a ship during military conflict, they are responsible for the upkeep of the officers' accommodation and dining areas, where they hone their skills in the hotel services area so that the officers can concentrate on the military task in hand.

Rather than being trained in using an arsenal of different weapons, the Royal Navy have informed me that Acting Stewards, of which Osborne briefly was, 'are specially trained to carry out a range of hospitality tasks, including the organisation, preparation, serving and accounting for food and drink of all kind'. In short, Gordon Osborne was a waiter or porter who had failed to make the grade.

I have stated on more than one occasion in this book that I do not know if Ricky Percival is guilty or innocent. After reading this, who can honestly say that they disagree? I did not write this book just for Ricky Percival's benefit. I believe that the Tretton family, Jenny Dickinson, the manager of the Wickford snooker club and last, but by no means least, Beverley Boshell deserve to know the truth. Beverley has already endured one traumatic hoax.

When Alvin appeared in court to stand trial for her son's murder, she prepared herself to face the man police said was his killer. Eleven months later, Beverley was back in court and being asked to believe that Percival had murdered her son. What will Beverley face after yet another trial, featuring not only Percival but also a whole host of previously unheard witnesses? There must be another trial – no civilised society would permit a young man to spend 28 years in a prison cell based on the evidence of some of the witnesses who did and did not testify against Percival.

Epilogue

ALVIN'S *COUP DE GRÂCE*

Apart from Damon Alvin and a handful of Essex police officers, there were few smiling faces at the conclusion of Percival's trial. Mrs Boshell walked out of Chelmsford Crown Court still unsure about who had taken her son's life and why. Percival and Walsh were taken to prison and Griffiths went home to try to rebuild her life. Percival's parents were left to face up to the reality that their youngest son may never be freed in their lifetimes.

Damon Alvin and his family ceased to exist. They were given new identities and disappeared into the witness-protection programme to begin a new life. Nobody thought for one moment that Alvin would ever surface again. All he had to do was attend court after the Christmas holiday and be sentenced for the numerous crimes that he had admitted to carrying out. Despite assurances by the police that his assistance in clearing up so many serious crimes would undoubtedly be rewarded by the sentencing judge, Alvin was not so sure. A 50 per cent discount on a twenty-year prison sentence might sound good, but the prospect of serving ten years is only marginally more appealing. Alvin knew from past experience that he would have to ensure that the judge would be left in no doubt about his regret and desire to make good in the future if he was to earn maximum credit. One would assume that Alvin had no more cards with which to play his games, but he could always be relied upon to come up with a solution when his liberty was under threat. Before Percival's trial had even ended, he was already planning his next move.

Alvin had sat down and penned a letter to Beverley Boshell, the lady whose life he had already made a misery. When finished, Alvin's letter mirrored the speech that he had read out to the judge prior to his being sentenced for possessing the kilo of cocaine. It was full of woe, promises of an industrious future and insincere remorse. Alvin wrote:

Dear Mr and Mrs Boshell,

I will start by saying that I will understand if you don't want to read this letter, but I hope you will understand why I had to write it. Sorry is a word easily used by many but truly meant by a few. I hope that you can believe that I am one of these few. I am truly sorry for everything that's happened and for what I've put you and your family through. I know how strongly you must feel towards me because I know how I feel about myself – hate and ashamed are just some of the words I would use.

I first met Dean in Chelmsford prison in 1998 and we struck up a friendship and would often clown about to pass the time away. I had a lot of time for Dean, he could be very humorous. For the two years that I knew Dean, we got on very well and we never once fell out. He never had a bad word to say about anyone and he was keen to be helpful. He helped me more in the two years that I had known him than any of my other friends had in all the years I had known them. Dean would often talk about his family and he had told me that there had been bad times for you all, but it was clear that his family was a big part of his life. It was clear that he felt lost and guilty at times because of his past behaviour. It was obvious that he was desperate to meet somebody and settle down. He was always keen to make new friends and would often surprise me with the different girls he would meet. Unfortunately, it was me and my friends that he came to befriend and become close to.

As you may be already aware, the three of us met up on the night of Dean's death to commit a somewhat simple theft of cannabis from a barn in which nobody needed to get hurt. I am in no way trying to justify this crime. I just want you to know that I didn't expect Dean to come to any harm that night. I can swear to you that had I had any inclination that he would be harmed, then I would have done everything I possibly could to prevent it happening.

On 27 February 2001, you lost a son and I lost a 'friend', if that's a word I'm allowed to use. I use it lightly because a true friend wouldn't have done what I did. I feel that I am as much to blame for his death as the person who pulled the trigger because I lied to protect him and myself and it was because of me that

EPILOGUE

Dean was there that night, and this is something I will have to live with as well as the memories of what happened.

Not a day passes when I don't think of Dean. There are reasons for my continued lying for that three-and-a-half-year period, but these are simply reasons and in no way excuses. There is no excuse for continuing this nightmare and denying you the truth and justice a family rightfully deserves. I can't begin to imagine how much upset and pain we have put your family through and I pray that I never have to find out. I wish I could, but I can't change what happened to your son, but I hope that I can help you get justice.

The past six years have been my hardest and saddest. That night changed many people's lives and continues to do so. My decision to come clean has split me and my brothers, devastating my parents, as well as my wife's family. At times I wonder if there will ever be an end to the upset that's been caused, but I have to acknowledge that at least I do still have a life to live. Only now do I truly realise how my actions and criminal ways devastate people's lives and hurt the people who least deserve it: the innocent.

I have led a life of crime since a young age and some of it has involved violence, but I'm taking this opportunity to confess to all the criminal offences that I've been involved in. I expect to receive a lengthy prison sentence for them and accept this. I want to assure you that when I am finally released I will take this second chance being given to me to live a law-abiding life. I don't ever again want to be involved in the pain families and friends suffer because of the consequences of crime. I don't know what I expected to achieve by writing this letter but I felt it was necessary and the right thing to do. I don't seek forgiveness, as I don't believe that I could give it if I was in your situation. I just wanted to apologise from the bottom of my heart and tell you how sorry I am for your loss. I hope this trial will bring closure for the both of you and your families.

Yours sincerely,

Damon Alvin

When Alvin appeared at Woolwich Crown Court to be sentenced, Judge Christopher Ball QC, who had presided over both Alvin's and Percival's murder trials, was reminded of not only Alvin's cooperation with the police but also 'the genuine remorse that he had expressed to those his crimes had affected'. Before passing sentence on Alvin, the judge told him, 'You took an extraordinary step in confessing what you had done over many years. It is in the public interest that what you have done should be recognised, as a very dangerous offender has been convicted. The public is now safer for what you have done.'

In total, Alvin was sentenced to 24 years' imprisonment for an orgy of violence that had ruined the lives of numerous people over many years in Essex. Standing in the dock, Alvin barely flinched whilst the sentences were read out. He wasn't concerned because he knew he had not yet been rewarded for the assistance he had given the police.

Finally, his payday arrived. The judge told Alvin that each sentence he had been given was only a third of what he would normally have received and all the sentences would be served concurrently. In his view, he said, Alvin should be considered for early release after 50 per cent of time served. The longest term of imprisonment handed down to Alvin had been five years. Because all his sentences were to run concurrently, this meant five years was the longest time that he could serve. With a 50 per cent discount, that sentence was further reduced to two years and six months. After deducting the two years and three months that he had already spent in and out of custody, Alvin was left with just twelve more weeks to serve.

After Alvin had been sentenced, the letter he had written to Mrs Boshell was hand-delivered to her by Essex police. They told her that if she wished to reply, a sealed letter would have to be hand-delivered to him by them. For security reasons, they were unable to give Beverley his address to reply to directly.

I have my own thoughts as to why Alvin might have wanted to write to Mrs Boshell and I did wonder if she would agree with them. When I visited her home, I took the opportunity to ask her what she had thought when Alvin's letter had arrived. With a look of total disgust on her face, she almost spat out her reply.

'Load of crap – they are the first words that entered my head after reading Alvin's pathetic letter. If it was his intention to make me feel better about what had happened, then he failed miserably. If anything, it made me feel more hateful towards him. Alvin isn't worried about how I feel. It's obvious that he wrote that letter to show it to the judge before he was sentenced. That's why the judge commended him for the remorse he pretended to show. It's sick, bloody sick.

'Alvin's now just trying to make himself feel better about Dean's death. This is the so-called man who transformed his prison cell into a makeshift crime scene investigation office where he rehearsed his lines. Why would anybody wanting to tell the whole truth and nothing but the truth need to do that? Alvin had also planned to insult my son's memory by claiming he was some sort of paedophile who had been murdered by a fictitious victim's family.

'In court, Alvin claimed that Dean was the only friend he had who would ring him up and go out socially with him. If Alvin truly believes that Dean was his best friend, I really wouldn't want to be his enemy. This is the same person who arranged for a wreath to be stolen from a grave and caused God knows how much upset to grieving loved ones. Alvin did this so that he could send it to his wife and "prove" to a judge that he was being threatened in the hope he would get a reduced sentence. It's apparent that Damon Alvin is only worried about one thing: Damon bloody Alvin.

'In the letter, Alvin talks about not being able to tell the police who had murdered my son for various reasons, but he fails to give one. The 12-week sentence Alvin had to serve was, in my opinion, diabolical. He pleaded guilty to conspiracy to pervert the course of justice, burglary, conspiracy to steal, possession of a firearm with the intent to commit an indictable offence and two counts of causing grievous bodily harm, and yet he was released just a few weeks later.

'The judge told Alvin that he hoped other criminals would follow his example and come forward to inform on their associates. It would make me and a lot of other people happier in Essex if the police stopped using the soft option of employing supergrasses to convict people. More often than not they are no better than the scum they are giving evidence against, yet they are treated like pillars of society.

'What happened to all the evidence the police had when they first charged Alvin with Dean's murder? I take it they discarded it when he agreed to blame Percival. That's not justice, because I have been deprived of knowing what really happened to my son and why. I honestly do not believe Alvin's versions of events and I also believe the police and the prosecution do not either.

'During the trial, they didn't question him about sensitive matters, such as what happened to the gun used to shoot Dean. Why would Percival lure a man to an area surrounded by houses, including his own, to commit a murder? Why would Percival, a reasonably streetwise guy, hide a gun in allotments where people naturally spend all day digging and foraging about? Alvin claimed Dean was going to be the getaway driver for a robbery that night, but he didn't have his glasses with him and Dean's eyesight was at best appalling. When this was pointed out, Alvin said that Dean was going to follow the white lines on the road. It was supposed to be a murder trial, not some Laurel and Hardy comedy sketch, but they allowed him to say it without the absurdity of what was said being questioned. I can only conclude that Alvin was permitted to lie unchallenged so that his evidence would fit the agreed story and exonerate him from any involvement in Dean's murder. The police were happy because they had somebody for Dean's murder, the Locksley Close shootings and the Wickford robbery, which looks good on their record.'

It was apparent to me that Beverley Boshell had a lot of questions that she needed answering. In the genuine hope that I could help this grieving mother achieve some sort of closure regarding her son's death, I suggested that she reply to Alvin. In his apparent virtuous state of mind, Alvin might have felt obliged to answer all the questions to which she sought answers.

After spending literally hours trying to write the words she felt she needed to say to Alvin, Mrs Boshell gave a letter to the police to pass on to him. They later confirmed that he had received it, but Alvin, true to form, had lied again. He didn't, as promised, bother to reply. There was nothing for him to gain by doing so, therefore I imagine that he couldn't see the point. The 'genuine remorse' commented on by the judge that he had 'expressed to those his crimes had affected' was apparently exhausted.

Alvin was not the only one holding his tongue in the hope that this case would go away. In a statement issued by Essex police following Percival's conviction, they said that they would be reviewing evidence of criminal matters raised at the trial. That review, if it ever did take place, doesn't appear to have resulted in a single independent witness, old or new, being interviewed. It is as if the review has never taken place.

Despite the hurdles erected by the authorities to hamper my enquiries into the case, I managed to unearth enough evidence to prove beyond doubt that Ricky Percival did not receive a fair trial and may very well be innocent of all charges. The authorities know that and I know that the authorities are not happy about it. I can state this with confidence because on Friday, 14 December 2007 I posted Percival all the new evidence that I had discovered. This was immediately seized by the security department at HMP Full Sutton and Percival was told that he would not be allowed to read or even catch sight of it. Prison staff then implemented an immediate and total ban on communications between Percival and me. He was told that in addition to the visiting ban that was already in place he could no longer telephone or write to me and I could no longer write to him.

When asked why such a draconian ban was being imposed, Percival was given what can only be described as a pitiful excuse: 'It's because you are collaborating on a book with O'Mahoney,' they told him. I say it is a pitiful excuse because the prison services, who have monitored all our calls and letters, and received an undertaking from me, know that Percival has not collaborated with me in the writing of this book. Even if he had, it is not illegal or forbidden for prisoners to assist authors with books of this nature.

Having read this book, you will know that the victims' families have not only assisted me but Beverley Boshell has also benefited from the proceeds of it after I agreed to pay for Dean's memorial.

There is nothing in this book that glamorises crime. The only quotes from Percival in this book relate to the evidence against him and so it cannot be said that he is using this book to justify his conduct or denigrate people that he dislikes. Less than ten years ago, the House of Lords ruled that a ban on prisoners talking to journalists was unlawful. Bans on prisoners receiving visits from journalists unless undertakings were given were also ruled unlawful. Freedom of speech, we were told, was 'the lifeblood of democracy'. Maybe so, but the laws of this land do not appear to apply to prisoner NE5377 Mr Ricky Percival. Democracy where Percival is concerned appears to have been bled dry.

We should all hang our heads in shame after seeing what the system has done and continues to do to this young man. The victims of crime and their loved ones undoubtedly deserve justice. The perpetrators of crime undoubtedly deserve their punishment. But no human being deserves to spend 28 years in prison deprived of hope and assistance from the outside world after being denied a fair trial.

The truth will always out, they say. I just hope for Mrs Boshell, the Percival family and in particular Ricky Percival that they are right and the truth does emerge sooner rather than later.

Essex Boys

A Terrifying Exposé of the British Drugs Scene

by Bernard O'Mahoney

Available now
ISBN: 9781840182859
£7.99 (paperback)

Essex Boys is the true story of the rise of one of the most violent and successful criminal gangs of the '90s, whose reign of terror was finally terminated when its three leaders were brutally murdered in their Range Rover one winter's evening. On their way to the top, they had built the drug-dealing organisation that supplied the pill that killed Leah Betts. They were responsible for a wave of intimidation, beatings and murder. Until, it seems, they took one step too far. Now there is compelling evidence that those convicted of shooting the dead men are innocent. Which means the real murderers are still at large.

Bernard O'Mahoney was a key member of what became one of the most feared gangs of the decade. His inside account of their cold-blooded violence reveals that facts can be more terrifying than fiction.

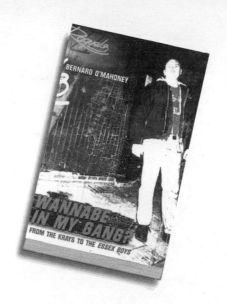

Wannabe in my Gang?

From the Krays to the Essex Boys

by Bernard O'Mahoney

Available now
ISBN: 9781840187670
£9.99 (paperback)

Kray gang boss Tony Lambrianou – who served a life sentence for the brutal murder of Jack 'the Hat' McVitie – has threatened to 'kill him by smashing a hammer through his head'. 'Dodgy' Dave Courtney, who claims to have murdered two gangland rivals, tried 'to put him out of his misery'. And 'the most dangerous man in the country', John 'Gaffer' Rollinson, has vowed to kill him 'when he finds him'. But Bernard O'Mahoney, former key member of the Essex Boys Firm, isn't concerned about their boastful threats because he knows the truth about wannabe gangsters.

For the first time ever, O'Mahoney exposes the gangland myths that have made legends of those who claim to be responsible for mayhem and murder. He reveals the sordid secret of one of Britain's most infamous gangsters and tells the truth about the imposters who make a living selling stories and writing books about events that have never even happened.

Wannabe in my Gang? is the book that many in the underworld never wanted the public to read.

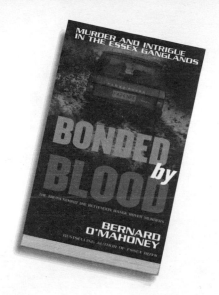

Bonded by Blood
Murder and Intrigue in the Essex Ganglands

by Bernard O'Mahoney

Available now
ISBN: 9781845961640
£9.99 (paperback)

Blood-soaked corpses and the faces of three teenagers poisoned by Ecstasy are the images that flash through Bernard O'Mahoney's mind when he closes his eyes and recalls his past. O'Mahoney was a key member of the Essex Boys Firm – one of the most violent criminal gangs in Britain. In December 1995, the three leaders of the firm were executed as they sat in their Range Rover down a deserted farm track. For many, this meant that the horror of the gang's brutal reign was over. For Jack Whomes and Michael Steele, the nightmare had just begun.

Convicted of the murders on the word of a supergrass, these two men have spent a decade in prison for crimes they claim they did not commit. In *Bonded by Blood*, O'Mahoney goes back to exorcise his ghosts and lay the past to rest. He returns to the scene of the murders and relives the bloody encounters that marked his time as a gang member. Divided by greed, bonded by the blood of their victims, the Essex Boys' rise to the top of the criminal underworld was as dramatic as their final fall.

AUTHOR BIOGRAPHY

Bernard O'Mahoney is a former key member of the Essex Boys Firm. He was the head doorman at Raquels nightclub in Basildon – the setting for many of the gang's lucrative enterprises and bloody encounters. Following the death of 18-year-old Leah Betts, who died after taking an Ecstasy pill that was supplied by his associates, O'Mahoney decided to leave the firm. His decision to quit was met with death threats from his former friends Tony Tucker, Pat Tate and Craig Rolfe. Two weeks later, all three were found shot dead in their Range Rover.

Having laid down his weapons and picked up the pen, O'Mahoney went on to write the bestselling *Essex Boys*. He is also the author of *Wannabe in my Gang?*, *Soldier of the Queen*, *The Dream Solution*, *Bonded by Blood* and *Hateland*, in which he describes his abusive and violent childhood through to his dark days as a football hooligan, right-wing thug and South African prisoner.

He has three children – Adrian, Vinney and Karis – and currently lives alone in Harborne, Birmingham.